The Ethics of D

Learning from Law's Morals

Do citizens have an obligation to obey the law? Do legal systems claim citizens have such an obligation? This book challenges the currently popular view that law claims authority but does not have it by arguing that the popular view is wrong on both counts: Law has authority but does not claim it. Though the focus is on political obligation, the author approaches that issue indirectly by first developing a more general account of when deference is due to the views of others. Two standard practices that political theorists often consider in exploring the question of political obligation – fair play and promise-keeping – can themselves be seen, the author suggests, as examples of a duty of deference. In this respect, the book defends a more general theory of ethics whose scope extends to questions of duty in the case of law, promises, fair play, and friendship.

Philip Soper is the James V. Campbell Professor of Law at the University of Michigan Law School.

Cambridge Studies in Philosophy and Law

Some other books in the series:

The Ethics of Deference

Learning from Law's Morals

Philip Soper

University of Michigan Law School

CAMBRIDGE
UNIVERSITY PRESS

PUBLISHED BY THE PRESS SYNDICATE OF THE UNIVERSITY OF CAMBRIDGE
The Pitt Building, Trumpington Street, Cambridge, United Kingdom

CAMBRIDGE UNIVERSITY PRESS
The Edinburgh Building, Cambridge CB2 2RU, UK
40 West 20th Street, New York, NY 10011–4211, USA
477 Williamstown Road, Port Melbourne, VIC 3207, Australia
Ruiz de Alarcón 13, 28014 Madrid, Spain
Dock House, The Waterfront, Cape Town 8001, South Africa

http://www.cambridge.org

First published 2002

Printed in the United Kingdom at the University Press, Cambridge

Typeface Times Roman 10/12 pt.   *System* LATEX 2_ε [TB]

A catalog record for this book is available from the British Library.

Library of Congress Cataloging in Publication data available

ISBN 0 521 81047 7 hardback
ISBN 0 521 00872 7 paperback

For My Children

Contents

Preface

. . . in general and ordinary cases, between friend and friend, where one of them is desired by the other to change a resolution of no very great moment, should you think ill of that person for complying with the desire, without waiting to be argued into it? – Jane Austen, *Pride and Prejudice*[1]

It would not be wicked to love me.
It would to obey you. – Charlotte Bronte, *Jane Eyre*[2]

To be servile to none – to defer to none – not to any tyrant, known or unknown. – Walt Whitman, *Leaves of Grass*[3]

In most cases, comity and respect for federalism compel us to defer to the decisions of state courts on issues of state law. – *Bush v. Gore* (Rehnquist, J., concurring)[4]

Sometimes when people disagree, conflict can be avoided by walking away. But going one's own way, following one's own lights, though it avoids conflict, does not resolve it. Nor is it likely to be an appealing or even available option when those who disagree are also connected – in a relationship, in a community, in a cooperative venture, in a state. It is in these cases, where context does not permit easy escape, that moral theory has its natural home, guiding argument and discussion and providing the theoretical basis for resolving disagreements through reason rather than force. In the ideal case, argument and discussion lead to consensus, which avoids conflict through a happy coincidence of views with the question of the correctness of those views temporarily relegated to the background. At other times, disagreement may continue beyond the time one can reasonably wait for consensus. Decisions must be made, actions taken, while the question of who is right remains undecided. If walking

---

[1] Jane Austen, *Pride and Prejudice*, ed. Frank W. Bradbrook (London: Oxford Univ. Press, 1970), 43.

[2] Charlotte Bronte, *Jane Eyre* (New York: Modern Library, 1997), 473.

[3] Walt Whitman, "A Song of Joys," in *Leaves of Grass*, eds. Harold W. Blodgett and Sculley Bradley (New York: New York Univ. Press, 1965), 181.

[4] 121 S. Ct. 525 (2000).

away and waiting for agreement are both impossible or impractical, another option may suggest itself: Perhaps one should defer to the views of those with whom one disagrees, even though one remains convinced that those views are incorrect.

Giving deference to the views of others is a familiar enough phenomenon, particularly in legal contexts. Appellate courts defer to the factual findings of lower courts, federal courts (usually) defer to state court interpretations of their own statutes, and state and federal courts often give deference to the views of agencies whose actions or statutory interpretations are challenged. Similarly, in nonlegal settings – close personal relationships, for example – one partner may defer to the other in order to resolve an impasse. Sometimes such concessions, as in Jane Austen's hypothetical, are "of no very great moment," in which case they may serve as examples of simple acts of courtesy, smoothing personal interactions and confirming that parties who care for each other will not hesitate to grant a partner's request and even "change a resolution" without demanding justification. On other occasions, deference may require action of greater moment – action one believes to be morally wrong. In these cases, if one defers despite serious normative disagreement, the action one takes, though prima facie wrong, is presumably justified in the end by the case that can be made for deference: The need to act before moral truth can be established provides reasons to act that outweigh the reasons for doing what would otherwise be the correct action.

The context that is most familiar in political theory as a possible occasion for deference of this latter sort is that of the citizen or subject confronting a legal norm he or she believes to be immoral. This conflict of normative judgment between citizen and state is a central focus of this book. And the point of this preface, in part, is to explain how the approach I take here to this classical problem of political obligation differs from standard approaches and justifies, I hope, yet another examination of a long mooted problem.

Consider, first, terminology. It is not uncommon and would not be odd to ask whether one has "reason to defer" to legal authorities in much the same way that one asks whether one has an "obligation to obey" the law. Indeed, as we shall see, the language of deference is often quite naturally in play when one explores the nature of authority and the various reasons for acting in compliance with the advice or requests of those who claim authority. Since political authority is one kind of authority, it should not then surprise that the language of deference could as easily be used in this context as the language of obedience. Certainly those who insist that there is no obligation to obey the law can do so as easily with the language of deference, as the quote from Whitman suggests, as with that of obedience. But this apparent interchangeability of "obedience" and "deference" does not hold in all contexts. Note how odd it would be to suggest that appellate courts, when they defer to the judgments of lower courts, are obeying the inferior court. Similarly, though marriage oaths today may still ritualistically invoke duties to "love and obey," one does not need to confront the peculiar problem of Jane Eyre (discovering that the man she was about to marry was already married) in order to conclude that "obedience" in this context is out of place: Modern sensibilities rightly balk at viewing a partnership as intimate as that of marriage as resting on promises to obey rather than on a mutual willingness to explore reasons for deference when conflicts arise.

To hazard a guess about what makes obedience in some of these contexts inappropriate we might say that obey, with its military connotations, is most at home when commands and orders are being given. Lovers and inferior courts do not typically issue orders; they make judgments, to which others should, perhaps, defer. But if this guess is close to the mark, then there may be reason to switch to the language of deference in the case of political theory as well. For as we shall see in later chapters, most legal theorists today agree that law is not accurately represented as a purely coercive system. Legal systems are normative systems: They make normative claims about their right to coerce and typically present their laws as normative judgments about what ought to be done. It is possible that these recent advances concerning the normative nature of law have outpaced, and so are not yet reflected in, the language we use to talk about political obligation. It is possible that by shifting from the language of obedience to that of deference, we can avoid the potentially distorting implications that arise when the conflict between citizen and state is presented simply as a matter of how one should respond to orders and threats.[5]

The preceding suggestion about terminology points to a second respect in which the study of political obligation in this book differs from other standard treatments. Though my interest is primarily in political obligation, Part I of the book is concerned exclusively with legal theory. While it is common these days to acknowledge the connection between these two subjects, it is also common to continue to treat them separately. Questions about the nature of law, even for theorists who defend a connection between law and morality, typically appear in a separate literature from the literature discussing the obligation to obey. But the recent turn in legal theory toward normative models of law has resulted in a curious position about the nature of law that makes exploring the connection between political and legal theory in a single work particularly appropriate now. The curious position, which I examine in later chapters, maintains that

---

[5] One influential article arguing against the existence of an obligation to obey the law begins by quoting H. A. Prichard's remark that "the mere receipt of an order backed by force seems, if anything, to give rise to the duty of resisting rather than obeying." See M. B. E. Smith, "Is There a Prima Facie Obligation to Obey the Law?" *Yale Law Journal* 82 (1973): 950 (quoting H. A. Prichard, "Green's Principles of Political Obligation," in *Moral Obligation* [Oxford: Clarendon Press, 1957], 54). Whether this vision of law as pure force influences Smith's conclusion that there is no obligation to obey is unclear. What is clear is that in the context in which the quotation occurs, Smith's use of the Prichard remark, and the largely discredited vision of law it implies, are essential to his claim that a "reflective man" might naturally assume that there is no obligation to obey.

legal systems are essentially characterized by claims of authority that cannot be supported by political theory. The oddity of this position, ascribing to law a normative posture inconsistent with political theory, provides the motivation for, and the connection between, the two parts of this book. In Part I, I focus on the kinds of normative claims that are essential to law. In Part II, I explore whether law, whatever its normative claims, has authority. The currently popular view that law claims authority but does not have it is here reversed on both counts: I argue that law does not claim authority but has it. I defend the first thesis in Part I, the second in Part II.

The third respect in which this work differs from other treatments of political obligation is revealed by the title. Though my focus is on political obligation, I approach that issue indirectly by first developing a more general account of when deference is due to the views of others. Indeed, I argue here that two standard moral practices that political theorists often consider in exploring the question of political obligation – the practices of fair play and of promise-keeping – can themselves be seen as examples of a duty of deference. In this respect, the book describes and defends a more general theory of ethics whose scope extends beyond the particular question of political obligation. But the ethical theory is only partial, and the description of the theory forms a large part of its defense. The theory is partial in two respects. First, it supplements, rather than supplants, existing moral theories and thus is not intended as a rival to them. Second, it does not purport to be a comprehensive theory, in the way that utilitarian or Kantian theories often do. It does not, that is, purport to be a guide applicable to every situation in which one might want to know what one ought to do. Instead, the theory focuses on four persistent areas of human interaction that have long served as central cases for inquiries into moral obligation – four situations in which persons often disagree about what to do and why. The aim of the study is to show that these four cases (raising questions of duty in the case of law, of promises, of fair play, and of friendship) share common features that are best illuminated by the concept of deference.

To claim that a concept or theory illuminates existing practices or institutions is not the same as claiming that the theory is correct; existing institutions and practices may, after all, be morally defective. In this respect, the account presented here may appear largely descriptive or conceptual. But the theory is also normative. For reasons explained more fully in Chapter 1, I assume that descriptive or conceptual approaches to the investigation of moral theories are necessary and important ingredients in the defense of such theories. I also assume that an explanation that illuminates existing practices in a common and prized tradition participates in the defense of that tradition, and in that sense is also normative, or "normative-explanatory."[6] Indeed, in the absence of any

---

[6] Joseph Raz, *The Morality of Freedom* (Oxford: Clarendon Press, 1986), 62–4.

clear consensus about what makes an ethical theory true, the only arena left for judging moral theories may be that of coherence; Which theory best explains long-established practices, considered judgments, widely shared intuitions?

The central thesis of the book was conceived some time ago during one of a number of leaves made possible through funds provided by the University of Michigan and the Law School. I am particularly grateful, in this respect, to the Cook Trust at the University of Michigan Law School for its generous support, as well as to the Terry and Ruth Elkes Fund for Faculty Excellence. Giving shape to the book's initial conception, however, proved more difficult than expected. One cause of the difficulty was the discovery that my own views changed over time in ways that required modifying or revising work in progress. In earlier work, I focused on legal theory and what I took to be the implications of H. L. A. Hart's description of law as a normative system. I suggested that this view of law made sense only when set against a background assumption that citizens have an obligation to obey the law. Today, the normative character of law seems widely accepted by most theorists, while the claim that there might be a general obligation to obey law remains increasingly suspect. My own views during this time have also changed, but in a direction different from that reflected in the current consensus. It now seems to me that the normative character of law is less robust than that suggested by much of the literature, leading me to a view of law not unlike, I think, one that Hart may have endorsed toward the end of his career. At the same time, my views about political obligation, only hinted at in previous work, have been reinforced and extended to areas beyond that of political obligation alone. The result is the present work, where the focus this time is mostly on moral theory, with legal theory providing the foreground.

The gradual change in views while the book progressed is reflected in some of the chapters. Chapter 2, for example, is an extensive revision of (and a slight departure from the views expressed in) "Legal Theory and the Claim of Authority," which appeared in *Philosophy and Public Affairs*, 210 (1989) and was reprinted in *The Duty to Obey the Law* (William Edmundson, ed.; Oxford: Rowman & Littlefield, 1999). Chapter 3 is a revised version of "Law's Normative Claims," published *in The Autonomy of Law: Essays on Legal Positivism* (Robert George, ed.; Oxford: Clarendon Press, 1996).

Another consequence of the time spent between conception and completion of this project is the growing debt I have incurred to increasing numbers of people over the last few years. Several chapters, for example, formed the basis for lectures or workshops given at law faculties in places ranging from Edinburgh to Osaka and Tokyo to Montreal. Some of the ideas in Chapter 5 were originally tried out on patient participants in a seminar on legal philosophy held a number of years ago at the University of Western Ontario. Comments and questions on each of these occasions invariably proved valuable, and have influenced and inspired the work in ways too numerous for me to recount in detail. I also thank several anonymous readers for Cambridge University Press, as well as the general editor of the series, Gerald Postema, whose comments on an earlier draft of this study corrected a number of mistakes and helped me reformulate poorly expressed ideas; the faults that remain obviously do so in spite of their efforts. Finally, I owe an immense debt to my colleagues at this Law School for their support and encouragement over the years, and to the many people in the field from whose published work I have benefited.

PART I

LAW'S MORALS

1

Introduction

Moral Inquiry and the Problem of Autonomy

Law's Morals

When we say of someone, "He has the morals of ... (an animal) (a saint)," we
engage in a commonsense way in the same activity that sociologists pursue in a
professional way: (1) we construct from the description of a person's behavior
the implicit normative principles that guide the person's actions; (2) we separate the descriptive parts of an inquiry (what *are* the principles guiding the
behavior?) from the ultimate evaluative issue (should this person's morals be
approved/condemned?). Of course, in the commonsense case, evaluation is
often just a step behind description – to say that someone has "the morals of an
animal" would normally serve to censure as much as to describe. It may even
be that most of the time when we talk this way about "the morals of a person,"
we implicitly intend to censure: We *could* say that someone "has the morals of
a saint," but it seems more natural, when praise is intended, to say simply that
someone "*is* a saint."

Putting aside this last question of whether a disparaging judgment is normally
intended, we can talk about "law's morals" in the same way that we do a person's
morals: We can describe the ways that legal systems present themselves to those
subject to them and reconstruct from that description the implicit normative
principles that underlie the legal system's actions. The additional puzzle that
is created by making "the law" the subject of the inquiry rather than a person
may be ignored so long as "the law" is understood as an institutional analogue
to a person engaged in self-conscious, purposive behavior. The "law's morals,"
we might say, are the implicit normative principles that individuals acting on
behalf of legal institutions – officials, for example – implicitly invoke whenever
they justify action "in the name of the law."[1]

---

[1] For further clarification of the personification of the law that seems to be entailed by these
discussions, see Chapter 3, 56–61.

The motivation for describing law's morals is much the same as the motivation for describing other people's morals. Apart from the lure of gossip for its own sake, we typically examine another's morals because (1) that person potentially affects us or those we care about in ways that make the person's principles relevant in determining how to interact with him or her ("the president's morals," "her fiancé's morals"); (2) even where no possibility of interaction exists, a person's morals may be useful in establishing a "moral" – an example, good or bad, that provides a guide to character or an aid to developing acceptable moral principles ourselves ("the morals of a Don Juan," "the morals of a Mother Theresa"). In each of these cases, as the examples suggest, description is usually followed closely by evaluation: characterizing another's morals is the preface to an implicit or explicit judgment, approving or censuring the person's behavior or character.

So, too, with law – with one significant difference. Unlike persons who can often be avoided if we disapprove of their morals, the law does not permit easy escape from its actions. One can move to another country or change one's citizenship, but in the modern world, neither course will avoid the confrontation with law. This inability to escape law's reach explains why so much jurisprudence is devoted to the study of legal systems in general: The aim is to characterize the phenomenon of organized state coercion that individuals inevitably confront, regardless of the particular form such coercion may take in particular societies. Moreover, the impossibility of avoiding law's morals ensures that the step from description to evaluation is even more natural than in the case of persons. If law's morals, for example, reveal a commitment to certain normative claims about the right to coerce others, we have much more at stake in the critique or approval of that commitment than in the case of casual encounters with strangers.

Describing law's morals has been the goal of a good deal of modern legal theory, particularly the branch of jurisprudence that considers the nature of law and legal reasoning and that is most prominently on display in the extensive literature discussing positivism and natural law. This literature, I shall argue, contains two mistakes. One mistake is now widely acknowledged; the other is not. The first mistake is the suggestion that law has no morals at all – not in the sense in which we might say of a person that "he has no morals at all" (meaning that he is immoral) but, rather, in the sense in which law is characterized as not being a normative system in the first place, but only a system of organized and effective coercion. The second mistake errs in the opposite direction. Most theorists, including legal positivists, now reject the coercive account of law and endorse instead the view that law is a normative system: Law makes implicit moral claims purporting to justify the coercive actions it takes. But moral claims come in two sizes. What might be called an "ordinary" moral claim is a straightforward claim about the content of a normative prescription. A person who claims that abortion is wrong (or permissible) makes an ordinary moral claim about a particular kind of action; the claim will be true or false, depending on whether abortion really is wrong/permissible. To be distinguished from ordinary moral claims are what I shall call "strong" moral claims. A strong moral claim usually entails an ordinary moral claim but includes in addition the peculiar claim, often associated with the concept of authority, that an action is wrong/permissible in part just because someone else (an authority) says it is. If I make a strong moral claim that one should not have an abortion, I imply two things: (1) one should not have an abortion because this action is wrong (the ordinary claim); (2) regardless of whether abortion really is wrong, one should not have an abortion because I (or some other appropriate authority) so declare.

As we shall see, many legal theorists currently describe law as making this latter strong moral claim about its directives. Sometimes this is expressed by saying that law claims authority, or that law claims that persons are to obey just because something is required by law, regardless of the merits of the law. I examine and criticize this characterization of law's morals in Chapter 3. For now, in light of the popularity of the view that law makes this strong claim, I point out in the remainder of this chapter some of the problems created by this view of law's morals.

Society's Morals

Just as we can talk about the morals of an abstract entity like law, we can and do talk about established normative practices within a society that are not necessarily enforced by state coercion. Philosophers call such practices "conventional norms": "conventional" to emphasize, once again, that we are dealing with description rather than evaluation (what *are* the established patterns of conduct in this community, and what do they reveal about the community's implicit moral principles?); "norms" to call attention to the distinction between practices that have an implicit, self-critical aspect as opposed to patterns of behavior that, though predictable and regular, do not depend for their maintenance on critical justification.

The extensive literature in legal theory describing law's morals does not have a precise counterpart in the case of society's morals. In part, that is because modern societies often appear too diverse and heterogeneous to permit confident descriptions of norms that underlie or guide patterns of group behavior. Conventional norms, typically stand out as objects for study in three cases: (1) when the group whose norms we are describing is a relatively homogeneous society or societal subgroup; (2) when the norm is embodied in formal documents, as in the case of particular legal norms; and (3) when the norm is so vague that it can command assent among diverse groups precisely because the level of abstraction is sufficiently great to avoid disputes about how to apply the concept in concrete cases.

The first case speaks for itself: Where groups are homogeneous and small, anthropological studies of a familiar sort can often describe the group's customs and compare and contrast them to more familiar moral ideas. The second case is also familiar. Conventional norms may be revealed in documents accepted as authoritative sources of legal norms within a society. We might call these norms "law's morals writ small." Unlike the concept of law's morals discussed in the previous section, which refers to the characteristics of legal systems in general, societal norms revealed by legal documents are particular to that society: They reveal norms sufficiently widely accepted to underlie the legal structure of that society, whether or not they are found in other legal systems. We use "law's morals writ small" whenever we characterize particular societies by reference to differences in their fundamental frameworks or constitutions or by reference to variations in the day-to-day laws enacted and enforced in the society. Thus constitutional documents that vary in the protections accorded property rights lead to descriptions of societies as "socialist" or "capitalist," just as varying constitutional procedures for enacting laws can reveal a society to be "democratic" or "totalitarian." Because these descriptions of a society's morals stem from authoritative sources, the task of description is somewhat easier than in the case of informal custom, and thus permits tentative descriptions of conventional morals of this sort even in societies made up of large and diverse groups.

The case of vague social norms illustrates the third possible way of describing a society's morals even in a complex and diverse community: One may sometimes succeed in describing conventional norms in a heterogeneous society by sacrificing specificity for accuracy of description. It may be accurate, for example, to claim that respect for privacy is a conventional norm in the United States, with weak or no counterparts in other countries. But explaining precisely what this vague norm entails in particular cases (e.g., abortion) would be difficult or impossible (there may be no conventional norm in particular cases), even though one might be able to describe with some precision the legal norm concerning abortion.

As the last example illustrates, legal and social norms can diverge in obvious and familiar ways. But this divergence between particular norms within a society must be distinguished from divergence between law's morals and society's morals. Law's morals are those normative principles that underlie the general attempt to justify imposing sanctions on others "just because it is the law." A society might be sharply divided about the content of particular norms and yet agree that the law is justified in acting as it does. It is society's morals on *this* issue – the issue of the legitimacy of state coercion – that poses the more radical problem in the event of divergence. If law implicitly operates on a theory of legitimacy inconsistent with the theory accepted by society, the need for reconciliation is more compelling than in the case of particular legal norms temporarily out of step with the times. In the latter case, divergence leads to legal reform or to a change in societal norms; in the former case, divergence leads at best to disrespect for law or, at worst, to civil unrest or revolution.

True Morals

If descriptive inquiries into the morals of others are typically preliminary steps toward evaluation, sooner or later one confronts the problem of evaluation: how to justify moral judgments. By comparison, that problem makes the difficulties that confront descriptive or conceptual inquiries pale. One reason for the difficulty is the continued influence of the view that factual and moral judgments are radically different sorts of things, with the concept of "truth" more easily explained and applied in the former case than in the latter. Moreover, even those who accept that truth has meaning in ethics often insist on maintaining a divide between facts and values that can be crossed, if at all, only very cautiously. It is not that facts are irrelevant in the construction of a true moral theory. A true moral theory must be a theory about how *humans* should act in *this* world; it is not a theory for super-beings in a science fiction setting. Moral theory must accordingly be based on intelligent judgments about facts: facts about what people are like and what the world they confront is like.[2] This much, it seems, any good moral philosopher will concede. What is difficult to concede is that facts *about other people's moral views* have any bearing as such on moral truth. Another person's morals, society's morals, law's morals – all three are examples of conventional or individual norms that have no necessary connection with true norms: Conventional norms are simply another kind of fact that true moral theory must evaluate.

For most objective moral theories, this view about the lack of connection between convention and truth functions almost like an axiom whose strength is hard to overestimate. The autonomous individual may be well advised to listen to others in developing his or her own moral views; but in the final analysis, autonomy requires individuals to make their own judgments about the merits of opposing views and about the correct action to take. No religious, legal, or social system has any legitimate claim (as opposed to causal influence) on one's allegiance except as one's independent, mature judgment determines.

It is this "principle of autonomy," as it is sometimes called, that seems often to present an insurmountable obstacle to attempts to justify deferring to the normative views of others. If deference requires, as I shall argue it does, acceding to the views of others even when one's own personal judgment is that the recommended action is wrong, how could deference ever be consistent with autonomy? In traditional discussions of political obligation, this alleged conflict between autonomy and authority is famously illustrated by Robert Paul Wolff's claim that "for the autonomous person there is no such thing as a command."

---

[2] It is this connection with the facts of the natural world that makes it hard sometimes to know how natural law moral theories are any different in the end from any other objective theory of ethics. See Philip Soper, "Some Natural Confusions about Natural Law," *Mich. L. Rev.* 90 (1992): 2393. See also William K. Frankena, "On Defining and Defending Natural Law," in *Law and Philosophy*, ed. Sidney Hook (New York: New York Univ. Press, 1964), 200.

If one decides, for example, to follow the orders of the captain of a sinking ship who is directing the manning of lifeboats, one is not acknowledging the captain's authority, but simply making one's own autonomous judgment about the best course of action under the circumstances:

[I]nsofar as I make such a decision, I am not obeying his command; that is, I am not acknowledging him as having authority over me. I would make the same decision, for exactly the same reasons, if one of the passengers had started to issue "orders" and had, in the confusion, come to be obeyed.[3]

This study concedes the principle of autonomy as a claim about the necessity for individual judgment in deciding how to act. But that concession does not entail the conclusion that deference to the views of others can never be justified. The principle of autonomy is open to two interpretations: One is harmless; the other is false or, at best, unproven. The harmless interpretation is simply the truism that autonomous individuals must, in the end, make judgments for themselves – including judgments about the circumstances in which authority is legitimate. Individual views about the foundations of morality and the ethical life are necessarily *individual* views, personally developed and rationally defended against the contrary views of everyone else. Where starting points are thought to be inevitable, as they always are in moral theory, that thought too is presented as a matter for others to share and acknowledge. There are, in short, no givens in ethics, no prescriptions about what one should do that are immune from the critical examination of individual reason.

One can, however, interpret the principle of autonomy in a second way: as a substantive claim that extends beyond the truism that autonomous individuals think for themselves. The substantive claim, under this interpretation, is a denial that deference *could* ever be justified for an autonomous individual. But this claim, if it is to be more than an unproven assertion, requires for its defense a confrontation with the arguments within political theory aimed at demonstrating that rational individuals do, sometimes, have reason to defer to the views of others, including the state, in deciding what to do. The major point of this study is to explore and describe circumstances in which individuals have just such reasons for deference – even if the views to which they defer are wrong. To the extent that the study succeeds, the principle of autonomy will remain untouched and the claim that the principle is inconsistent with deference will be proved false: Reasons for deference will be reasons that any autonomous individual should acknowledge.[4]

---

[3] R. P. Wolff, *In Defense of Anarchism* (New York: Harper & Row, 1970), 14.

[4] I follow here a treatment of the problem of autonomy similar to that found in Josepn Raz, *The Authority of Law: Essays on Law and Morality* (Oxford: Clarendon Press, 1979), 25–7. See also Tom Campbell, "Obligation: Societal, Political, and Legal," in *On Political Obligation*, ed. Paul Harris (London: Routledge, 1990), 120, 146–7.

Deference: An Overview

The Practice of Deference

Before examining possible reasons for deference, it may be helpful first to note some examples of the practice. Several familiar features of our moral life point to a more complicated picture of the relationship between convention and truth than is admitted by the view that "true morals" are necessarily independent of conventional norms. These features suggest that deference to the views of others does in fact occur in a variety of contexts, including the context of political authority, in ways that help motivate a study designed to understand whether such deference can be defended. I shall introduce these examples of deference (1) by considering the connection between law's morals and true morals; (2) by considering the connection between society's morals and true morals; and (3) by considering the dependence of a true moral theory itself on the morals of others.

LAW'S MORALS: THE PROBLEM OF COMPETING NORMATIVE SYSTEMS. Current attitudes toward law display two features that strongly suggest that many people believe, rightly or wrongly, that there are reasons to defer to political authority. First, as noted earlier, the currently popular view about law's morals is that legal systems make strong normative claims for their directives: Law prescribes conduct without any apparent concern for individual evaluation of the merits of its prescriptions. If this view about the nature of law is correct, it would be natural to assume that the legal claim coincides with background social understandings: Why would we continue to accept a concept of law that commits law to claiming authority if, in fact, we do not believe such a claim is defensible as a matter of political theory? Second, even the most conscientious person, committed to the necessity of autonomous judgment in deciding what to do, exhibits in practice a tendency to accept the law's particular set of prescribed norms without serious objection. Each of these features provides an occasion for reexamining the possible connection between conventional (legal) norms and true norms and for considering what reasons might justify deference to law. The first feature states a descriptive or conceptual claim about law's morals; the second feature represents an empirical claim about the way most people respond to law's morals – a claim about society's morals, as reflected in commonplace attitudes toward law. Both features, but particularly the first, will be examined more closely in the course of this study. For now, I want only to describe these two features as vividly as possible in order to show that there is here, in the phenomenology of the ordinary confrontation with law, an unresolved problem – a problem that would be solved if there are in fact reasons to defer to law.

The descriptive or conceptual claim is that the legal system – any legal system – purports to deny exactly what I have suggested the principle of autonomy assumes: the relevance of individual evaluation to the validity of its norms. Much of this book is about the problems created for moral theory in trying to reconcile this alleged posture of the law with the principle of autonomy. We have already seen that in some ways this conflict has a familiar ring – how to reconcile authority and autonomy. But it is important to understand how this old, familiar issue of political theory differs from the contemporary problem that arises when one views law and morality as apparently competing normative systems. The "old, familiar issue," as usually treated, turns into just another occasion for the moral philosopher to determine whether and on what grounds the demands of law are justified. The contemporary problem is more complex than, though related to, this traditional issue: The current clash is not just a clash of content between what is prescribed by one putative normative system (law) and what is validated by the "true" methods of moral philosophy. The clash is between what appear to be two entirely different theories of morality, two views about the role of individual evaluation in the determination of what one ought to do. In order to demonstrate how this clash differs from ordinary disputes within morality or political theory, it may be helpful to review briefly the stages that led to the current situation in legal theory.

The first stage in legal theory embraced the view that law is not a system of norms at all, but a system of directives enforced by coercive sanctions. As previously noted, this view is no longer as popular as it once was. But the view illustrates one way of avoiding the apparent inconsistency of living within competing normative systems. Any moral theory must deal with the obstacles that the natural world poses to the achievement of one's aims. Rivers and mountains can impede travel, but so can hostile people. The view that law is just such a set of hostile threats renders its directives no different from other such natural obstacles that sensible persons must take into account in deciding what to do. Moreover, it is not just the actively hostile whose reactions must be considered; one must also consider the reaction of all those who accept or acquiesce in the law's demands and adjust one's own conduct accordingly. (Whatever one thinks about the authority of law, one has reason to stop on red and go on green just because there is a law to that effect that one knows others are likely to observe.[5])

This view of law as mere force or constraining obstacle avoids the conflict between law and morality and restores the autonomous individual's prerogative

---

[5] See Donald Regan, "Law's Halo," *Soc. Phil. Policy* 4 (1986): 15, 16. The contribution of law to solving such coordination problems is often noted. The contemporary discussion focuses on whether this contribution depends on recognizing the law's authority or is simply a result of law's providing a salient point that permits others to achieve coordination. The latter view (law simply provides salience) allows one to deny law's authority even in these apparently paradigmatic cases of coordination; the former view (law coordinates only because its authority is recognized and real) acknowledges the authority of law in coordination cases but not, apparently, in the many other cases where law also seems to claim authority. For further discussion, see Chapters 2 and 3.

to decide for himself how to act in the face of law's threats. But it does so only by ignoring persuasive arguments, developed during the second stage of modern legal theory, concerning the appropriate descriptive or conceptual account of law. Law makes moral claims – ordinary moral claims, at least – about its right to coerce. The hostile reactions encountered in law are not like the threats of a primitive tribe encountered in the jungle; they are reactions from one's own community, one's own neighbors, and they are reactions that presumably take place in a community that acknowledges that one cannot normally jail, fine, or otherwise invade significant interests of others without moral justification. It is this apparently moral nature of the claims made by legal systems that has led so many modern legal theorists in this second stage of development to reject the view that law is nothing but force.

Conceding that law makes moral claims, the legal theorist's next logical step would be to view law's claims like any other moral claim. The fact that two individuals disagree about what morality requires does not show that they operate within competing normative systems: It shows only that they are involved in an ordinary case of moral disagreement of the sort that sets the process of moral inquiry in motion. So too with law's claims: Those claims are conventional facts and represent, at most, a moral claim whose truth is to be established by moral theory.

This transformation of the legal claim into just another moral claim to be evaluated like any other would be unproblematic, consistent both with the principle of autonomy and with a continued denial of the existence of reasons to defer to the state. But a third stage of legal theory has recently added a striking additional feature to the descriptive account of law's morals. Law, we are told, does not simply claim that the content of its prescriptions is morally justified; law makes what I have labeled the strong moral claim, associated with the idea of authority: The actions it prescribes are morally obligatory just because the law so declares. Law, in short, makes precisely the claim about its ability to create moral obligations just in virtue of its existence whose truth moral philosophers debate, question, and regularly deny.[6]

At this point, the conflict between the alleged claims of law and the "true" claims of morality becomes problematic. If law made only ordinary moral claims about the contents of its norms, we would be faced with an ordinary case of deciding whether those claims were correct by reference to one's own autonomous moral views. But if law makes the claim that its norms obligate just in virtue of their existence, one is now confronted with an issue of political theory. The conflict will still be, on one level, just another ordinary case of moral disagreement, though the disagreement now is not about the content of

---

[6] I am repeating here a commonly accepted view about law – that it claims authority in the sense described here, even though that claim is not justified in many cases. As will become evident, I do not think that this is a correct view of law's claims.

any particular legal norm, but about the general ability of legal norms to obligate independent of content. But the evidence for the view that law makes a strong claim of authority is not easily confined to a dispute *within* political theory. The dispute quickly threatens to become a dispute *about* political theory – a dispute about who has the final say on this question of authority within political theory. Presumably, the evidence for law's strong claim is the fact that the law imposes sanctions and enforces its norms regardless of individual views about whether the content of its norms is justified. On the basis of this evidence, one concludes that law must be making a strong claim of authority, not just an ordinary claim about the content of its norms. But by reference to this same evidence, the law's claim appears even stronger. For whatever moral philosophers conclude about the question of political obligation, the law continues to impose sanctions and enforce its decrees, apparently in the continued belief that its decrees obligate just in virtue of their existence. The law, in short, by the same evidence that shows it claims the authority to enforce its norms independent of content, would also seem to be claiming the right to enforce its norms independent of political theory. If law claims to generate obligations that are content independent, then by the same token it also seems to be claiming that those obligations are political theory independent.

Putting the point this way brings out, I hope, the sense in which law and morality seem to confront each other according to these standard current views as distinct normative systems, resting on fundamental differences about the role of individual evaluation in determining what to do. One problem with this view of law's morals is its paradoxical quality. To suggest that law claims that its norms obligate, regardless of what political theory has to say about the matter, cannot be done: It only leads to the question of how such an assertion of legal authority could be justified if not through political theory. To undertake any justification is to embark on political theory. To undertake no justification makes the assertion arbitrary and no more than an exercise of pure power.

One possible conclusion from this discussion is that the autonomous individual should insist that law's strong moral claims be justified by political theory. Of course, there is another possibility. It may be that modern legal theory is mistaken in describing law as making strong rather than ordinary moral claims. If that is so, we would no longer face a conflict between apparently competing normative systems. If law claims only the right to coerce, without necessarily claiming a correlative duty to obey, then the question of whether law obligates just in virtue of its existence will remain a question of ordinary political theory for the individual or moral philosopher to evaluate. However that issue is resolved, no conflict with the claims of law will result. Law's morals and society's morals will coincide.

The point to be emphasized is that one of these resolutions – a revision of currently popular political theory to make it coincide with law's strong claim or a revision of current legal theory to reduce law's claims to the status of ordinary moral claims – is essential in order to avoid the unhappy stalemate of apparently competing normative systems. That such a stalemate is an unhappy one from the point of view of both legal and moral theory should be clear. Legal and moral points of view are not developed in isolation as if each view were unaware of the other. Philosophers may not often become kings or judges, but they can surely consider what they would do if they did occupy such roles and what principles they would implicitly be endorsing whenever they sent people to prison on the sole ground that they had violated specified laws – laws whose merits they never stop to consider in carrying out their judicial role. Conversely, judges should and presumably do accept the principle of autonomy in their personal lives, recognizing (and teaching their children, no doubt) the value and necessity of exercising individual judgment in determining what to do. The competing normative systems of law and morality, in short, present the classical problem of consistency in thought that should motivate attempts to seek reconciliation from both sides.

SOCIETY'S MORALS: CONNECTIONS BETWEEN CONVENTION AND TRUTH. Put aside for the moment the problems that arise from contemporary descriptions of law's morals and consider the second feature that characterizes current attitudes toward law – the empirical claim about how most people react to law's norms. I said that most people do not seem to object strongly to finding themselves in a system that purports to prescribe actions without regard for individual evaluation of the merits of such action. The truth of this claim can be partially assessed by contrasting the ordinary person's reaction to law with the likely reaction to any other normative system that purported in similar fashion to preempt individual reason in determining what to do.

Imagine that you have been raised in a nonlegal normative system, say a religion, that you have now begun critically to question. You also accept the principle of autonomy concerning the role of individual judgment in determining what to do. You have read enough works on ethics to have a set of favorite moral philosophers and a rough general theory that you use to evaluate the more serious demands that are made on you by your religion. As you compare the demands of your religion with the ethical prescriptions supported by your own moral theory, you begin to find examples of divergence, some serious, some not so serious, between what you think, morally, you should do and what your religion tells you to do. Sometimes you are able to reconcile this conflict because your own moral theory justifies deferring to religious norms on occasion even when they diverge, on the surface, from what morality seems to require; that is to say, your initial moral evaluation of some action is adjusted by a deeper moral theory that explains why occasional deference to a competing religious norm is permissible or required. Where this possibility of reconciliation does not exist, you ignore the religious norm. Where it does, you continue to have a place, it seems, for both your moral theory and your religion. On reflection, however, you realize that you no longer share the same basic attitude toward these religious norms as do others around you. In particular, others (believers) do not think, whereas you do, that the validity of the religious norms and their priority over conflicting prescriptions depends on your moral theory. The role left to religion in your life is simply due to the place assigned to it within your moral theory; it no longer operates for you as the normative foundation for prescribing action in the way that it does for everybody else. Whether or not you leave the church, you no longer, it seems, accept its authority. Suppose, finally, that as a result of finding yourself in such a fundamentally different position from other believers, you decide to leave the church but discover you can't. The church, that is, continues to impose its norms on all persons within a certain territory, punishing those who transgress whether or not they are believers. Escaping the church's power is possible only by leaving the country, and that is not an easy thing to do even if you were inclined to uproot your family and leave your friends, community, job, and all the rest.

I present this patently transparent analogy between a religion and a state not to aid or evade analysis, but to support the empirical claim about the inconsistency between the presently popular view that legal systems do not have authority and what I take to be the general practice of most people. What would be the ordinary reaction to a system that imposed and enforced its norms on one with no possibility of opting out in the manner of the religion just described? "Righteous indignation" or anger are not implausible suggestions for answers to that question, even if in many cases the inability to alter the situation might lead to quiet resignation or despair. Indeed, it is precisely because of the power of the principle of autonomy in the lives of all of us that normative systems like religions are typically voluntary associations, with entry and exit determined by each person on the basis of his or her own values and reason. Why, then, do so few people react with the same sense of moral affront when faced with the demands of the law?

The claim that few people do react to law in the way one would expect, *if one assumes that law claims more authority than it has*, is, as I said, an empirical claim. No doubt, there are some (maybe most ordinary people) who have no reason to be offended by law's moral stance because they believe law's claims are justified. Such people implicitly accept a political theory that endorses law's claimed authority in the same way that many people accept, after reflection, religious authority. People in this category, who believe law's strong claims are justified, will not be test cases for the empirical claim.[7]

---

[7] That most people believe that there is an obligation to obey the law (which would mean that a strong moral claim of authority by the law would be legitimate) is a proposition that is often acknowledged even by those theorists who do not share the belief and who argue against political obligation. See, e.g., Raz, *The Authority of Law*, 235 ("most people believe themselves to be under such an obligation"); A. John Simmons, *Moral Principles and Political Obligations* (Princeton, N.J.: Princeton Univ. Press, 1979) ("many people feel, I think, that they are tied in a special way to their government, not just by 'bonds of affection,' but by *moral* bonds"); M. B. E. Smith, "Is There

Even the most law-abiding citizen, however, may on occasion strongly disagree with particular legal norms, as the history of civil disobedience attests. This latter class of people – those who disagree on occasion with (and are willing to disobey) particular laws – *are* potential tests of the empirical claim.[8] Such persons are similar to those whose religion just coincidentally happens to prescribe norms that, most of the time, coincide with norms one accepts as valid on independent moral grounds. Such persons do not necessarily accept law's authority if they do not also accept law's claim about its right to impose its decision about what to do on each individual. The conflict between law and morality when law is viewed as making strong moral claims is a conflict of method, not results: a conflict about how to determine what to do. Even if both methods concur most of the time in their substantive recommendations, one ought to resent the idea that one method purports to make and enforce its recommendation without regard for individual evaluation. Preserving one's outrage only for cases of strong substantive disagreement ignores the underlying reason for the conflict and allows the particular disagreement to obscure the more fundamental one about how to determine what to do in the first place. (An imposed religion would not be any less outrageous just because it happened, by and large, to prescribe conduct one would have thought obligatory or appropriate in any event.)

But the best test cases for the empirical claim are those who, after due reflection, conclude as a matter of their own considered political theory that

---

a Prima Facie Obligation to Obey the Law?" *Yale L. J.* 82 (1973): 975 ("I am not contending that reflective and conscientious citizens would, if asked, deny that there is a prima facie obligation to obey the law. Indeed, I am willing to concede that many more would affirm its existence than deny it" [But see the preface, footnote 5, noting Smith's suggestion in the same article that, released from "conventional views," the reflective man would likely doubt the existence of any such obligation]). Theorists more sympathetic to the existence of political obligation also assume that the "average person in the Western world accepts that one has a general moral obligation to obey the law...." George C. Christie, "On the Moral Obligation to Obey the Law," *Duke L. J.* 1990: 1311, 1312. See also id., 1336 ("Given the failure of [current arguments against political obligation] I am forced to conclude that if ordinary people believe that there is a moral obligation to obey the law, who is to say that they are wrong?"); George Klosko, *The Principle of Fairness and Political Obligation* (Lanham, Md.: Rowman & Littlefield, 1992), 68 ("I take it as intuitively obvious that most individuals believe they have political obligations ... and that their governments are legitimate").

[8] People who disobey laws that they think are misguided or unjust may do so either (1) because they think their prima facie obligation to obey the law is outweighed in a particular case by a greater duty or (2) because they think there is no obligation to obey law qua law, so they may (must) act as conscience guides with only the sanction (no countervailing moral duty) to worry about. This study defends the first explanation for civil disobedience (almost no philosopher suggests that the obligation to obey the law could be absolute). But note that the law as it is currently pictured by modern legal theorists does not make this distinction between prima facie and absolute obligation. Those who think law claims authority describe the claim as absolute, leaving no room for individual weighing of competing moral duties. Under this description, every act of civil disobedience is always in defiance of the law's claim, which should at least prompt some concern about the divergence between individual and social norms, on the one hand, and law's morals, on the other.

law has no intrinsic power to create a moral obligation to obey. This group, which includes the increasing number of contemporary political theorists who deny that there is any prima facie obligation to obey the law,[9] seldom exhibit in practice, I suspect, what the logic of their position seems to require. Most, I suspect, continue to obey most laws – even those they think are misguided or unjust.[10] And even if they don't have moral qualms when they do disobey particular laws, they probably accept the resulting fine or sanction, if caught and punished, with some grace. Of course, there are many explanations for such conduct that would be consistent with continued rejection of legal authority – just as there would be in cases of continued compliance with, or resigned submission to, a religion one could not escape. But possible rationalization is not the point: The point is the absence of the feeling of outrage that often is a better guide to an internalized moral theory than abstract discussions on the printed page.

The empirical question is, of course, for each individual who does not accept law's claims of authority to decide for herself. Only introspection will determine how one reacts to law's stance and whether that reaction is consistent with one's understanding of what is required by autonomy. Objections to the empirical claim are easy to imagine. It might be thought, for example, that the analogy between law and an imposed religion (which is intended to give the claim some

---

[9] In a recent work, Leslie Green suggests that this position, if not exactly an emerging consensus, is "shall we say, a significant coalescence of opinion." Green, "Who Believes in Political Obligation," in *For and Against the State*, eds. John T. Sanders and Jan Narveson (Lanham, Md.: Rowman & Littlefield, 1996), 1. Green is also one of the few philosophers in this emerging group who challenge the claim that most ordinary people, in contrast to the philosophers, believe that there is an obligation to obey (see footnote 7). For the most part, Green's challenge consists in raising doubts about how one would go about proving what is, after all, an empirical claim. He considers inconclusive, for example, a recent study that seems to bear out the claim about the ordinary person's view because some of the questions asked in the study (e.g., "Should people obey the law even if it goes against what they think is right?" [82% agreement]) fail to eliminate the possibility that people obey for prudential reasons rather than out of a sense of political obligation; other questions asked in the study are open to related objections. See id., 10–14 (reviewing the empirical study by Tom R. Tyler, *Why People Obey the Law* [New Haven, Conn.: Yale Univ. Press, 1990]). The upshot, for Green, is that the question of what most ordinary people think remains an open one. I have elsewhere suggested that one way to test the empirical question is to use a variation on a question suggested (for a different purpose) by M. B. E. Smith: Knowing that someone has broken a law, but not knowing what kind of law, would you say that the lawbreaker should at least come forth with a justification for what he did? See Philip Soper, "The Moral Value of Law," *Mich. L. Rev.* 84 (1985): 63, 68–9.

[10] It may be true that one can "find people of impeccable character who break the law and see nothing morally objectionable in so doing." J. W. Harris, *Legal Philosophies* (London: Butterworths, 1980), 209. But this commonplace fact, if it is one, is ambiguous evidence for the empirical question of whether people generally believe there is a prima facie obligation to obey laws. Such a belief, after all, is still consistent with disobeying the law whenever the prima facie obligation is outweighed by other considerations. (This ambiguity in inferring attitudes about the obligation to obey law from the mere fact of disobedience is avoided by the test described in footnote 9.) I return to this issue of the strength of the obligation to obey and how it might be overcome in the final chapter.

plausibility) is misleading or false, and that deference to the law – willing deference, not just grudging submission – is consistent with autonomy in a way that forced submission to a religion is not. Moreover, submission to law, even by those who do not acknowledge its authority, need not result simply from fear of punishment or weakness of will; the motive for submission could stem from more virtuous-sounding ambitions – the desire, for example, to express one's solidarity with a group regardless of the group's misguided claims of authority.[11] These various explanations for the empirical behavior are, no doubt, only a few of those that can be imagined and even defended as normatively appropriate. My main purpose in making the empirical claim is not to deny the possibility of such explanations but to provoke those for whom the claim rings true to think about why that is so. Is the analogy with religion inapt? Would a proper understanding of the basis for deferring to state authority show that autonomy is in fact consistent with routine submission to law in a way that it would not be in the case of an imposed religion?

TRUE MORALS: CONNECTIONS BETWEEN FACT AND VALUE. It might be thought that the empirical claim about society's tendency to defer to law, even if true, proves little about which perspective – society's or the skeptical philosopher's – is correct. But the empirical claim is not unrelated to this question. As I will explain more fully, there is at least one connection between description and prescription in moral theory that only the most self-confident moral philosopher would deny: Social behavior that remains impervious to moral criticism must raise doubts about the moral theory as much as it raises doubts about the integrity of the persons whose behavior is criticized. If most people do submit to law in ways that seem inconsistent with the contemporary philosopher's claim that law does not have authority, it is possible that the moral theory that underlies the philosopher's claim is not the morality of most people – and hence is not an adequate account of *our* moral life. In that case, it is moral theory that should adjust its conclusions to correspond more closely with observed behavior.

---

[11] This position appears to be that of Joseph Raz, who argues that one may *choose* to respect and obey the law as a means of expressing one's identification with one's community but that one has no *obligation* to do so. See Raz, *The Morality of Freedom*, 88–105. One should not confuse the point made in the text (about the peculiar combination of attitudes involved in believing that states claim authority they do not have) with the different (but related) question of whether one who simply denies that states have authority is necessarily committed to disobeying all laws or seeking the state's destruction. Those who deny that the state has authority will still have general moral reasons for action, some of which will often require compliance with the law. See A. John Simmons, "Philosophical Anarchism," in *For and Against the State*, 19. The questions that the "philosophical anarchist" needs to address are: (1) why should one accept living in a state that claims authority it doesn't have (i.e., why not at least demote the state's claims, even if one continues to tolerate its existence)? and (2) does rejecting the legitimacy of the state mean that one rejects the state's right to coerce or just the idea that such coercion creates a duty to obey? I return to these questions in Chapter 7.

The general question of what connections, if any, there are between accepted norms and true norms arises only because the principle of autonomy seems to require maintaining a sharp divide between convention and truth. There are many ways, of course, to challenge this divide. Those skeptical of the whole idea of moral truth will explain that conventional norms are as far as one can ever go in justifying or defending moral statements, thus eliminating the distinction between fact and value altogether by translating moral claims into factual ones. I do not tackle this large issue in this brief study. My goal is the more limited one of defending a partial theory of ethics for those who do accept as meaningful the idea of moral truth. The claim I shall defend is, roughly, that even a true moral theory must make more room than is commonly acknowledged for the moral relevance of the ethical views of others – even if those views are wrong.

The clearest example of a connection between convention and truth is what might be called the "evidentiary" connection, illustrated by remarks in the preceding paragraphs. When people fail to behave as moral theory says they should, one possible conclusion is that they are acting immorally. Another possible conclusion is that the moral theory that condemns the behavior is mistaken. Choosing between these alternatives requires comparing one's confidence in the correctness of one's moral theory with one's sensitivity to the fact that nonconforming behavior by others, at least where it is widespread, may be evidence that one's moral theory is wrong. This simple evidentiary point, rather than some more complex "fusion of fact and value," is all that is needed in order to defend at least one link between description and evaluation. Just as moral intuitions are relevant "facts" to consider in the development of basic moral principles,[12] so too with the facts of human behavior: Social practices that fail to conform to moral theory represent occasions either for applying the theory (thus condemning and trying to change the behavior) or for reconsidering the theory.[13]

Admitting an evidentiary connection between convention and truth is easy. The connection, after all, is simply a reminder that the difficulty of knowing what is true in morals makes the contrary views of others relevant as reasons for perhaps reconsidering one's own views. The evidentiary connection also leaves the principle of autonomy intact: The contrary views of others may make one more tentative about one's own conclusions, but those conclusions will in the end remain the operative determinants of what one should do, however much

---

[12] See John Rawls, *A Theory of Justice* (Cambridge, Mass.: Harvard Univ. Press, 1971), 48–53 (on "reflective equilibrium").

[13] For further discussion, see Philip Soper, "Law's Normative Claims," in *The Autonomy of Law: Essays on Legal Positivism*, ed. R. George (Oxford: Clarendon Press, 1996), 216. What I call here the "evidentiary" connection between practice and theory is not a theory of truth so much as a theory about the evidence that bears on truth. It is possible to make stronger claims about the relation between practice and theory, leading to a "coherence" theory of truth. For criticisms of such a stronger approach in this context, see "Who Believes in Political Obligation," Green, 2–5.

they differ from the opinions of others. Listening to others is one thing; but once one has concluded, on reflection, that others are wrong, autonomy, it seems, still requires acting on one's own views. There is a second connection, however, between the views of others and conclusions about what one ought to do that is more direct than the evidentiary connection. Sometimes, morality itself may require one to defer to another, even though one (correctly) believes the other to be wrong. Where this is the case, one can continue to embrace the principle of autonomy, but only by recognizing that the question of what one ought to do in the final analysis (the ultimate "moral truth") often involves a compromise between competing intermediate moral claims. We are familiar with this problem in the case of competing moral goods: A persistent strand in moral philosophy explains that one must sometimes balance the prima facie moral value of (for example) keeping one's promise against the prima facie value of protecting innocent life. If, in the end, we act in a way that would normally be immoral (by breaking our promise, for example), we nevertheless act correctly if the balance between these prima facie moral requirements has been correctly determined. The question is whether a similar moral weighing is justified where the choice is not between competing moral *goods*, but between competing moral *views* – your own and one that you believe to be (and, by hypothesis, *is*) morally wrong.

In some contexts, an affirmative answer to this question seems plausible, perhaps because we can translate the issue into the previous one of competing goods. Friendship provides the most obvious example. Persons in a close relationship may sometimes conclude that one ought to defer to the opinion of one's partner even though that partner's opinion is morally wrong. Such examples seem acceptable illustrations of the possibility that moral truth may sometimes require action in accordance with the (erroneous) moral views of another because we can recast this example as a case of competing moral goods: We weigh the prima facie value of maintaining the relationship against the prima facie dis-value of acting incorrectly and discover that sometimes the correct action (in the ultimate sense) requires a compromise of our own (correct) views about what to do.[14]

The purpose of this study is to suggest that this feature of our moral life, illustrated by the example of friendship, is far more widespread than is commonly recognized. I shall suggest that the moral views of others about what to do count, in the sense just described, in ways that explain a variety of puzzling moral problems, including the problem of why and how much promises

---

[14] For an economic model of the situation as it applies more generally, not just in personal relationships, see Robert E. Goodin and Geoffrey Brennan, "Bargaining Over Beliefs," *Ethics* 111 (2001): 256, 257 ("[Sometimes] disputes over beliefs get 'resolved' through negotiation rather than persuasion. Each still believes the truth of the proposition she was originally advocating, but each sees the need to 'get on with it,' so all agree to treat certain propositions 'as if true,' for the particular purposes at hand").

obligate, the problem of explaining the basis for the obligation of fair play, and the problem of justifying legal authority. It is no coincidence that the primary examples I shall use to illustrate the ethics of deference are precisely those that have long been the major theoretical paradigms for establishing political authority. Classical political theory attempts to explain law's authority by invoking notions of consent and fair play. Most contemporary philosophers conclude that these attempts fail. It may be, however, that they fail because they begin at the wrong end. It may be that we should not try to explain political authority by reference to consent or fair play because the explanation for why promises bind or when obligations of fair play arise is itself dependent on political theory. It may be that when we understand the circumstances under which deference to the views of others is morally required, we will better understand some of the puzzles of promise, fair play, and the like.

The Concept of Deference: Form and Substance

How do reasons for deference compare to other reasons for action? How do they interact with other reasons to justify action that would otherwise, in their absence, be wrong? These are questions about the form or structure of deference. In addition to questions about form, one can also ask questions about substance: What kinds of reasons could justify action that would otherwise be wrong? In this section I offer a preliminary exploration of both kinds of questions by using the example of personal relationships mentioned in the preceding section. By considering how deference works in this context, one in which the concept is likely to be most intuitive and familiar, I hope to lay the groundwork for extending the analysis in later chapters to more controversial contexts, including that of political authority.

FORM. Consider the following cases. You are asked for money by (1) a stranger; (2) a neighbor who wants the money (a) to help him through a temporary setback; (b) to help him buy a luxury vehicle; (3) a friend, who does not explain why he wants the money. Does the request for money in each of these cases provide any reason at all for you to act as requested? One standard suggestion is that requests provide "content-independent" reasons for action, which are to be weighed along with the ordinary "content-dependent" reasons one may have for the action. Thus, in each of the preceding cases, if one decides not to give the money, the person requesting aid may be disappointed, but will understand that the request was considered and weighed along with other reasons: The reasons for not giving the requested aid proved stronger, on balance, even after including the reason provided by the request. In contrast to a "request," which simply adds another reason to be considered in the balance of reasons, an "order" to give someone money would normally be presumptuous: Orders imply that the request is to be given some special priority or weight, more than the normal weight of a simple content-independent reason – enough additional weight to possibly preempt or outweigh all other reasons that bear on the decision. For a stranger, a neighbor, or even a friend to order me to give money implies a relationship of authority that is absent and thus makes the order, but not the request, presumptuous. Orders, to use our current terminology, assume that deference is appropriate or even required; requests, in contrast, make no assumption about whether deference is due but simply add another reason to the existing reasons bearing on the action.

This distinction between orders and requests is a plausible starting point for explaining how reasons for deference work, but it needs to be amended in two respects. First, not all requests are reasons for action; second, requests can also be presumptuous. Consider again the beggar who asks for alms. Even if one decides to grant the request, it does not follow that the beggar's request provided a *new* reason for action. The general obligation to help others can be met in various ways. One way is by making contributions to established charities; another way, given the immediacy of the beggar's present claim and the apparent ability immediately to satisfy that need, is through instant donation. The point is twofold: First, we would not say that if one gives the requested alms, one has "deferred" to the beggar; second, we can explain why this action is not a case of deference: Rather than deferring to another's view about what to do, one has simply acted on one's own preexisting assessment of the extent to which aiding others is morally appropriate, using the information provided by the beggar's request as the minor premise in a previously established general argument about when and how to aid those in need. We could make the same point in more mundane contexts. The request to "pass the salt" does not need to be seen as presenting one with a *new reason* to act (in order to please the person who made the request); it can also be seen as simply providing the information needed to act on preexisting reasons one already has for acting appropriately in certain social settings.[15]

Why make this distinction? Why does it matter whether a request provides a new reason for action or simply new information that triggers the application of preexisting reasons? One answer is that it helps to explain how requests can also be presumptuous. Consider again the neighbor who asks me to give him money to help him buy a luxury vehicle. Though the plea here is only a request, not an order, it is equally capable of being presumptuous. It presumes

---

[15] Raz suggests that it would be wrong to think of requests as "mere communication of information that the speaker . . . needs or wants something." He notes that one might deliberately avoid making a request while still providing another with information about one's needs, because "while one would be pleased if one's need moves the friend into action, one would be displeased if it takes a request to do so." Raz, *The Morality of Freedom*, 36. The discussion in the text is not necessarily in disagreement: *From the point of view of the person making the request,* Raz is persuasive that the request always is *intended* to constitute a new reason for action. The discussion in the text aims to show that *from the point of view of the person addressed,* a request may provide no reason to act at all and may even be presumptuous.

that I have background reasons to help my neighbors buy luxury items when, in fact, no such presumption is warranted (not for *this* neighbor, at any rate). It presumes, in short, a relationship that does not exist. I may be presumed to have background reasons for helping neighbors in temporary need (as I can be presumed to have background reasons for sometimes helping beggars asking for alms), but to ask me to help you buy a yacht or a luxury car is presumptuous. (Even if I accede to the request, one would hardly say that I am deferring to my neighbor's wishes: Perhaps, taken aback by the presumption, I act for reasons of my own bemusement or for reasons based on my own calculations of what I can demand in return.)

We can make the point even more vivid by imagining presumptuous requests in the case of serious normative disagreements. Assume that you believe your children should go to private school; your neighbor, who strongly believes in public schools, requests you to send your children to public school. Does your neighbor's request provide any reason at all for acting as requested? If you believe, for example, that the reasons are equally balanced between public and private school, should the neighbor's request have the power to tip the scales toward the public school choice? The answer, I assume, is no: The fact that it would please your neighbor to know that you have sent your children to public school is not a reason for action at all for you. One might support this conclusion by suggesting that there could be many other neighbors who might feel differently and "one can't please them all." But I am making a stronger claim: Even if all your neighbors were united in their views, pleasing them is not a reason for action because it is none of their business. Asking me to base a decision about my children on your preferences as my neighbor is presumptuous because it assumes, falsely, that the relationship of neighbor warrants making your desires relevant to a decision that is not yours to make. Advice one may welcome, but the expectation that I will take into account the mere fact that you would be pleased if I act as you request is out of place.

In none of these examples so far is it appropriate to talk of deference. I may give alms to the beggar, I may give aid to my neighbor in need, and I may give money to a friend without asking why he wants it. (Depending on the nature of the friendship, the friend's request for money, even to help him buy a luxury item, need not be presumptuous.) But even if I act as requested in these cases, I am not deferring to the wishes or views of another; I am simply acting on my own understanding of what the balance of reasons, in this context, supports.

Deference suggests that I am acting in some sense contrary to the way I would normally act if I simply considered the balance of reasons (including any new information supplied by your request) that bear on the action. Examples are easy to produce. At one extreme, one may have reasons to defer to another even in the case of serious normative disagreement. If one disagrees with one's spouse about whether to send one's children to private or public school, the disagreement is now clearly one in which the views of each spouse are relevant and must be taken into account. Each will have reasons to defer to the other's views – reasons we will describe more thoroughly in the next section – with the question of whose view should prevail to be resolved through some mutually acceptable procedure – a rough comparison, for example, of the relative strength of each spouse's convictions. At the other extreme are less serious examples in which the inconvenience is slight. You invite friends to dinner knowing that they are vegetarians. Your own view of what is appropriate in such a case is that you should be able to serve your friends a vegetarian meal while you and others eat steak. But out of deference to your friends, you decide that you will serve everyone a vegetarian meal. Even if you think it is "super-sensitive" of your vegetarian friends to be offended by others' eating meat in front of them, it seems plausible now to speak of deferring (against your own judgment of what is normatively appropriate) to the views of your friends. In this particular case, of course, one may suggest that deference is more a matter of courtesy or civility rather than a serious moral requirement. But the form of deference in the case of courtesy is the same as in more serious cases involving moral disputes: Deference is justified by reasons that outweigh or override the normal reasons that bear on the action taken.[16]

Reasons for deference, then, are at the very least reasons to be weighed along with the preexisting reasons that bear on the action under consideration. But reasons for deference are not simply to be equated with the content-independent reasons for action provided by a nonpresumptuous request. Our previous discussion shows that some requests provide no reason for action (and may be presumptuous), while others provide a content-independent reason. But even if the content-independent reason in a particular case proves decisive, one is not, in acting on it, necessarily deferring to the person making the request. Deference implies acting against one's normal view of what is required after balancing both kinds of reasons, content-independent (where they exist) and content-dependent. How, then, do reasons for deference arise, and how do they differ from straightforward content-independent reasons?

Consider again the example of one's vegetarian friends. In that case, we said, if one decides to serve an exclusively vegetarian meal, it seems appropriate to speak of deferring to one's friends' sensitivities about meat-eating. This conclusion is reinforced if one's friends' views are based on strongly held opinions about the immorality of killing and eating animals. But how is this case different from that of granting a friend's request for money, which, we said, does not seem like a case of deference? Both cases, we may assume, present one with content-independent reasons for action: That is, both requests provide not just relevant information about one's friends' interests, but also a reason to act in

---

[16] For recent discussions defending a connection between courtesy and morality, see Cheshire Calhoun, "The Virtue of Civility," *Phil. & Pub. Affairs* 29 (2000): 251; Sarah Buss, "Appearing Respectful: The Moral Significance of Manners," *Ethics* 109 (1999): 795.

order to accommodate a friend's (nonpresumptuous) expression of interest or need. The difference seems to be that in the case of one's vegetarian friends, by hypothesis, one's own normative judgment (prior to the decision to defer) is that serving meat for others at the dinner is entirely acceptable – even after taking into account the interest in pleasing one's friends. Though your friends have strong views about the immorality of killing and eating animals, you do not share those views and you also think that, even considering their interests, it should be acceptable to make both meat and vegetarian dishes available at the same meal. To defer despite all of this to one's friends suggests that one has given extra weight to the interests of one's friends – more than one thinks is normally appropriate or required. With a slight alteration, we could say the same about the example of giving money to a friend. Suppose that my own calculation is that, even taking my friend's wishes into account, I do not think it appropriate to give her the money – but I do it nonetheless. Now it seems natural to say that I deferred to her judgment about whether I should give her the money – against my own better judgment that, for example, it would do her no good, or wasn't really in her interest, or could be put to better use by me. Reasons for deference, in short, appear to influence decisions by assigning extra weight to the content-independent reason represented by the request: I make the interests of my friend more important than I normally would in deciding what to do.

Substance: The Reasons for Deference

Given the preceding account of how reasons for deference work, we now need an explanation for why one might assign increased weight to the views of one's friend. What reasons warrant making another's views more important than I actually think they are?

To answer this question, I shall use the example of spouses disagreeing about where to send their children to school to present a tentative list of plausible reasons for deference. First, reasons for deference may be either instrumental or intrinsic. Instrumental reasons are the easiest to illustrate and (in appropriate cases) the easiest to defend as normatively appropriate. When I disagree in a close relationship about a serious normative issue, I need to consider more than just the normal weight I would assign to the interest of my partner in having the disagreement resolved as he or she prefers. I must take into account not only my partner's disappointment if I do not defer, but also the potential impact on the relationship. These two factors represent theoretically distinct kinds of instrumental reasons, though in some cases they may amount to the same thing: Disappointed spouses may be able to contain their disappointment in ways that avoid adverse effects on the relationship, but the possibility of such effects, extending beyond the immediate disappointment, must be considered. Instrumental reasons, in short, are typically of two kinds: The first kind points to the *positive* impact on the person I confront and whose interests are partly captured by the notion of a content-independent reason; the second kind points to the *negative* impact on the relationship if I fail to defer. Assessing the weight of these reasons requires much more than just calculating how much the other person in the relationship would be pleased if I defer; it requires as well a sensitive understanding of the nature of the relationship that makes the other person's wishes a content-independent reason for action in the first place.

Intrinsic reasons are more difficult to describe and more controversial. In some contexts, as in the relationships we are currently considering, it may seem unnecessary to look for intrinsic reasons for deference because of the obvious availability of instrumental explanations. But the tendency to think that intrinsic reasons are either nonexistent or always capable of collapse into instrumental ones should be resisted. Consider again one's vegetarian friends. One *could* explain deferring to their super-sensitive judgment on instrumental grounds similar to those described earlier: It is, after all, no great inconvenience to make and eat an exclusively vegetarian meal, and doing so will both please one's friends and avoid possible negative repercussions on the friendship. But there is something incomplete about this explanation. What counts is not simply that one's friends may be pleased; it also matters how and by whom they are pleased. What counts is not simply that, like manna from heaven, utility is increased or more preferences are satisfied by my act. What counts is also the fact that it is *my* act, *my* decision to defer. That *I* do this is a signal about how I value my friends and the ideal of friendship. Indeed, the very fact that I am acting against my better judgment turns my act into a particularly poignant symbol of respect – both for my friend and for the value of friendship.[17]

Intrinsic reasons for deference are also of two kinds. "Objective" reasons exist when deference serves as a sign of respect for a relationship that is in fact valuable. In the previous example, if one assumes that friendship is the kind of relationship that, correctly understood, warrants showing respect by deferring to one's vegetarian friends, then one has intrinsic objective reasons to defer. What if, however, one disagrees about the value or the nature of friendship? The committed hermit might claim that friendships are pernicious and rob people of self-sufficiency and independence. A tough-minded sergeant might believe that friendships are desirable, but that they are best understood as requiring one not to defer to super-sensitive friends: More candor and less fawning, one might say, makes for better friendships in the long run. Assume that you disagree with both of these latter views: You believe that friendship is an objectively valuable good, and you also believe that a proper understanding of the ideal will show that deference is a sign of respect, not an example of

---

[17] The suggestion that what matters is not only what is done but also who does it bears an obvious resemblance to suggestions that agent-relative moralities are superior to, and not compatible with, consequentialist theories. For an overview see Samuel Scheffler, "Introduction," in *Consequentialism and Its Critics*, ed. Samuel Scheffler (Oxford: Oxford Univ. Press, 1988), 1–13.

weakness or of toadying or condescension. If you are correct, then you have, in appropriate cases, an intrinsic objective reason to defer. But what if you are wrong, and moral philosophy eventually "proves" that the hermit's view or the sergeant's is correct? In that case, you no longer have an objective reason to defer because, by hypothesis, your understanding of the ideal of friendship is flawed. But you still have what I shall call a "subjective" reason to defer: Since you sincerely (but wrongly) believe that deference is a sign of respect for the value of friendship in appropriate cases, failure to defer is inconsistent with your own values. Deferral in this case is required not because it is actually (objectively) required for the sake of the friend or the friendship or some other valuable good, but because it is required to show *self-respect*. Objective reasons show respect for others – for friends and for the relationship; subjective reasons show respect for oneself in acting consistently with one's own values, even if moral theory might, in some ultimate sense, show those values to be indefensible.

In sum, intrinsic reasons to defer justify acting "against the normal balance of reasons" either because (1) they are necessary ways of demonstrating the kind of respect that is, in fact, required by a correct understanding of the relationship or context or (2) they are necessary ways of avoiding the "moral hypocrisy" of acting inconsistently with one's own values. The claim that subjective reasons for deference are legitimate reasons for action is, of course, open to a variety of objections that I shall not consider here in detail. The most obvious objection is that some limit must be placed on the idea that consistency itself is a moral virtue and a reason for action. Thus, if one honestly believes that murder and torture are permissible, it is not likely that one deserves any moral credit for acting consistently with such clearly erroneous views. What counts here, one thinks, is not consistency but truth. But this easy dismissal of consistency as a moral virtue per se is not so easily accomplished when the views one holds reflect one side of a widely debated issue over which society itself is divided and which involves not harming another (as in the case of murder) but deciding about the nature and value of certain basic social relationships. Consider, for example, the question of political obligation. Suppose you believe that states are valuable entities and that a correct understanding of the nature of the state and the resulting relationship between citizen and state is one that justifies the state's expectation that you comply voluntarily with its legal norms. Suppose, however, that the anarchist, who denies the value of the state, is correct. In this case, you do not, in fact, have objective (intrinsic) reasons to defer to the state; but you still have, I shall argue, subjective reasons to defer. Being consistent with one's own values when it comes to showing respect for entities one believes valuable may be a moral requirement, even though one is wrong about the underlying value judgment. Unlike the murderer, who has no moral duty to be consistent in acting on a view that results in harm to others, showing respect (even where it is based on an erroneous underlying value judgment) is itself a way of advocating one's views about value. One does not harm others by acting consistently with one's underlying value judgment, even though that judgment is wrong; one harms oneself (and indirectly the process of arguing for and establishing value) by not practicing what one preaches.[18]

A Road Map

Legal Theory: Law's Morals

We are now in a position to describe the arguments to be developed in the chapters that follow. As indicated in the preface, the two parts of the present study correspond to the two issues, one an issue of legal theory, the other an issue of political theory, that are currently in tension in contemporary discussions of the nature of law. The tension results from the possibility that law's morals conflict with true morals. Law, we are told, claims a kind of authority that political theory denies it has. Part I, which begins with this introductory chapter, examines the first part of this tension: the nature of law's morals. This part continues in the next chapter by examining the concept of authority and explaining how that concept can be understood in terms of the preceding analysis of reasons for deference. Chapter 3 shows that law does not claim political authority. Chapter 4 puts together the conclusions of the two preceding chapters to present an image of law that I briefly defend in light of recent controversies about the nature of law in the debate between positivism and natural law.

Political Theory: The Ethics of Deference

Part I having concluded with an image of law's morals, Part II moves to the political theory half of the current controversy: Even if law does not claim authority, is it possible that law actually has authority – that citizens always have reasons (which may be overridden) to defer to legal norms? The route to an affirmative answer to this question proceeds indirectly. Instead of assuming that theories of promise and fair play should be the starting points for an inquiry into political obligation and then trying to see whether those paradigms can be applied to law, I examine the basis for the obligations of promise and fair play. Chapter 5 explains how certain persistent puzzles about promissory obligation can be understood in terms of the ethics of deference. Chapter 6 does the same

---

[18] This sketch of the argument for deferring to the state (an argument for the obligation to obey) is more fully developed in later chapters. For now, it is worth emphasizing that the argument here establishes only a prima facie reason for deference. Obedience to bad laws often *will* result in causing harm to others; in that case, one must weigh the harm caused to others against the intrinsic reasons for deference provided by the argument here. No parallel argument can be made for the murderer who believes that murder is good: He does not have even a prima facie subjective reason to act on his belief because there is here only one action to evaluate: the harm caused to victims. There is, in short, no broader relationship or context that could serve as the subject of respect for the murderer when he acts on his subjectively erroneous views.

for obligations of fair play. Chapter 7 extends the analysis of these two chapters to the problem of political obligation and defends the conclusion that one always has reason to defer to legal norms, even if that reason is sometimes outweighed in particular cases by countervailing concerns.

That the obligations of promise and law stand or fall together is, of course, not a new idea, and Hume's observation to that effect[19] is often noted. In this respect, the approach of the current study both resembles and differs from that of Hume. The study resembles Hume's in arguing that standard political theory mistakenly assumes that the moral force of promise can be taken as given, with consent serving as a kind of first principle for the evaluation of the authority of law. The study also endorses Hume's suggestion that the solution to both political and promissory obligation is to be found in principles that underlie and explain both kinds of obligation. But the study departs from Hume's in its conclusion about the nature of this deeper explanation and how it supports political obligation. The more general explanation for the force of promise that this study supports is not necessarily utilitarian: The reasons for deference to the promisee as well as to legal norms, I shall argue, are primarily intrinsic, not instrumental. Moreover, the deference-based explanation for the force of promise that I develop here is applied directly to law, without assuming that an intervening promise to obey is a condition of political obligation. In this respect, this study indirectly reverses the standard order of dependency between the explanations for the authority of laws and of promises. We are more likely to understand how consent itself works only by first understanding why deference to the views of others with whom we are connected might be required, even if those views are wrong. That problem is the classic problem of political obligation. Consent theory, in short, depends on political theory rather than vice versa.

Methodology

Disputes about the nature of law are notorious for fostering disputes about methodology, with the latter often upstaging the former. In recent discussions, these disputes in legal theory seem aimed at establishing the same general point: the impossibility of resolving underlying substantive arguments about the nature of law by reference to anything other than subjective or verbal criteria. In the same way that persistent disagreement about moral issues often leads to skepticism about the objectivity of moral judgments, continued disagreement about the nature of law seems to lead to claims that the entire dispute is meaningless. The best response to such skeptical claims probably lies in demonstrating, through studies such as this, that common practices often can be illuminated by considering and comparing competing descriptive, conceptual, and normative

---

[19] See Hume, "Of the Original Contract," in *David Hume's Political Essays*, ed. Charles Hendel (New York: Liberal Arts Press, 1953), 43, 55–6.

claims about such practices. In light of the recent resurgence of skepticism about these standard methods of analysis, however, a brief explanation and defense may be in order.

DESCRIPTIVE AND CONCEPTUAL CLAIMS. The move from confronting a social practice to understanding how it works begins with description – a simple listing of features that characterize the practice or that are commonly associated with it. This claim, that description is the starting point for analysis, will seem obvious to many; but the claim has been called into question recently by proponents of normative or "interpretive" theories eager to show that descriptive enterprises inevitably reflect the subjective, and thus arbitrary, interests of the theorist.[20] On its face, this assertion seems implausible. We are accustomed to describing things, ranging from our house to the structure of our government, in part because we want to draw attention to features of our house or our government that we do or do not like. It is because one can say "I approve/disapprove of this feature of (my house, my government)" that descriptive and evaluative enterprises appear distinct: Description does not entail endorsement of the object described.[21]

[20] See Stephen R. Perry, "Interpretation and Methodology in Legal Theory," in *Law and Interpretation*, ed. A. Marmor (Oxford: Clarendon Press, 1995), 112–21; id., "Hart's Methodological Positivism," *Legal Theory* 4 (1998): 427. See also Gerald Postema, "Jurisprudence as Practical Philosophy," *Legal Theory* 4 (1998): 329–58. (For a persuasive critique of Perry's and Postema's views and a defense of conceptual or descriptive/explanatory analysis, see Michael S. Moore, *Educating Oneself in Public* [Oxford: Oxford Univ. Press, 2000], 6–18.) The question of whether theories about the nature of law are objective, and in what sense, should not be confused with the question of whether particular legal decisions within a legal system have objective answers. The latter issue, raised largely in response to Dworkin's theory of adjudication, has now become the focus of an ever-burgeoning literature. For general discussions see, e.g., Kent Greenawalt, *Law and Objectivity* (New York: Oxford Univ. Press, 1992); Jules L. Coleman and Brian Leiter, "Determinacy, Objectivity and Authority," *Univ. Pa. L. Rev.* 142 (1993): 549. For two particularly insightful recent discussions, see Brian Leiter, "Objectivity, Morality, and Adjudication," in *Objectivity in Law and Morals*, ed. Brian Leiter (Cambridge: Cambridge Univ. Press, 2001), 66; and Gerald Postema, "Objectivity Fit for Law," in id., 99. I return briefly to this question of the objectivity of legal standards in Chapter 4. For the most part, however, the main theses in this study are independent of the debate about the objectivity of legal norms: The claims about law's authority that I consider are claims made even in the "easy case," where all but the most radical skeptic will concede that there is a determinate answer to the question of what a particular legal norm requires of its subjects.

[21] Sometimes the claim that description is necessarily normative confuses endorsement of the object described with two other respects in which the descriptive analyst may bring values to bear on his or her project. First, the motives for selecting a particular social phenomenon for study no doubt reflect the analyst's values in deciding what phenomena are worth investigating. Second, as noted in the text, description is often a prelude to making an evaluative claim about the object described. Both of these possible connections with normative judgments are consistent with the basic idea that description itself does not require appraisal of the object described. See Leslie Green, "The Concept of Law Revisited," *Mich. L. Rev.* 94 (1996): 1687, 1713 ("A description of something . . . is a selection of those facts that are taken to be for some purposes important, salient, relevant, interesting, and so on. This is not to say that a description is an appraisal of its object. . . ." [footnote omitted]).

I suspect that the attack on descriptive jurisprudence does not intend to deny this general possibility of separating description from evaluation, but insists that, at least when it comes to the case of law, nothing *interesting* can result from description alone. Description, if it is to be more than a simple listing of observed features of the world, must have a point; but the only point that emerges from disputes about the nature of law is a value judgment about the features or functions *important* to law. It is these claims of importance that are essentially normative and that cannot be resolved by closer inspection of the facts. In order to assess this claim, we need to consider more carefully just what the point of description might be.

In addition to serving as a prelude to evaluation, descriptive inquiries have often been preludes to three distinct, nonnormative claims about the object described. One may claim that the features described are *important* in the sense of illuminating how a particular social practice works[22]; one may also claim that the features are *essential* to the practice; finally, one may claim that the features are potentially inconsistent with other social practices, thus requiring one practice or the other to be modified in order to achieve coherence.[23] These three objectives of description are not mutually exclusive and may be pursued simultaneously within a single study.

In the study at hand, I shall not distinguish between the second and third goals of a descriptive enterprise, but shall view them as essentially similar attempts to establish *conceptual* claims about a practice or concept. In other words, to claim that a particular feature of an enterprise is essential to the concept means, for the purposes of this study, only that the feature is required in order to avoid inconsistency with other existing concepts or practices. The difference between claiming that a particular feature is important in understanding a concept and claiming that it is essential can be illustrated by considering the connection between laws and sanctions. To say that the organized sanction that backs the state's directives is an important feature of legal systems is to do no more than claim that the sanction significantly affects widely shared human interests. It

---

[22] See Brian Bix, "Conceptual Questions and Jurisprudence," *Legal Theory* 1 (1995): 465, 472 (suggesting that the goal of establishing what is important about a practice is one of the purposes of a conceptual claim).

[23] For further elaboration see Philip Soper, "Alternative Methodologies in Contemporary Jurisprudence: Comments on Dworkin," *J. Legal Educ.* 36 (1986): 488; see also Soper, "Legal Theory and the Problem of Definition," *Univ. Chic. L. Rev.* 50(1983): 1170, 1185–92. The goal of achieving coherence here between our concepts and our practices should be distinguished from a coherence theory of adjudication. The latter is a theory about how to find the law in particular cases. See, e.g., Ken Kress, "Why No Judge Should Be a Dworkinian Coherentist," *Texas L. Rev.* 77 (1999): 1375. As I make clear in this chapter, my goal here is to analyze the concept of law, an enterprise I view as distinct from a theory about how to find the law in particular cases, just as an analysis of the concept of "religion" is different from a theory about how to discover the precepts in a particular religion. Coherence as a methodology is simply the familiar philosophical attempt to reconcile apparently inconsistent or conflicting views in established social practices.

is a means of social control that stands out from other forms of social control because of its institutionalized and monopolistic character. Holmes' "bad man" aphorism makes the point: The bad man is, of course, not a *morally* bad man, but only a character who serves to remind us that, whatever other features of law might interest people, the potential sanction addresses a fundamental area of human concern (of course, for Holmes, it was also the only concern that was important in *identifying* the law). There is nothing in any of this to implicate the analyst's own values: A detached observer oblivious to sanctions could still note that this particular means of social control is important *for most people* who encounter legal systems – a report about others' values, not about the analyst's own. Suppose, now, that one says that the sanction is not just important but essential to the concept of law or legal system. This move to a conceptual claim about law may be controversial for two reasons. First, we might not know exactly what to say to the question of whether we would still call a system "legal" where no sanctions were employed because, never having encountered such a case, we have not had to decide whether something significant in our existing classificatory scheme is lost if we extend the term to include this case.[24] Second, if we do attempt to decide whether a sanctionless system can still be legal, we may find ourselves in disagreement because it is not clear what is at stake: If the disagreement is only about whether to extend the concept to include the sanctionless case, we seem to be engaged in stipulating definitions, an exercise of little interest.

In contrast with the concept of sanction, which seems important but not necessarily essential to law, consider now two examples of plausible conceptual claims – plausible claims about features that are not only important but also essential in the sense defined previously. The first example concerns the normative claims of law. As I explain in more detail in Chapter 3, the thesis that law makes certain normative claims for its directives is largely a conceptual thesis: To deny that law necessarily makes such claims (to assert that legal systems are indistinguishable from coercive systems) leads to inconsistencies with the language of guilt and blame that we associate with lawbreaking. Thus such normative claims are not only important but also essential features of legal systems. A second example of a conceptual claim about law can be found in recent positivist theories that insist that law must have a social source. The basic conceptual argument for this position can be put fairly simply. We begin by recognizing that among the many functions that law might be thought importantly

---

[24] It is sometimes argued that sanctions would have to be present for a state to operate, even in a society of perfectly virtuous citizens. See Gregory S. Kavka, "Why Even Morally Perfect People Would Need Government," in *For and Against the State*, 41. If true, this contingent feature of states and humans could help ground a conceptual claim that sanctions are essential to law, but it need not: A conceptual claim is about the meaning of a concept and thus could still distinguish between properties that are thought to be indispensable to the concept semantically from properties that are empirically indispensable.

to serve, one in particular is fundamental, namely, the function of communicating standards of conduct – explaining what is to be done, usually on pain of sanction. This function of guiding conduct must precede arguments about whether it is also essential to law that it present the motivations for complying with legal standards as primarily moral or coercive. Until one knows what is expected, one cannot know why it is expected or what additional claims about the motives for compliance might accompany the law's demands. This simple argument from a basic function of law seems to me to be another plausible candidate for an essential feature of law, a conceptual claim about the concept that cannot be denied consistent with claiming that we are still dealing with a legal system.[25] It is, in fact, probably better seen as a definition of what it means to be a system rather than a legal system: Directives that cannot communicate what is to be done with some clarity will necessarily be unable to coordinate and regulate activity in the way that is required to distinguish systems of social control from arbitrary exercises of ad hoc and unpredictable power.

Two points should be noted about this demonstration of the plausibility of conceptual and descriptive jurisprudence. First, the fact that an argument is based on an allegedly important function or purpose of law does not turn the argument into a normative or evaluative claim. While this point may seem obvious, there is a tendency to think that any argument about *purposes* is inevitably a normative argument that relies on the values of the disputants themselves. This is a mistake. Arguments about which purposes are important or essential to a concept are arguments about what those who use the concept of law find important for purposes of their own classification scheme; they are not claims about the analyst's own values, but about the existing purposes of others.[26] Second,

---

[25] Joseph Raz is the best-known proponent of what appears to be a conceptual defense of the argument that law must be derived from social sources (facts rather than values). See Raz, *The Authority of Law*, 37–52. Though Raz's argument seems to rely on an argument about the implications of what it means to claim authority, the simpler argument in the text seems to me to convey the same idea and avoids imputing to law a claim about authority that this study disputes. Anthony Seebok describes Raz's argument as relying on both a functional claim about law and a conceptual claim about the concept of authority. See Seebok, *Legal Positivism in American Jurisprudence* (Cambridge: Cambridge Univ. Press, 1998), 278–80. Jules Coleman at one point seemed to view Raz's argument as a practical argument concerned with law's effectiveness, rather than a conceptual or theoretical claim about the essence of law. See Coleman, "Incorporationism, Conventionality, and the Practical Difference Thesis," *Legal Theory* 4 (1998): 381, 386, and n.10; see also id., "Authority and Reason," in *The Autonomy of Law*, 287, 302–14. Others who come close to making a conceptual claim similar to the one in the text include Scott Shapiro and Larry Alexander. See, e.g., Shapiro, "The Difference That Rules Make," in *Analyzing Law*, ed. Brian Bix (Oxford: Clarendon Press, 1998), 33, 56–9; Shapiro, "On Hart's Way Out," *Legal Theory* 4 (1998): 469; Alexander, "With Me, It's All er Nuthin: Formalism in Law and Morality," *Chi. L. Rev.* 66 (1999): 530, 548 ("[Legal] rules can fulfill their function only if they are determinate rules, not indeterminate standards"). See also Larry Alexander and Emily Sherwin, *The Rule of Rules* (Durham, N.C.: Duke Univ. Press, 2001).

[26] One of the most eloquent defenders of the possibility of descriptive or conceptual jurisprudence seems at one point to suggest that arguments about law's essential function *would* be normative rather than conceptual. See Jules Coleman, "Incorporationism, Conventionality, and the Practical

one should note the limited reach of the argument about law's guiding function. The argument establishes that legal systems must have standards that, for the most part, are determinable. But it does not resolve the question of whether all legal standards must be determinable or whether some standards can, or even must, be moral standards even though such standards are indeterminate. I address these questions at greater length in Chapter 4; the general conclusions defended in that chapter are these: (1) Soft (or inclusive) positivism – the notion that law can incorporate moral standards – is a plausible account of law *if* one can explain what other function, apart from guiding conduct, might be served by incorporating such standards and *if* one can explain how such standards can be said to play a role in adjudication that distinguishes judges from legislators. (2) Legal systems necessarily include at least one overriding moral principle according to which standards that otherwise meet the tests for law will not qualify as law if they are so unjust that one cannot defend even the minimal moral claim of law (the right to coerce).[27]

DESCRIPTION AS RE-PRESENTATION. The preceding discussion, in addition to illustrating the uses of descriptive inquiries, also serves as a review of current controversies in legal theory that are implicated in the course of this study. But the general thesis I defend is not simply a thesis of legal theory and a claim about the nature of law. I argue (1) that law does not claim authority but (2) that law has authority. The first claim is the subject of legal theory and results from a combination of descriptive and conceptual claims and coherence arguments. The second claim is a claim of political or moral theory and thus necessarily involves normative argument. But even here the normative argument relies heavily on a descriptive prelude and on arguments for coherence. As indicated in the last section, I suggest in this study that familiar practices of promising and fair play may be better understood when recast as examples of

Difference Thesis," *Legal Theory* 4 (1998): 381, 386, 390. This concession is unnecessary and appears to be considerably modified by Coleman in other writings. See id., *The Practice of Principle* (Oxford: Oxford Univ. Press, 2001), 205–8. When Lon Fuller, in a famous episode, once argued that concepts that were defined by function or purpose inevitably combined facts and values, and that law, in order to perform its guiding function, must conform to procedural principles that he called an "inner morality" of law, he was met by the uniform response that "purposes" were not necessarily "moral." This response applies equally to those who think that arguments over the purpose of law can only be normative arguments: As long as they are arguments about the conventional purposes that underlie existing classification schemes, the arguments will not be normative. I have defended this claim elsewhere in "Legal Theory and the Problem of Definition."

[27] The argument for these two claims is developed in Chapter 4. I put the latter claim in this stark way in order to make it clear that this study defends what might be called a classical form of natural law, according to which law that is too unjust is no law at all. Unlike Dworkin, I do not rely on a theory of adjudication to suggest that legal standards are complex combinations of fact and value; I rely instead on conceptual, descriptive, and coherence arguments about the concept of law itself.

the ethics of deference. It is this additional use of description, inviting new views of familiar subjects, that warrants a brief additional discussion.

Descriptions are presentations of phenomena, highlighting particular features for one or more of the purposes just discussed. When a familiar phenomenon is recast to emphasize different and unexpected features, I shall call this new description a "re-presentation." The distinctive point of a re-presentation does not differ from the point of description in general except in the implication that (1) the new description differs in unexpected ways from familiar descriptions and (2) the new description fits the facts of the practice it describes at least as well as more familiar descriptions, but provides a better solution to coherence problems or affords greater insight into what is important or essential to the practice. Thus, though I shall defend the ethics of deference on normative grounds, the primary defense is still based on a claim of greater coherence with existing practices. Description as re-presentation derives its force largely from attempts to make existing practices coherent rather than from reexamining the ultimate normative foundations for those practices. An example of this use of description is found in Chapter 5, where I attempt to re-present promises as analogous to laws: The re-presentation helps show how the obligation of promise can be seen as analogous to the obligation to defer to the norms of the state. A somewhat similar, though perhaps less novel, re-presentation of the idea of fair play is found in Chapter 6. The insight gained in these two chapters lays the foundation for the arguments for deference to the state, found in Chapter 7.[28]

---

[28] For another example of re-presentation, applied not to a particular social practice but to a cultural icon in the literature of political theory, see Philip Soper, "Another Look at the *Crito*," *Am. J. Jurisp.* 41 (1996): 103 (re-presenting the familiar Platonic dialogue as an example of the ethics of deference).

2

Understanding Authority

Theoretical and Practical Authority

This chapter and the next consider in turn two questions about authority: (1) What do we mean by authority? (2) Does the law claim authority? Both chapters are preludes to a third question to be considered at the end of Part II: (3) Does law have authority? That these are distinct questions may not seem obvious; if, for example, law has authority, it might seem natural to suppose that legal systems necessarily claim authority. As indicated in the preface, however, I argue here not only that these are distinct questions but that they deserve distinct answers: Law has authority but does not claim it. But, though the questions are distinct, the first question concerning the nature of authority is closely connected to each of the latter two questions. That is because conclusions about whether law has or claims authority may depend on what one means by "authority." This chapter thus begins with that question: What does one normally mean when one ascribes authority to a person or to the state?

Philosophers who discuss this question commonly begin by distinguishing theoretical from practical authority. Theoretical authority, it is usually said, is authority about facts, about what is the case; practical authority is authority about action, about what one ought to do. Theoretical authority does not provide one with new reasons for action but only with new reasons for belief (which may, of course, be relevant to action); practical authority, in contrast, provides new reasons for action.

Using the approach developed in the preceding chapter, it is easy to see both how deference to theoretical authority works and what kinds of reasons typically justify such deference. Compare the case of my vegetarian friends, to whose opinions I defer in deciding what kind of meal to serve, with the case of my doctor friend, who advises me about the health effects of certain foods. Deference in the former case, we said, results from concluding that the reasons to defer, which may be instrumental or intrinsic, outweigh other reasons that bear on the action in question. In contrast, if I defer to the doctor's opinion on the assumption that he is, and I am not, an expert on the nutritional value of food, I do not normally weigh the doctor's opinions against my own view of the matter; rather, I make no calculation about the matter at all. The doctor's views do not *outweigh* mine; they *replace* mine. Deferring to theoretical authorities is like *delegating* to the authority the task of making the judgment that I recognize I cannot accurately make myself.[1] Moreover, the reasons that justify such deference are typically instrumental: Relying on legitimate theoretical authority is no different from relying on a calculator or computer; deference is justified in exactly the way that one justifies using any tool as the best means of achieving one's predetermined ends.

Practical authority, in contrast, seems to present a considerable initial problem of justification. If practical authority is authority about what to do – requiring submission to another's opinion about values rather than facts – it is not obvious how such submission could ever be consistent with the principle of autonomy. One common way of justifying such submission is to re-present practical authority as just another instance of theoretical authority: Where one has grounds to think that other people are wiser about what is good for one in a particular case, deference may be justified.[2] But in ordinary life, the occasions on which one could defend this collapse of practical into theoretical authority seem limited for two reasons. First, the view that others have more accurate knowledge about one's own good seems plausible only in unusual situations – cases in which one's judgment is systematically or temporarily impaired by factors that interfere with clear thinking. Children are commonly thought to have systematic reasons to defer to the opinions of appropriate adults; persons temporarily confused by excessive drinking may be best advised to defer to a bartender who insists on calling a cab instead of allowing them to drive. But such cases warrant deference to another's view only because they are extreme, resting as they do on background assumptions of paternalism that do not apply

---

[1] The claim that deference to theoretical authority typically works by replacing, rather than outweighing, one's own views is not meant to deny the possibility that sometimes deference even here could involve weighing an expert's views against one's own. Consider, for example, two experts disagreeing about a factual issue – two doctors disagreeing, say, about a diagnosis. One doctor might defer to the greater expertise of his colleague by according extra weight to his colleague's opinion rather than by completely substituting his colleague's judgment for his own.

[2] Heidi Hurd defends a version of law's theoretical authority derived not from a legislature's greater expertise, but from the possibility that law might serve as a sign pointing to reasons for believing that action in accordance with law is correct. See Hurd, *Moral Combat* (Cambridge: Cambridge Univ. Press, 1999), ch. 6. It seems unlikely, however, that the instances in which law has this kind of epistemic authority will be any greater than the instances in which it has epistemic authority based on its greater expertise. Hurd admits that the question is an empirical one and confines her examples primarily to cases involving coordination; thus even this account results in a view of law's authority that seems just as restrictive as Joseph Raz's competing account of practical authority examined later.

in most ordinary cases.[3] Paternalistic explanations, in short, have no application in the ordinary case of adults who are admittedly free of impediments to normal reflection.

Second, any attempt to go beyond cases of paternalism in justifying practical authority as an instance of theoretical authority confronts the problem of the difference between facts and values: We are less inclined today to think that there are experts about moral matters. If one does believe there are such experts, then practical authority is justified in the same way as theoretical authority. But that view (that there are moral experts) would itself have to be defended by individual judgment – just as one defends the decision to rely on a computer in making a calculation. The claim that practical authorities are moral experts is not often heard today except, perhaps, in the context of religious authorities. In particular, when one confronts the apparent demands of legal authorities, it seems unlikely that demands for deference to law's view about what to do could be justified on the ground that "the law knows best." Perhaps some values are particularly connected to the good of a nation in ways that might conceivably be better discovered by government officials, through hearings and official investigations.[4] Whether, for example, a country should provide special benefits to veterans may be a question not just about the factual consequences of such preferential treatment, but about the importance to the country of honoring veterans – a value judgment that, one might suggest, the legislature is best able to make. But, as this somewhat strained example illustrates, the instances in which one concludes that the legislature has such special expertise about values are likely to be few in number – nothing approaching the routine reliance on a calculator or computer or on expert judgment about factual matters. Most individuals are likely to insist that even if there is agreement on the factual issues about a particular governmental policy (e.g., what are the consequences of winning or losing this war?), the normative issues that remain (should resources be devoted to prosecuting this war?) are not questions that legislatures are better able to decide than individuals (which is why Thoreau's writings have such appeal for those who resist governmental authority[5]). Thus, it seems, legal

---

[3] Furthermore, even these examples beg the question of who is to decide the underlying jurisdictional issue that warrants paternalistic intervention in the first place: Is the child really still a child and is the drunk really too drunk to decide? For an excellent discussion, concluding that law will seldom have the necessary expertise to justify authority on these grounds, see Hurd, *Moral Combat*, 133–40.

[4] For the suggestion that democratic decision procedures can justify attributions of epistemic authority to legislation, though no such attribution would be warranted if one considered only the motives or expertise of individual lawmakers, see Jeremy Waldron, "Legislators' Intentions and Unintentional Legislation," in *Law and Interpretation*, ed. Andrei Marmor (Oxford: Clarendon Press, 1995), 329–56.

[5] See David Lyons, "Moral Judgment, Historical Reality, and Civil Disobedience," *Phil. & Pub. Affairs* 27 (1998): 31, 40–2.

authority – where it cannot be characterized as a case of theoretical authority – presents a problem.

Two Concepts of Practical Authority

My main interest in the remainder of this chapter is to compare and contrast two accounts of practical authority in light of the preceding preliminary discussion about the difficulty of justifying such authority. One view of practical authority, which I shall call the "restrictive" account, makes the justification of authority simple, but it does so only because it weakens and understates the concept of political authority as understood by most people. This account is restrictive in two senses: (1) it restricts the grounds that will justify practical authority to essentially the same grounds that justify theoretical authority (that is why the justification is easy); (2) as a result of this restriction on how to justify authority, it restricts the instances in which practical authority is legitimate to far fewer occasions than most people normally acknowledge (that is why the thesis is out of line with society's views about the nature of political authority). The alternative account, which I shall call the "expansive" account, displays features that are the precise counterpart of the restrictive account: (1) the expansive account purports to justify submission to practical authority on grounds that are fundamentally different from those that justify theoretical authority (that is why this theory of justification is controversial); (2) but the expansive account captures more closely the ordinary understanding of what it means to have practical authority, at least in the context of political authority.

The Restrictive Account

One version of the restrictive account, associated primarily with the work of Joseph Raz, assumes that deference in the case of practical authority works in the same way that it works in the case of theoretical authority: To acknowledge that one has practical authority is to acknowledge that one should abandon one's own attempt to balance reasons bearing on the recommended action against the reasons for deference and should, instead, delegate the decision entirely to the authority.[6] An alternative version, defended by those who find this degree of deference both unwarranted and an unnecessary feature of authority, is that something less than complete "preemption" is required. Legitimate authorities provide one with new reasons for action that have considerable weight – enough, perhaps, to be conclusive in many cases; but it is not necessary to think that such authorities intend the individual to defer entirely to the authority's judgment. Thus it is always open to subjects, and it is consistent with the concept of

---

[6] See Joseph Raz, *The Morality of Freedom* (Oxford: Clarendon Press, 1986), 53–69. For the most part, the text follows Raz's account in describing the features of the restrictive conception.

authority, to override the authority's directions in cases where the balance of reasons seems strongly to favor such action.[7]

I shall argue in the next section that this latter view of authority, in which reasons to defer do not replace but are weighed against other reasons, is a better model of the standard conception of political authority. This difference between the two accounts, however, is not a particularly critical one for several reasons. First, in many cases, there will be no difference in result: Where reasons for deference are strong enough to outweigh countervailing considerations, one will not easily detect the difference between a conception that views authority as preempting one from considering other reasons and a conception that views authority as outweighing such reasons. Second, even the preemption account makes an exception for "clear" cases in which the directions of a legitimate authority may be overridden or ignored. Thus, to use Raz's example, a column of added numbers with one and only one decimal fraction that yields an integer as sum can be seen to be clearly wrong, without requiring one to do the addition oneself.[8] Though not everyone is persuaded that the distinction between clear mistakes and unclear but "great" mistakes is a tenable one,[9] the main point is that even the restrictive account, it seems, is open in some cases to comparing the reasons for deference against one's own views of the correct action to take. Finally, regardless of one's view about whether legitimate authorities preempt individual judgment or only provide a strong countervailing reason for deference, the major normative question of political theory remains unaffected. The problem of justifying deference to authority, in other words, is not made easier because of the degree of autonomy that is sacrificed.[10]

---

[7] For arguments opposing Raz's preemptive account of authority, see Stephen Perry, "Judicial Obligation, Precedent and the Common Law," *Oxford J. Legal Studies* 7 (1987): 215; Michael Moore, "Authority, Law, and Razian Reasons," *S. Cal. L. Rev.* 62 (1989): 827, 895; Frederick Schauer, *Playing by the Rules* (Oxford: Clarendon Press, 1991), 88–93; Hurd, *Moral Combat*, ch. 3.

[8] Raz, *The Morality of Freedom*, 62.

[9] Donald Regan argues that Raz appears to "express no opinion" on whether authorities still deserve deference in the case of "clear" mistakes, a position that Regan finds puzzling. See Regan, "Authority and Value: Reflections on Raz's Morality of Freedom," *S. Cal. L. Rev.* 62 (1989): 995, 1030 ("Raz's indecision about cases of clear error reveals the tension in his whole analysis of authority"). See also Hurd, *Moral Combat*, 85–93 (concluding that this concession about clear mistakes contributes to the incoherence of Raz's concept of practical authority). In many respects, Regan's analysis of authority, which distinguishes indicator reasons from intrinsic reasons and generally denies that authorities provide reasons to obey of the latter sort, is a more consistent example of a restrictive account of authority than Raz's. See Regan, "Reasons, Authority, and the Meaning of 'Obey': Further Thoughts on Raz and Obedience to Law," *Can. J. Law Jurisp.* 3 (1990): 3. See also Regan, "Law's Halo," *Soc. Phil. & Policy* 4 (1986): 15.

[10] As Raz notes in his debate over this issue with his critics, whether normally valid reasons are outweighed, or excluded by authorities requires an explanation in either case of how normally relevant moral reasons can be defeated: Whichever side one chooses in this debate, the moral problem results in a "symmetrical quandary." Raz, "Facing Up," *S. Cal. L. Rev.* 62 (1989): 1153, 1166. (See also Hurd, *Moral Combat*, 93–4.) It is perhaps worth noting that the quandary here is

More critical to the distinction between the restrictive and expansive accounts of authority is the difference in the kinds of reasons needed to justify each kind of authority. The restrictive account requires practical authority to be justified on the same grounds as theoretical authority: namely, by showing that following the authority is more likely to result in correct action than if a subject tried to deliberate directly about what to do.[11] This account of the reasons that justify deference leads directly to the question we considered briefly in the previous section: If practical authority "shares the same basic structure"[12] as theoretical authority, how is it possible that practical authority could ever be justified? Absent assumptions of paternalism, why would one ever think that deferring to the state (much less allowing one's own judgment to be preempted by the state) is more likely to result in correct action than thinking for oneself? For that matter, if the justification of practical authority resembles that of theoretical authority, how can such authorities ever provide one with reasons for action rather than, as in the case of theoretical authority, reasons for belief?

The answers to these questions typically focus on one kind of case: the case of coordination.[13] To use the standard example, one may have no reason to drive on either the right or the left side where there is no legal or other convention; after the law makes a choice, one now has a reason to conform to that choice. Thus, we have an example of law exercising practical authority under the restrictive account – providing new reasons for action, not just reasons for belief.[14] This

---

the result of the restrictive account's limited view of how to justify authority: One must show that following the authority is more likely to lead to correct action than acting on one's own. Thus, whether one follows the authority a little bit (the balancing view) or blindly (the preemptive view), the problem of explaining why one should follow at all remains. The quandary disappears in the expansive account of authority because the expansive account claims that there are reasons to defer even assuming that one knows that the authority's recommendation is incorrect. If that account can be defended, the main problem is solved. How much to defer (partially or totally) will be a minor issue, resolved by reference to the reasons for deference in the first place.

[11] Raz calls this the "justification thesis," claiming that it is the normal way that one justifies practical authority.

[12] Raz, *The Morality of Freedom*, 53.

[13] See id., 48–52. Actually, Raz discusses three types of cases where practical authority makes a difference under his restrictive account: (1) cases where the correct action is underdetermined, prior to the law's speaking (taxes could be paid annually or quarterly, with the law's determination being decisive); (2) cases of coordination ("Drive on the right"); and (3) prisoner's dilemma cases (I have no reason to install pollution control devices on my car when I doubt whether others will, too, until the law makes the "selfish" free-riding problem unlikely by threatening sanctions). I agree with Don Regan that all of these cases seem to be either variations of the coordination case or cases that do not significantly affect the analysis of how authority works. See Regan, "Authority and Value," 995, 1031–3n.79.

[14] This attempt to stake out at least a minimal domain for practical authority in coordination cases must confront the increasingly common view that even in these cases, law does not give new reasons for action in the strict sense but simply provides the salience that enables coordination to occur: One drives on the right because, once the law has spoken, one can predict the behavior of others and thus achieve coordination. The reason for the action, however, is the practice; the law is merely the device that enables successful prediction of the practice. This view about how law achieves coordination without exercising practical authority has the virtue of remaining true

explanation also helps explain how a concept of authority can depend for its justification on being a better guide to correct action than individual calculation while at the same time preempting individual determinations about what to do. The explanation draws on the same arguments that rule utilitarians use to explain why one should follow a rule designed to promote certain values rather than calculate directly in each case the effect of contemplated action on those values.

Unfortunately, for reasons suggested in the preceding section, this analogy to the justification for rule-following in moral theory isn't easily transferred to legal authority. First, the debate between rule and act utilitarians usually assumes that the rules that are to guide conduct are those that the philosopher or the enlightened individual can justify as more likely to produce optimal conduct than any other. But in law, the rules are designed by legislators or other authorities who are no better at practical reasoning, by and large, than other individuals. Moreover, even in the best of governments, there are probably some individual citizens who are better able to judge practical matters than the legislature and who, thus, according to the restrictive account, should no longer view law as binding when it affects their particular fields of expertise.

Raz, in fact, accepts these consequences of the restrictive account. He concedes that under this account:

[a]n expert pharmacologist may not be subject to the authority of the government in matters of the safety of drugs [and] an inhabitant of a little village by a river may not be subject to its authority in matters of navigation and conservation of the river by the banks of which he has spent all his life.[15]

---

to the core idea that only theoretical authority can ever be justified. For an early example of the argument, see Gerald J. Postema, "Coordination and Convention at the Foundations of the Law," *J. Legal Studies* 11 (1982): 174. For a later example, see Regan, "Authority and Value," 995, 1019, 1024–32 (arguing that a correct interpretation of what Raz calls the "recognitional conception" of authority can explain how coordination through law is possible, without ascribing authority to the law). See also Hurd, *Moral Combat*, ch. 6. For the argument that law generates moral reasons to comply through its choice of a coordinating solution see John M. Finnis, "Law as Co-ordination," *Ratio Juris* 2 (1989): 101–2. Raz's response to the salience argument seems to create fresh problems for his attempt to distinguish practical from theoretical authority. Thus Raz suggests that law does not simply provide the point that allows random action to achieve coordination – law actually determines when coordination is desirable:

It can instruct me better than I can myself when [coordinating] practices are justified and how I should contribute to them.... [A]uthorities are [also] useful as a means of securing the continuity of coordinative practices in the face of changing populations ... [and] by relying on the authoritative directives I am spared the need to judge for myself if the coordinative practice exists (a task at which I am no expert). Raz, *The Morality of Freedom*, 1192, 1194.

This response suggests that law can also play the expert's role in determining whether coordination is needed in the first place. But since the expert role *is* paradigmatically the role of a theoretical authority, not a practical authority, the reply reinforces the view that the only justifiable authority, under the restrictive account, is theoretical authority.

[15] Raz, *The Morality of Freedom*, 74.

We could, no doubt, add indefinitely to this list of examples: Motorists who have expert knowledge about the roadworthiness of their cars will not be subject to laws requiring periodic safety tests, and parents who know their children better than the government (and what parent doesn't?) will not be subject to laws regulating day-care hours and so on.[16]

Finally, even if a particular legislature is more likely to be right in its judgment about the best laws to enact in a particular area, laws by their generality operate far too grossly to allow one confidently to assert that second-guessing is always likely to be worse than blindly following the rule. A favorite example of philosophers discussing the obligation to obey the law is the red light in the desert when nobody is around, but one can also use the speed-limit example to make the point that most people will be able to make a plausible claim that the law is clearly wrong far more frequently than is suggested by the example of adding several integers and one fraction and getting an integer as the sum. The 55 mph speed limit represents a general solution to the balance of interests involving fuel conservation, safety, and speed that only by the most implausible assumption will be the correct balance for all individuals in all circumstances. Even if one adds to the account the expense and energy of making an individual calculation each time, there must surely be many instances when my need to get somewhere fast, coupled with my safety record as a driver and the absence of significant traffic, make it clear that the legislature's judgment about how fast I should drive is not more reliable than mine.[17]

So far, I have been suggesting that the restrictive account of authority has the consequence that many instances of apparent legal authority will in fact be unjustified. That may be a consequence one is prepared to accept. Raz, for example, accepts it, though he admits it is paradoxical: Political officials and legal systems generally make claims of unlimited authority that the justification thesis simply does not support.[18]

---

[16] Id., 78.

[17] See Larry Alexander, "The Gap," *Harv. J. L. Pub. Policy* 14 (1991): 695; Alexander and Emily Sherwin, "The Deceptive Nature of Rules," 142 Pa. *L. Rev.* 142 (1994): 1191 (legal authorities must inevitably make "deceptive" claims about the extent to which rules should be followed). For a full treatment of the issue, incorporating the arguments from both of these articles, see Larry Alexander and Emily Sherwin, *The Rule of Rules* (Durham, N.C.: Duke Univ. Press, 2001), pt. II.

[18] Raz, *The Morality of Freedom*, 76–8. The common reasons that justify legal authority also apparently explain why legal systems inevitably claim more authority than they have. States have legitimate authority, most commonly, whenever they (1) have greater expertise; (2) can calculate correctly, with less chance for bias; (3) can save individuals time and trouble in calculating themselves; (4) can coordinate and/or avoid prisoner's dilemma problems; and (5) can provide an indirect strategy for achieving correct results. If these are the situations in which states have legitimate authority, why do they inevitably claim more authority than they have? Presumably, legal authority fails (1) when the legislature's expertise on policy matters is suspect or less than that of particular individuals (the "expert pharmacologist . . . in matters of the safety of drugs") or (2) when, due to the necessity of administering on a broad basis, laws that are unimpeachable in

The Expansive Account

The concept of authority we have been examining resolves the problem of reconciling authority and autonomy almost entirely in favor of the autonomous subject. Raz calls this the "service" conception of authority. The fundamental problem with the service conception is that it rules out an entirely different conception of authority that has long been at the center of attempts to justify political authority. The restrictive account limits the authoritative state role to that of the expert or the traffic cop who *serves* others by helping them attain their own preexisting goals. But there is an alternative conception of authority that embraces a very different image: that of the authority who *leads* others by making and enforcing normative judgments about what ought to be done – even if those judgments conflict with an individual's own goals.

To see the difference between these two conceptions, consider the state's authority in the case of taxation, to take just one example. The restrictive account explains how law can have authority and provide new reasons for paying taxes by setting definite times for, and amounts of, payments – thus facilitating the preexisting moral duty to make contributions to the welfare of others. While one may have a general moral duty to share resources with others or help allay the expenses of the state, until a scheme is in effect that provides for taxation, one has no reason to make voluntary tax contributions. Thus the tax laws can provide new reasons for action in line with the coordinating explanation of the restrictive account.[19] But what is left out of this explanation of how law can act as a practical authority is the matter that is usually most controversial and that is equally the subject of legal enforcement: the norms of distributive justice that underlie a particular tax scheme. What seems most to require justification, and at the same time is most characteristic of the state, is not the decision about whether payments will be made quarterly or annually, but the decision about the underlying theory of justice that determines whether and how taxes are to be levied in the first place. Are taxes just only if proportional to wealth? Only when raised in support of the minimal state rather than the redistributive state? Only when levied on consumption rather than income? These substantive issues of policy and morality are the critical issues that underlie any particular taxing scheme and on which the state takes a stand and enforces its own view. None of these matters seems to fall within the realm in which the state, under the restrictive account, could possibly have legitimate authority.

---

their general goals fail to apply to particular cases (the speed limit that, under the circumstances, does not describe for a particular case the optimum driving speed):

[B]ecause of the bureaucratic necessity to generalize and disregard distinctions too fine for large-scale enforcement and administration, some people are able to do better if they refuse to acknowledge the authority of [the] law. Id., 75.

[19] Id., 48–52.

The taxation example can be generalized to include many others. It may even be that most of the decisions that governments make in law represent a resolution of controversial moral disputes where "there does not appear to be an independent criterion of success."[20] In these cases, the assumption that the legislature has superior deliberative ability or is simply "coordinating" action is unwarranted. Justifying authority in these cases, where the law is setting and enforcing moral norms rather than acting as a policy expert or traffic cop, has always been the central problem of traditional political theory. The problem is not to explain why one might have a reason to follow the state's judgment about tolerable levels of toxic wastes or about how to drive so as to avoid accidents at busy intersections – that problem is too easily solved. The problem is to explain why one would ever have reason to defer to state judgments – even when one believes them to be erroneous – about substantive and controversial moral issues. It may well be that this expanded concept of authority could never be justified and, hence, that the only concept of authority that could be defended as legitimate is the restrictive account. But whether that is the case is a question of political theory that must be confronted directly, not ruled out in advance on conceptual grounds about what we mean by authority. The next two sections expand on this alternative account of authority, comparing it with the restrictive account in terms of both the structure of the decision to defer and the reasons for deference.

STRUCTURE. Consider again the examples of deference discussed in the previous chapter. Though this study assumes that authority can be explained in terms of deference, that assumption is not reversible: Not every case of deference can be viewed as a case of acknowledging another's authority. If one spouse defers to another's view about how the children should be educated, it is not because one is acknowledging the other's authority. Even less so in the case of deferring to one's friends: If I have reason to defer to requests of friends, I am not normally doing so in acknowledgment of their authority.

To see what turns a simple case of deference into a case of authority, imagine the spouses in our earlier example deciding that for reasons of fairness or efficiency, each spouse will assume responsibility for distinct family decisions: One spouse, for example, will decide issues involving education, the other issues concerning health care. In this case, it is far more plausible to describe each spouse as having authority to decide issues within the allocated area – not because of any greater expertise but because of the reasons that justify the allocation (and the resulting agreement) in the first place. An even better example is provided by the last of the quotations that head the preface to this study: When courts defer to the judgments of another court or agency, we may plausibly describe the situation as one that involves recognizing the subordinate

---

[20] See C. McMahon, "Autonomy and Authority," *Phil. & Pub. Affairs* 16, no. 4 (1987): 308.

institution's authority to make an initial determination, not necessarily because of greater expertise but because of a prior decision to allocate the "right to decide" to particular institutions.

This view of authority, as based on reasons that require allocating the right to decide to some final institution or person, rather than on reasons that suggest greater expertise or coordinating ability, is far closer to the traditional vision of political authority than the restrictive account of authority. It is also a vision of authority that potentially encompasses far more instances of governmental action than does the restrictive account. And this view differs from the restrictive account both in the way that deference operates and in the reasons that justify deference.

In regard to the difference in structure, we have already indicated that the expansive account of authority typically operates by giving additional weight to the views of the authority rather than by allowing those views to replace entirely one's own reasoning. Examples of this kind of deference within legal institutions are familiar and easy to find. When appellate courts defer to agency interpretations of their authority, they do so unless the agency's determination is clearly erroneous. When judges defer to juries' findings, they do so unless the facts are clearly against the weight of the evidence. When common law courts view prior precedents as authoritative, they do not mean that precedents can never be overruled; they mean only that one must make an unusually strong case that the precedent is wrong and that expectations will not be unduly disappointed in order to justify overruling the prior decision. All of these examples share a common feature: It is not enough for the deferring institution to disagree with the judgment it confronts; deference requires that extra weight be given to the authoritative decision and thus requires one sometimes to act in ways inconsistent with one's own view of the correct judgment.[21] At the same time, however, the authoritative judgment can be avoided if it is sufficiently outweighed by the reasons that favor a different result. As will be clear, this is the typical structure of deference that we described in the preceding chapter: One's own judgment is not preempted, but only balanced against the reasons for deferring to the views of another.

Notice that this view of the structure of deference also coincides with standard views about the possibility of legitimate state authority. Few people suggest that the obligation to obey the law is absolute; the argument, instead, is over whether there is even a prima facie obligation to obey – reasons to defer that may, perhaps, be overridden in particular cases. The expansive account of authority accommodates this possibility. The restrictive account dooms the possibility of establishing a prima facie obligation to obey from the start by insisting that

---

[21] For an excellent analysis, recommending a model of legal reasoning from precedent that requires judges sometimes to reach decisions they would not otherwise make, see Alexander and Sherwin, *The Rule of Rules*, ch. 7.

authority, when it is legitimate, must be absolute, that is, must preempt entirely the subject's own views of correct action.

There is a second difference between the expansive and restrictive accounts of authority that can best be seen by considering a normative claim about how authority works. The restrictive account, in addition to suggesting that authority preempts individual calculation, also entails what Raz calls the "dependence thesis" – the thesis that authority, in order to be legitimate, must base its decisions on the same reasons that would apply independently to the subjects of the directives.[22] At first glance, this seems like a fairly strong constraint. It seems to ensure that, while subjects may be preempted from doing their own calculations, at least they will not be subjected to directives designed to advance interests completely foreign to their own.

The appearance of constraint, however, is problematic for two reasons. First, the dependence thesis does not require that authorities act in the "interests" of their subjects, but only that they act "for reasons which apply also to the subjects."[23] Thus a military commander complies with the thesis when he orders a soldier, in the interest of national defense, to take action that is inconsistent with the soldier's interest in personal safety. That is because soldiers *ought* to put their country above their own interests, whether they do in fact or not. Second, the dependence thesis ignores the problem of disagreement about what reasons *are* applicable to subjects. The typical posture of the law when it enforces its norms is that the question of which reasons apply to a subject is itself a question that the legal authority has the right to decide. Under the expansive account of authority, the dependence thesis would thus require only that an authority act on reasons *that the authority believes* its subjects ought to acknowledge, whether or not they in fact do so. Under this interpretation, the modest constraint of a jurisdictional limit on the types of reasons that may be considered disappears given the ability of the authority to decide for itself whether it has exceeded the limit.

The dependence thesis provides a constraint on legitimate authority only if it is interpreted to require that the reasons on which the authority relies apply to the subject in fact, that is, as a matter of an objectively correct normative view about what reasons individuals ought to consider or what areas of individual life authorities can properly control. Thus, in the case of the soldier, the military command would be consistent with the dependence thesis under a restrictive view only if the commander (and his superiors in turn) were objectively correct in their conclusion that citizens ought to participate in a particular war. But if this is what is intended by the dependence thesis, it underscores the difference between the "service" and "leader" conceptions of authority. Under the leader conception, a legitimate authority is entitled to deference regardless of whether

---

[22] Raz, *The Morality of Freedom,* 42.
[23] Id., 15.

it is correct in its evaluation of the pros and cons of particular action; that being the case, it also seems to follow that deference is due to the determinations of such authorities about what reasons ought to apply to and be considered by its subjects. It would be odd, for example, to suggest that the government's authority survives mistakes in its calculation about, for example, the legitimacy of a war but does not survive mistakes in its decision about what reasons individuals ought to consider in deciding whether to fight.

In short, under the leader conception, the likely response of the state to the suggestion that its authority is limited by the dependence thesis is, at best, to agree, but to insist that it has the same right to be wrong in deciding what reasons citizens ought to consider as it does in deciding the content of the law. The government no doubt will claim that its laws are based on reasons that apply to its subjects, but it will insist that its authority is not conditional on having correctly determined what those reasons are or how they apply to particular cases. Thus the dependence thesis, under the expansive account of authority, must be reformulated to reflect more accurately the extent to which it serves as a normative constraint on the exercise of authority. All that is required under this account is that the authority act in good faith in the interests of the general welfare or of justice as it sees it, defending that general pursuit of the public welfare as based on reasons that all individuals should take into account. This formulation is, no doubt, sufficiently general to include almost any set of reasons, some of which include the interests of particular individuals and some of which do not. It is also broad enough to include the range of contested positions within political theory about the proper range of interests that governments may appeal to in justifying constraints imposed on individuals. In fact, all that seems to be ruled out by this reformulation are cases of purely self-interested tyrants who rule solely in their own interest, with no belief that their self-interest coincides with broader goals of justice or the public good with which individuals too should be concerned.[24]

SUBSTANCE. What then is the justification of authority under the expanded conception? What reasons could one have for deferring to the law's judgment about the merits of action, regardless of any likelihood that following the judgment would more likely accord with correct action than following one's own lights? That question will be examined throughout this study, but two initial

---

[24] I do not meant to suggest that this constraint, which requires authorities to issue directives thought to be in the public interest or in the service of a general theory of justice, is no constraint at all. To the contrary, the requirement of sincerity and the need to justify, even if by reference to a theory of justice that is in fact erroneous but is believed to be correct, will provide some limits on what may be proffered as the grounds for an authoritative decision, if only because of the constraint of consistency. It should, however, be recognized that the constraint is consistent with almost any form of government from the divine rule of kings to the democratic rule of a small city-state. I discuss the potential constraints of this requirement at greater length in Philip Soper, *A Theory of Law*, (Cambridge, Mass.; Harvard Univ. Press, 1984), 119–22, 133–43.

points emerge from the current discussion. First, the kind of answer that might be and has been given by classical political theorists to this question differs radically from the justification of theoretical authority. The justification of theoretical authority, and of the related restrictive account of practical authority, is instrumental: A government exists because (and has authority just in case) it does a better job of advancing the aims of the governed (what "ought to be their aims") that they could do on their own. Under the expanded conception, government exists because (and has authority just in case) it provides necessary direction in default of agreement about what *are* the aims of the governed. The justification of political authority under this conception rests on the possibility that other values are at stake in the decision to defer – values that offset or outweigh one's own values and that designate as the "correct" action (in the ultimate sense) an action that may in fact be wrong if assessed only by the reasons that bear directly on the action.

Raz suggests that the restrictive conception represents the "normal" justification thesis. It *is* the normal justification of theoretical authority; but it is doubtful that it is the normal justification of practical authority within traditional political theory. It may be that classical political theorists who argued for an expanded view of state authority were wrong and that no theory could ever justify the expansive concept. In that case, the restrictive conception will become the normal one by default. But it is to substantive political theory, not conceptual analysis, that one must turn in order to decide that question; until then, it remains an open question which account should be viewed as the default or normal account.

Collapsing the Two Conceptions

The distinction between these two conceptions of authority raises the possibility that some more fundamental theory can explain one in terms of the other, thus collapsing the competing theories into a single theory. This possibility is a real one and repeatedly surfaces in political theory. The justification for authority under the leader conception draws on two persistent ideas: (1) that decisions about the best action to take are often deeply controversial and (2) that we cannot avoid giving some persons in society the power to resolve these disputes – including disputes about the limits of their own power.

This explanation suggests that the role of the state in setting moral norms may, in fact, simply be another instance of coordination. The reasons one has to acknowledge the authority of the state are the same as those one has to acknowledge the authority of the policeman directing traffic or the arbitrator settling a dispute. In the latter case, for example, the arbitrator may announce the norm that she believes controls the issue; but one's reason for acknowledging her authority may still be largely instrumental: Even if one thinks the arbitrator is wrong, the impasse that led to the arbitration cannot be avoided in any other way than by acceding to the arbitrator's decision. This view has, of course, been a persistent explanation for the justification of state authority at least since the time of Hobbes.[25]

The attempt to collapse the leader account into the service account in this fashion fails for two reasons. First, the standard argument that deference to state normative judgments is justified in order to avoid the even worse catastrophe of returning to the state of nature strikes most people as implausible. It is possible that failure to defer to the state's decision about some highly controversial issue in society could lead, particularly if others did the same, to disruption and disorder in ways that would justify deference to the state in a particular case for the reasons emphasized by the restrictive account. (The state would have authority here under the restrictive account because, to further one's own goals in achieving security, the state's lead must be followed.) But it is highly unlikely that this explanation would ring true in many or even most cases.[26]

There is a second reason, though, why this attempt to collapse the expanded account into the restrictive one fails. Even if one thought that all instances of deference to law's norms could be justified instrumentally in terms of one's own interest in security, that explanation for deference does not reflect the state's own vision, and that of most other subjects, about what the state is doing when it decides controversial moral issues. If the only goal were to settle moral controversies, all such decisions could be treated like rules of the road, where what counts is only that some position be adopted, with the particular position itself being irrelevant. The state could just as easily (and at far less cost in terms of debate and discussion) flip a coin in deciding, for example, whether to permit abortion or whether a flat tax scheme would be fair.[27] That the state does not act as if it is simply coordinating activity in these cases by making any old decision seems clear: The state purports to be resolving issues on their merits,

---

[25] For a contemporary example of the argument, see W. S. Boardman, "Coordination and the Moral Obligation to Obey the Law," *Ethics* 97 (1987): 546.

[26] Christopher McMahon tries to rescue the restrictive account of authority and its justification thesis along these lines by suggesting that when the state decides controversial moral issues, the state's authority is justified on the same grounds as when the state helps resolve a prisoner's dilemma: It is better to go along with the legislative determination, however wrong or controversial, because failure to cooperate could lead to the even worse result of the state of nature. See McMahon, "Autonomy and Authority," *Phil. & Pub. Affairs* 16 (1987): 308, 310–19. Most theorists, including Raz, whose account of authority McMahon is discussing, reject this claim. See Raz, *The Morality of Freedom*, 101 ("it is a melodramatic exaggeration to suppose that every breach of law endangers, by however small a degree, the survival of the government, or of law and order"). I shall not evaluate McMahon's intriguing attempt to rescue the state-of-nature explanation, but note only that it is the kind of argument that would have to be made in order to show that the expansive conception of authority is really only a subspecies of the restrictive account. Even if the argument were successful, as the text indicates, it would misrepresent the law's own claims about what it is doing when it makes controversial moral decisions.

[27] Or, to use Ronald Dworkin's famous example, it could enact "checkerboard" statutes that give proponents on both sides of a controversial issue a victory in alternate years. See Ronald Dworkin, *Law's Empire* (Cambridge, Mass.: Harvard Univ. Press, 1986), 176–86.

applying its own vision of what justice requires to the controversy before it. For Dworkin, of course, this attitude toward the state's laws rises almost to the level of a defining feature of law as well as a fundamental principle of political morality: In order to be consistent with the ideal of integrity, the state must act on principle, as any conscientious single agent would. Whether such action also helps solve a coordination problem is secondary to the requirement that one actually struggle with and decide the issue on principled grounds. For our purposes, we do not need to decide whether this attitude is morally required or conceptually connected to the idea of law. Indeed, one can imagine unusual situations where the state might explicitly avoid taking a substantive position on a controversial issue while at the same time regulating the issue to avoid dispute and controversy.[28] For our purposes, it is enough to establish as a descriptive matter that the implicit attitude behind such state action is one that endorses the legal norm based on its content and recommends that others comply *because* the content is claimed to be just.

Arguments that attempt to collapse the expanded concept of authority into the restricted concept fail to distinguish the reasons that justify creating the state in the first place from the reasons that justify an individual's acting in accord with state directives. The critical issue for political theory has always been whether one has any reason to follow authority if, in particular cases, the reasons for establishing authority in the first place do not seem to be implicated by a particular act of disobedience. Even if the primary motivation for creating the state is the need to achieve coordination or to solve a prisoner's dilemma problem, the means subsequently used by the state are not confined to coordinating activity. The state's claim that its norms are justified is in most cases a claim about the content of legal norms, not a claim that following the laws, whatever their content, is the only or best way to avoid instability.[29]

---

[28] See Kent Greenawalt, *Conflicts of Law and Morality* (Oxford: Clarendon Press, 1987), 19 (discussing a hypothetical settlement on Mars where religious divisions among the settlers lead to a deliberate decision to let the state make laws that regulate religious disputes but that explicitly do not represent a state position on the merits of the dispute). Greenawalt's point, presumably, is that whether the state must be seen as endorsing the merits of controversial legislation is an empirical question, not a conceptual one. But the artificial nature of the example helps make the point that this situation is unusual: As a purely descriptive matter, states usually do purport to be making decisions about moral issues on the merits as they see them.

[29] Lon Fuller, in a somewhat different context, made a similar observation. In discussing two conceptions of democracy, he urged that one reject the view that democracy is founded on the negative idea "that there is no such thing as justice . . . [and that] majority rule is preferred not because it is most likely to be right, but because it is most likely to be obeyed." Lon Fuller, *The Law in Quest of Itself* (Boston: Beacon Press, 1940), 121.

3

Claiming Authority

Introduction

In Chapter 1, I suggested that current legal theory, confronted with law's apparent moral claims, tends toward two mistakes. The first mistake is to demote law's claims, making them accidental rather than necessary features of legal systems. Under this view, legal systems are essentially coercive. The fact that many such systems make normative claims for their directives is no more critical to the understanding of the concept than the fact that legal systems make different *kinds* of normative claims, reflecting the different ways in which state power can be organized. No one would suggest, for example, that the concept of "legal system" properly applies only to those systems that make a particular type of normative claim about their right to coerce – democratic claims, say, rather than totalitarian ones. In like fashion, it is suggested, we should not limit the concept to just those systems that make normative claims in general of whatever type: What counts in deciding that systems are legal is the organized coercion that distinguishes legal systems from, say, religious and moral systems.[1]

The second mistake in current characterizations of law's claims errs in the opposite direction by promoting those claims to what I previously described as strong moral claims. It is easy to see how this promotion might occur. Modern positivists recognize that the normative claims about law's moral force are presented as serious (at least by insiders); but since it must be obvious, even

---

[1] This view of law, sometimes called the "classical" version of positivism, is most commonly associated with the legal theory of John Austin. See Austin, *The Province of Jurisprudence Determined* (London: J. Murray, 1832). H. L. A. Hart's disagreement with Austin on this point became the basis for the turn to "modern" positivism and the insistence that an accurate legal theory model law's normative claims as well as its coercive power. Although most recent positivists have followed Hart's lead, disagreeing only about how to characterize law's normative claims, recent discussions appear to revive some aspects of the Austinian account of legal obligation. The most notable such revival is found in recent work by Matthew Kramer. See Kramer, *In Defense of Legal Positivism* (Oxford: Oxford Univ. Press, 1999), 101 (defending the possibility of legal systems working by "sheer imperatives," making no pretensions to moral worthiness). I consider Kramer's arguments later in this chapter.

to insiders, that officials can make mistakes and that *particular* norms can thus (however unwittingly) be unjust, the claims about law's moral force must be about the duty to obey law *just because it is the law*: Law must, in short, claim practical authority. In the terms of this study, law claims that there are reasons to defer to legal norms even if those norms are wrong or unjust.

For a positivist, the latter conclusion, however sensible as a re-presentation of ordinary attitudes toward law, is not easily accommodated within a legal theory that requires all claims of legal validity to be resolved by purely factual tests ("social sources" or empirically verifiable rules of recognition). The result is a paradox within positivist legal theory. The paradox, which others have also observed,[2] results from the combination of two theses: One is a thesis in legal theory about what law must claim in order to count as law; the other is a thesis in political theory about what law is entitled to claim. The legal theory claim is that

[n]o system is a system of law unless it includes a claim of legitimacy, or moral authority. That means that it claims that legal requirements are morally binding, that is that legal obligations are real (moral) obligations arising out of the law.[3]

The accompanying political theory claim is that: "Even reasonably just states claim more extensive authority than they are entitled to. . . ."[4]

---

[2] See W. J. Waluchow, *Inclusive Legal Positivism* (Oxford: Clarendon Press, 1994), 123 ("According to Raz it is in the very nature of legal systems that they necessarily claim justified authority over a population. This claim is, somewhat paradoxically, almost always false, but it must be made by those who represent the legal system, if what they represent is truly to count as law"). See also R. Shiner, *Norm and Nature: The Movements of Legal Thought* (Oxford: Clarendon Press, 1992); Jeffrey D. Goldsworthy, "The Self-Destruction of Legal Positivism," *Oxford J. Legal Studies* 10 (1990): 449. I have discussed aspects of this apparent paradox before. See Philip Soper, *A Theory of Law*, (Cambridge, Mass.: Harvard Univ. Press, 1984), 46; id., "Making Sense of Modern Jurisprudence: The Paradox of Positivism and the Challenge for Natural Law," *Creighton L. Rev.* 22 (1988): 67, 85 ("the problem is that even if positivism is true, it cannot be believed to be true. Insiders must act as if positivism is false, i.e., they must believe that there is a connection between the sanctions they impose and their ability to justify them, just because it is the law, even though positivism claims that this belief about the connection between law and morality is false"); id., "Legal Theory and the Claim of Authority, *Phil. & Pub. Affairs* (1989): 18 209; id., "Legal Systems, Normative Systems, and the Paradoxes of Positivism," *Can. J. L. & Jurisp.* 8 (1995): 363, 375–6 (Critical Notice, reviewing Shiner, *Norm and Nature*).

[3] Joseph Raz, "Hart on Moral Rights and Legal Duties," *Oxford J. Legal Studies.* 4 (1984): 123, 131. See also Leslie Green, "Law, Legitimacy, and Consent," *S. Cal. L. Rev.* 62 (1989): 795, 797.

[4] Joseph Raz, *The Morality of Freedom*: (Oxford: Clarendon Press, 1986), 70. See also id., 77 ("[Law] claims unlimited authority, it claims that there is an obligation to obey it whatever its content may be. . . . [but] there has hardly been any political theorist in recent times who has shared this view"). See also Leslie Green, *The Authority of the State* (Oxford: Clarendon Press, 1990), chs. 3, 8, 9; R. Flathman, *The Practice of Political Authority* (Chicago and London: Univ. of Chicago Press, 1980), 227 ("the overwhelming preponderance of known political associations that have claimed or now claim authority did not or do not come close to meeting the requirements [for justifying those claims]"); David Lyons, *Ethics and the Rule of Law* (Cambridge: Cambridge Univ. Press, 1984), 208–14; R. George Wright, "Does Positivism Matter?" in *The Autonomy of Law: Essays on Legal Positivism*, ed. Robert P. George (Oxford: Clarendon Press, 1996), 57, 59

In this chapter, I examine the legal theory claim, and in subsequent chapters I examine the political theory claim. The general account I shall defend is the following: (1) The legal theory claim is false; it is not the case that a correct account of law must portray law as claiming authority in the sense of an obligation to obey directives just because they are the law. In the terminology of this study, law does not claim that subjects always have reasons to defer to legal norms, regardless of the correctness of their content. (2) The political theory claim is also false: Even though law does not essentially *claim* authority, law *has* authority; moreover, it has authority of a kind far more extensive than the restrictive account would justify: It has expansive authority that does not run out in the way that it inevitably must under the restrictive account.

Before turning to the legal theory issue, two additional comments about the general strategy of the following chapters may be in order. First, the combination of legal and political theory claims just described (law has authority but does not claim it) may seem to produce its own air of paradox, in part because the moral half of the argument for this position must be postponed to the next part of this study. Note, however, that if one accepts that people (or legal systems) can have authority even though they do not claim authority, the position defended here restores unity to both political and legal theory in a way that avoids the paradox that modern positivists confront. It is not conceptually odd, after all, to suggest that one might be an expert without claiming to be; whether for reasons of humility or because of doubt about what qualifies one as an expert, the possibility that one can actually have theoretical authority without claiming (or knowing) it is a possible and even familiar one. The same is true of deference to the normative judgments of others. I may have reason to defer to my friend's vegetarian views on particular occasions or to my spouse's views about how to educate our children. But those reasons will be drawn from moral theory independently of whether my friend or spouse actually claims that I should defer. Indeed, in the common situation of serious normative disagreement between close friends or spouses, opposing views are more likely to be presented for consideration without an accompanying claim that one's partner is obligated to concede or has reason to defer to one's wishes. The decision to defer is derived from background theories of morality of the sort explored in this study; they do not depend on, and may even be more likely to apply in the absence of, the accompanying claim that deference is required. Thus no paradox results from the combination of claims supported in this study similar to that which results when law is pictured as essentially claiming what political theory denies it is entitled to claim. For similar reasons, one can accept the arguments about legal theory in this chapter, while rejecting those in Part II about law's moral authority, without being left in the curious

---

("Probably the current majority position among Anglo-American legal philosophers is that there is no general prima facie moral obligation to obey the law").

position of counting systems as legal only if they make claims branded as false by political theory. Whatever one thinks about the arguments in Part II, the classical question of political theory – is there an obligation to obey the state? – will permit resolution in a way that does not affect or conflict with the characteristic claims of legal systems.

Second, it is worth bearing in mind that "authority" in common usage is notoriously ambiguous. One can talk about the state's authority to coerce, or the authority to rule, or the authority to decide, where all one may mean is a "right" to coerce, or rule, or decide – without necessarily implying a correlative "duty" to obey by those subject to the state's rule.[5] In order to keep these alternative conceptions of authority in mind, I shall call the stronger view of authority (which implies a correlative duty to obey) "moral authority"; the weaker view (claiming only a right to coerce) I shall call "coercive authority." Both kinds of authority are to be distinguished from purely coercive power (which makes no moral claim either to a right to enforce or a duty to obey). With these distinctions in mind, the thesis defended in this chapter and in the next part is this: The only claim one can derive from the concept of law *as a matter of legal theory* is the weaker claim of coercive authority; in particular, the only reasons law claims citizens have for following the law are content-dependent ones (obey the law because the content is just) or coercive ones (obey the law because we have the right to impose sanctions if you don't). Law does not claim that citizens have content-independent reasons to obey or that citizens have reasons to defer to the law just because it is the law.

Finally, it is also worth noting how the distinction just drawn between coercive and moral authority relates to the two conceptions of practical authority discussed in the preceding chapter. The distinction between restrictive and expansive accounts of authority is a distinction about the *meaning* of authority. The restrictive account insists that, as a conceptual or normative-explanatory matter, to claim "practical authority" is to claim roughly the same thing that we claim in the case of theoretical authorities (i.e., the claim of authority entails only the claim that there are "indicative" reasons for compliance). To claim expansive authority, on the other hand, is to claim that there are "intrinsic" reasons to follow the authority, not merely indicative reasons.[6] The distinction between

---

[5] The thesis that legitimate assertions of authority entail correlative duties on the part of subjects to comply has been called the "correlativity" thesis. See John Simmons, "Voluntarism and Political Associations," *Va. L. Rev.* 67 (1981): 19, 20; see also Raz, "Authority and Consent," *Va. L. Rev.* 67(1981): 103. As I explain in the text, I accept the correlativity thesis as a thesis about expansive authority. That means that since legal systems, as I argue, do not claim expansive authority, neither do they claim that subjects have reasons to defer. But to conclude that states actually have expansive authority, as I do in Part II, entails that there are always correlative reasons to defer to the state's normative judgments.

[6] The distinction between indicative and intrinsic reasons for following authority is developed by Donald Regan in his analysis of Raz's attempt to defend practical authority by the analogy to theoretical authority. Theoretical authorities, in Regan's terms, provide at best only indicative

coercive authority and moral authority is a substantive distinction within political theory that overlaps this conceptual distinction. To claim coercive authority is to claim only the right to enforce – not necessarily a correlative duty to obey. To claim moral authority is to claim that there *is* a correlative duty to obey – a duty to follow the (legitimate) authority's prescription, in part, just because the authority has so prescribed. Claims of moral authority are necessarily claims of expansive authority. But claims of coercive authority are not necessarily claims of practical authority of any kind (restrictive or expansive). They are claims that one has a right to enforce the norm even if a subject correctly concludes that there are no reasons – indicative or intrinsic – that justify the subject's acting as the norm prescribes. It may be that such a claim is *justified* only if the authority *believes* there are reasons (indicative or intrinsic) for complying with the prescribed action (a conclusion that this study endorses). But that possibility still makes claims of coercive authority, as a conceptual matter, distinct from claims of practical authority of either the restrictive or expansive kind. In the previous chapter, I defended a stronger general account of authority than that implied by the restrictive account as the kind of authority that states may well have and that political theorists investigate. In this chapter, I suggest that when the state makes what may in ordinary language appear to be a claim of authority, it is really only (essentially) claiming something like the right to coerce or decide, without implying a correlative duty to obey – coercive authority rather than moral or practical authority.[7]

---

reasons that bear on the decision about what to do; they do not provide intrinsic reasons for action. See Regan, "Authority and Value: Reflections on Raz's Morality of Freedom," *S. Cal. L. Rev.* 62 (1989): 995 (Raz's theory is largely consequentialist) and id., "Reasons, Authority, and the Meaning of 'Obey': Further Thoughts on Raz and Obedience to Law," *Can. J. L. & Jurisp.* 3 (1990): 3 (Raz's theory wrongly suggests that law provides intrinsic rather than simply indicative reasons to obey). What I defend in Part II as the expansive account of authority is an account that claims that authorities do provide intrinsic reasons for action, not just indicative reasons. Regan's own view of authority would not accept this account; as previously noted, his account of authority is an even more consistent version of the restrictive account than one finds in Raz. Regan would apparently agree that law has what I call here "coercive authority"; see Regan, "Authority and Value," 1020 ("[g]overnment may justifiably coerce in some cases where it lacks authority") but would deny that it has "moral authority."

[7] In the terminology that has developed in the literature, the thesis I defend here is that the only claim the state makes is the claim of a "justification right" (the right to use coercion to enforce its norms), which need not entail a further claim of a duty to obey law qua law. See R. Ladenson, "In Defense of a Hobbesian Conception of Law, *Phil. & Pub. Affairs* 9 (1980): 134, 137–40. (For a recent discussion of the difference between a justification right and a claim right, see William A. Edmunson, *Three Anarchical Fallacies* [Cambridge: Cambridge Univ. Press, 1998], 39–44.) This view of authority is also defended in R. Sartorius, "Political Authority and Political Obligation," *Va. L. Rev.* 67 (1981): 3, 4–10. As I argue more fully in this study, I believe Ladenson and Sartorius are correct as a matter of legal theory (law does not make a claim of authority any stronger that what is entailed by the conception of a justification right), but they are wrong as a matter of political authority (law does possess political authority in the sense that it creates a duty to obey.) See John Finnis, "The Authority of Law in the Predicament of Contemporary Social Theory," *Notre Dame J. Law, Ethics, & Pub. Policy* 1 (1984): 115, 116n.4 ("[Sartorius] fails to show that arguments capable of justifying a claim to moral authority to make and enforce the law

The Minimal Normative Claim: The Claim to Justice

How Does "the Law" Make Claims?

Although my primary interest in this chapter is the law's claim to authority, I begin by considering a weaker normative claim that legal systems typically make. I do so in order to illustrate the connection between descriptive, conceptual, and normative inquiries in legal theory and to clarify certain potentially troublesome preliminary issues. One such preliminary issue is the problem of explaining what is meant in referring to the "claims" of a legal system. Although the idea of the law making claims might seem as mysterious as reference to the intent of corporations, legislatures, or similar groups, legal theory, by and large, has not been concerned with this potential problem, and I shall spend little time on it as well. I shall make the same assumption that seems to be shared in the literature: To refer to what the law claims is to refer to what any sensible individual, putting himself or herself in the position of a representative of the legal system – for example, the officials who are responsible for the implementation and enforcement of the system's directives – ought to recognize as the implicit claim that accompanies such official action. The claims of the law, in short, are the claims (implicit or explicit) of those who accept and enforce its norms in their capacity as representatives of the legal system. Undoubtedly, more needs to be said than this, and I shall say more later as the issue becomes important. For now, one point should be emphasized: The attempt to characterize the law's "self-image"[8] requires distinguishing between the claims of the law and the claims of any particular official or set of officials, such as judges, who may operate as the law's agents. Officials may make claims about law in their private capacity, just as moral philosophers do. These claims may differ from and even contradict the implicit claims of the legal system in which they function. Roughly, what needs to be kept in mind is the distinction between an official who represents the legal system in the sense of speaking for (on behalf of) the law and an official who makes personal claims about the law in the same way that any citizen might.[9]

Establishing the Minimal Claim

The manner in which descriptive or conceptual inquiries combine with normative inquiries in legal theory, and the manner in which one establishes what the

---

would not equally (or by addition of only uncontroversial premises) justify the claim that there is a generic moral obligation to obey that law").

[8] This term is used by Leslie Green; see Green, *The Authority of the State* (Oxford: Clarendon Press, 1990), ch. 3.

[9] As should by now be clear, I do not distinguish in this study between "law," "state," "government," or other similar terms that in common usage refer to the official institutions that create legal norms and enforce them through the relative monopoly on force that is characteristic of a legal system.

law claims, can both be illustrated by beginning with the minimal claim that legal systems make. Law claims that its actions are morally defensible. The "actions" that are the object of this claim include both the establishment of legal norms (the right to decide) and the enforcement of those norms through the use of the state's unique apparatus for imposing sanctions (the right to enforce). The minimal normative claim of the law is about both of these kinds of actions, but since it is the sanction that impinges on others and thus seems to require justification, the right to enforce may seem the more basic claim. As long as it is recognized that the right to enforce entails a claim about *what* one is enforcing (the state's view about the appropriate content of the legal norm), it will not matter which formulation is used. For purposes of this study, I shall use a third formulation of the basic claim, namely, the "claim to justice," as a shorthand way of referring to either the right to decide or the right to enforce. This formulation helps draw attention to the essential normative component of the claim, namely, that when the state acts, it does so in the belief that it has chosen morally appropriate norms for enforcement, as reflected, for example, in the claim that "it is right" to act as legal norms prescribe or "it is just" for the state to enforce these norms.

That the law makes such a minimal claim, variously described in the ways just suggested, is no longer particularly controversial as a descriptive thesis about legal systems. Indeed, it is almost the defining characteristic of modern positivism to insist that it was this attitude of the law toward its norms that was overlooked in classical positivism's exclusive focus on the state's coercive power.[10] However obvious the point may seem, it is worth pausing to consider how one might defend this descriptive thesis about the law's normative posture if challenged. The natural response to one who suggests that law makes no such claim is simply to call attention to common features of social life: the kinds of things that law does when it imposes sanctions – taking property, liberty, or life – are such serious invasions of another's interests that it is impossible to exempt them from the normal assumption that a morally conscientious agent will commit such acts only in the belief that they are justified. Only if one thought that the law did not purport to be a morally conscientious agent (if it purported, for example, to be no more than a "gunman writ large") could one fail to see that the practice of law belongs in the same category of other social practices that purport to be morally defensible.

Recognizing that law makes claims different from those of the ordinary gunman was Hart's way of making the point; but there are other ways of making the point that depend less on the contrast with gunmen and more on the analogy with any ordinary person who expects to be taken seriously in attempting to communicate and interact with others. Neil MacCormick, for example, notes that the law has Acts that are labeled the "Administration of Justice Act," but

---

[10] See generally H. L. A. Hart, *The Concept of Law* (Oxford: Clarendon Press, 1961), 79–88.

that no legal system is likely to pass an "Administration of Injustice Act."[11]
The insight that underlies this observation is, of course, hardly peculiar to
law: Governments do not enact Administration of Injustice Acts, but neither do
parents announce "Unjust Demands for Bedtime" or friends or neighbors proffer
"Silly Advice for Improving Your Garden." The point is simply the truism about
human behavior that conscientious people (unless they are engaging in some
odd joke of the Monty Python sort) do not offer advice, much less issue demands
or take action that affects others, unless they implicitly believe that what they are
doing – advising, acting, ordering – is based on morally defensible (sincerely
held) beliefs about what it is permissible or right to do.[12]

Consequences and Aspects of the Claim

However expressed, the point about the law's minimal normative stance, once
made, seems to many to be sufficiently obvious that it causes confusion, not
because it is overlooked but because too much is made of it: Recent discussions
often suggest that the law's normative claim is somehow inconsistent with
positivism's insistence on the separation of law and morality.[13] But the fact that

[11] Neil MacCormick, "A Moralistic Case for A-Moralistic Law," *Valparaiso Univ. L. Rev.* 20
(1985): 1, 28.

[12] Hart's later apparent retreat on this issue – denying that officials must be seen as implicitly
expressing a belief in the justice of the rules they accept and enforce (see Hart, *Essays on Bentham*
[Oxford: Clarendon Press, 1982], 153–61, 262–8) – may be due to a failure to distinguish the
attitudes of particular judges, considered as agents, from the implicit attitude of the law whose
norms the judge is asked to enforce. Hart is correct that particular judges may have any view of
the merits of the laws they enforce, including conscious and explicit disapproval of the law; see
id., 158–9. But the individual judge's situation differs from the law's in the same way that the
situation of an agent, who did not choose the content of the instructions he has been given, differs
from the situation of his principal. In both cases, it is possible for the judge or agent to form a
different view of the merits of the law than that formed by the principal, who is responsible for
the content of the law. The point can be illustrated by imagining a judge deciding a case where
the judge *is* responsible for the content – as when the judge has discretion (in what Hart would
call the "penumbral" area of a case). For such a judge to exercise his discretion and choose
the norm to create and enforce, while still denying that he approved of the norm, would at best
be strange, at worst "pragmatically self-defeating" or "logically inconsistent." MacCormick,
"A Moralistic Case," 2. For an interpretation of Hart's final word on this subject, see Philip
Soper, "Two Puzzles from the Postscript," *Legal Theory* 4 (1998): 359, 379–80 (suggesting that
Hart may have been endorsing the same weaker view of law's normativity that is defended here
as the claim of coercive authority).

[13] This mistake (confusing the implicit moral judgment that the law makes with an essential
connection between law and morality) seems to me to be implied by the title of, and much of
the argument in, Deryck Beyleveld and Roger Brownsword, *Law as a Moral Judgment* (1986).
For other examples of the mistake, see Michael J. Detmold, *The Unity of Law and Morality*
(1984), 21–7; Robert Alexy, "On Necessary Relations Between Law and Morality," *Ratio Juris*
2 (1989): 167–83. The problem in all of these accounts stems from a failure to appreciate the
distinction between the implicit moral claims that underlie legal norms (which need only be
content-dependent claims that the norm is right, just, and so on) and claims about the concept
of law itself. The judge who sentences the defendant to death implicitly represents that the law
believes the sentence is just, but that does not entail that the judge also represents the sentence as

conscientious persons believe they act correctly does not prove that they do, and this distinction between what is claimed (or believed) and what is the case is apparently all that the modern positivist needs for his or her continued denial of a necessary connection between law and morality.

In order to provide a contrast with the question to be considered subsequently, it may be worth briefly considering why the preceding description of law's minimal claim does *not* diverge from what moral theory accepts as a plausible claim, in the way that many think the claim to authority does. That there is no radical divergence here between description and evaluation follows from the arguments made in defense of the descriptive thesis. The claim to justice is no more than what is implied by the analogy to ordinary individuals engaged in sincere and serious attempts at communication or interaction. In making the same claim that any individual might, the state is not operating differently or more autonomously than any ordinary person. The claim to justice does, of course, imply a subsidiary claim: namely, that the state has a right to exist in the first place, but that claim, too, I shall assume, is not one that diverges from what political theory would accept as justified or plausible.[14]

This view of the state as making claims about its actions that are no different in kind from those of any ordinary conscientious individual leaves room, of course, for differences in the content of the claim that the state makes compared to other individuals. The content of the state's claim to justice will be informed by the peculiar kind of entity that the state is and the peculiar kinds of actions that it takes. In the case of law, the claim of justice presumably entails further claims, drawn from political theory, about why a state has the right to interfere at all with the interests of others. Though various political theories will give different explanations for this right, with accompanying differences in the limits recognized on the state's power, the state's posture is that it must act on its own lights in this area (as regards the correct political theory), just as it does in all other areas.[15]

---

just because it is the law. The latter claim is a claim about the concept of law itself and its implicit connection with morality; the former is simply a claim about the content of the act prescribed or permitted by law. Legal systems (officials) implicitly make the former claim; it is then legal theory that must show (as I try to in this study) that such implicit official claims about particular legal norms reveal a connection between the concepts of law and morality as those concepts are understood in the community. The mistake also appears in Roger Shiner, *Norm and Nature: The Movements of Legal Thought* (Oxford: Clarendon Press, 1992). For further discussion see Philip Soper, "Critical Notice: Legal Systems, Normative Systems, and the Paradoxes of Positivism," *Can. J. L. & Jurisp.* 8 (1995): 363, 366–73.

[14] The state's minimal normative claim *would* be out of line with prevailing moral or political theory if, for example, the state could not justify its right to exist. In this respect, legal systems differ from individuals: No one challenges an individual's right to exist in the way that some theorists (anarchists) challenge the state's right to exist. The anarchist's challenge, however, does not have enough adherents among contemporary moral and political theorists to create a problem of divergence in this respect between the practice of law and contemporary political theory.

[15] See MacCormick, "A Moralistic Case," 5 ("no law without supporting ideology"). It is possible, of course, that in a society sharply divided over ideology or over critical aspects of an ideology, no

So, too, with disputes within a particular version of political theory. In a society that accepts, for example, the view that a state exists only to realize the interests of citizens, further disputes may occur about *how* the state best serves citizens – by letting them lead their own lives as much as possible or by forcing them to lead "virtuous" lives. However this dispute is resolved, the state in such a society is likely to frame the implicit defense of its actions in terms that individuals normally do not use – for example, in terms of the "public interest," or the "common good," or, again as I call it, simply a "claim to justice." I do not intend, then, any sharp distinction between these various expressions (the "public interest," the "common good," or "justice"), nor do I intend these expressions to refer necessarily to an objectively identifiable "common good." I use these expressions as interchangeable ways of drawing attention to the fact that the state must morally defend its actions by reference to its own conception of how state power should be used. The law's claim to justice is, in short, open to the same variety of arguments about what justice is that characterize all of moral and political theory; so long as the state's implicit position on these issues is compatible with the range of contemporary moral debate about the matter, the state's posture will not be inconsistent with accepted moral or political theory.

In addition to taking an abstract position on what justice means (for a state), the law's claim to justice typically comprises two major subsidiary claims: (1) claims about the content of the law and (2) claims about the procedures by which the content is determined. Claims about content are made whenever the substantive purposes of legal rules are essential to the normative defense of the rule: The law's posture in such cases is that it has made its best judgment about the underlying substantive purposes and has reached a conclusion that reflects the law's view about how the issue should be resolved. Sometimes content claims are uncontroversial (murder is wrong); sometimes they are not (abortion is/is not permissible). Sometimes the claim about content is the minimum "content claim" that can be made, namely, that the actual substantive choice reflected in a legal rule is less important than that some choice – any choice – be made (rules of the road).[16]

implicit substantive position of the state on the ideological issue need be assumed; in such cases, presumably, the state's claim to justice will fall back on familiar arguments from political theory about the state's right to act despite (because of?) failure to achieve consensus on underlying moral issues. This possibility was recognized in the previous chapter; see Chapter 2, p. 50, footnote 28 (discussing Greenawalt's example of a hypothetical settlement where religious divisions among the settlers lead to a deliberate decision to let the state make laws that regulate religious disputes, but that explicitly do not represent the state's position on the merits of the dispute).

[16] In the previous chapter, I considered the suggestion that all norms might be viewed by the state as responses to coordination problems, See Chapter 2, 48–50. Under this view, presumably, all content claims become what I call in the text the minimum content claim that is possible, similar to the claim made about rules of the road. In societies where the state's underlying ideology denies the state power to take action except to resolve coordination or prisoner's dilemma problems, the state will presumably remain officially agnostic about the

Procedural claims are the state's implicit fallback response to the possibility that content claims might be wrong. Procedural claims – that the state has proceeded in a morally defensible fashion to determine the truth of a substantive dispute about the content of legal rules, or that it has fair procedures for determining the guilt or innocence of persons accused of violating such rules – are an inescapable part of the claim to justice. Just as procedural claims purport to shield the state from moral blame when it is later determined, for example, that a person was wrongly convicted, such claims also purport to protect the state from blame when it is decided that a legal rule, once thought to be defensible, is no longer so regarded: Past convictions (and sanctions) under the law will remain morally defensible so long as the state acted in good faith at the time.[17]

Doubts about the Minimal Claim: The Continuing Influence of Austin

The preceding arguments aim to establish a connection between law and certain minimal moral claims that any legal system must implicitly make. The arguments show why a classical form of positivism like John Austin's distorts the meaning of law by ignoring salient features of legal systems that are necessary in order to distinguish legal systems from coercive systems. In this respect, the argument bolsters the general position of Hart, and of modern positivists who followed Hart, in criticizing the Austinian account. But modern positivists who agree with Hart about the need to include the normative element in an account of law often disagree among themselves about how to model that element. And Hart himself, following the appearance of the *Concept of Law*, expressed views about the nature of law's normativity that seemed to retreat from what some positivists took to be the implications of his critique of Austin. I shall explain in later sections of this chapter how the minimal claim of law just described bears on this intramural dispute among positivists about how to model law's normative claims. The main argument I shall make, as already indicated, is that

content of the norm, claiming only that, like rules of the road, some norm had to be chosen and that the choice in the particular case was made in a fair manner.

[17] For the complications and paradoxes that result if one assumes, instead, that the state is justified in punishing only those who are guilty *in fact* (as respects both the immorality of the prohibited act and the factual proof that the act was committed by the defendant), see Heidi Hurd, "Justifiably Punishing the Justified," *Mich. L. Rev.* 90 (1992): 2203. That this is not the state's posture seems clear: The state is a human institution and thus claims not infallibility, but only lack of culpability when it makes mistakes, so long as it acts in good faith. See Philip Soper, "Some Natural Confusions about Natural Law," *Mich. L. Rev.* 90 (1992): 2393, 2418–23. If the state's claim is simply lack of culpability rather than a claim that the state, when it errs, nevertheless has engaged in right action, then we need not consider here the fascinating problems that Hurd discusses. See Heidi Hurd, *Moral Combat* (Cambridge: Cambridge Univ. Press, 1999), 6 (distinguishing the claim that an action is nonculpable from the claim that an action is right). The state need not claim that both it and the innocent (whom the state may have mistakenly punished) are engaged in right action. Only one action was right, but the state's sanction was not culpable so long as it believed in good faith, after appropriate procedures, that the person punished was guilty.

no stronger moral claim than the one I describe here as the "minimal" claim
can be attributed to law. Thus positivists who suggest that law claims more than
simply the right to enforce (coercive authority) are wrong; and Hart's apparent
retreat from a stronger account of law's normativity, I shall suggest, is best understood as a retreat to the thesis defended here: The minimal normative claim
is the only claim that can be ascribed necessarily to legal systems, and that
claim is sufficient to distinguish law from pure coercion.

Before proceeding to compare stronger and weaker accounts of law's normative claims, however, it is worth considering recent arguments aimed at denying
that any moral claim need be assigned to law. These arguments tend to make
mistakes that fall broadly into two categories: The first is the mistake alluded
to earlier in this chapter of failing to distinguish claims about the law and how
it implicitly presents itself from claims about what individual officials might
believe or claim as a matter of their own personal opinions. The second is the
mistake of failing to recognize that the claim about law's normativity is a conceptual claim, not just a descriptive claim, and thus requires for its evaluation a
consideration of whether and how it compares to competing conceptual claims
in terms of consistency with existing concepts and practices. I consider each
problem in turn.

DISTINGUISHING THE LAW FROM ITS AGENT. Consider first the problem of
distinguishing law from its agent, the judge or another official who enforces
the law in a particular case. It should be clear from the discussion about how
law makes claims that nothing in the preceding section assumes that individual
judges must actually believe in the minimal claim implied by the action they
take in a particular case. Individual judges who do not agree with the implicit
legal judgment that underlies the sanctions they impose will be like the priest
who, though he doesn't accept the church doctrines he preaches, must recognize
that when he pronounces those doctrines from the pulpit, he will be taken to be
presenting them as true religious propositions. The thesis about law similarly
requires officials to endorse or pretend to endorse the normative claim that what
law does is justified.

Once one recognizes that analogizing the law to any "conscientious" individual is a claim about the law, not about the beliefs of individual judges, it
is easy to avoid a number of mistakes. Matthew Kramer, for example, whose
defense of an Austinian version of positivism I consider in the next section,
suggests that judges and officials may have a range of attitudes toward norms
they enforce other than moral approval: They may have no moral attitude toward
the norm at all or an attitude of complete indifference; or their allegiance to
the norm may be based on purely prudential reasons for accepting a norm that
others view as moral.[18] All of these possible individual attitudes leave the basic

---

[18] See Kramer, *In Defense of Legal Positivism*, 103–5. Frederick Schauer has also recently suggested that law need make no normative claims. See Schauer, "Positivism Through Thick and

thesis about law's posture untouched. As long as the judge participates in a system that claims to justify coercion through law, he must recognize that he, by implication, will also appear to be endorsing that claim when he acts as law's agent in enforcing the law. If he does not personally agree with the law's claim and does not to wish to pretend, for example, that he shares the common official view that a particular legal norm can be justifiably enforced, he can, of course, make that disagreement known. In this respect, the judge is no different from any citizen who may disagree with the merits of the legal claim, the only difference being that the judge faces the additional dilemma in such a case of having to decide whether to continue to participate, as an agent, in a scheme of which he disapproves. None of these various individual differences in attitude toward legal norms affect the basic claim about law's general posture.

A problem related to the failure to distinguish law's claims from the beliefs of its agents can also arise from failure to understand the nature of the claim of justice that the law makes and that its agents, such as judges, implicitly endorse. This problem appears, for example, in Kramer's suggestion that particular norms may be based not on moral concerns, but on concerns to advance other, nonmoral values, such as efficiency or even the purely prudential interests of citizens or officials. "If the official believes that her choice of [a] particular norm will be doubtful morally but serviceable prudentially, then she may very well choose freely to adopt [the norm.]"[19] Kramer's observation misses the point. Judges, as agents, are not forced implicitly to claim that the laws of such officials, when they enforce them, are always and exclusively justified on moral grounds. Law's claim to justice, as indicated in the preceding section, is a claim about the right to coerce. Often, that claim *will* require, in order to be credible, a defense of the legal norm on moral grounds, but that need not always be the case. A legislature might justify a legal rule because it serves the interest of a particular political group and is enacted as a compromise among competing such groups. Obviously laws can also be based on considerations of efficiency distinct from strictly moral considerations – and can still be claimed to be appropriate bases for enforcement. For that matter, one can even imagine,

---

Thin," in *Analyzing Law*, ed. Brian Bix (Oxford: Clarendon Press, 1998), 73–4. Sometimes Schauer's argument, and the examples he uses of individual judges deciding particular cases, also seems to confuse the motivations and attitudes that an individual judge might have with the question of the implicit claims that the legal system (and the judge as representative of the system) makes when laws invade the significant interests of others. See Schauer, "Critical Notice," *Can. J. Phil.* 24 (1995): 495. As Kramer himself notes in a different context, when one behaves in a certain way "because one wishes to be seen to be behaving [morally], one thereby concedes that the mode of behavior in question is plausibly regarded as [moral]. Hypocrisy is the homage that vice pays to virtue." Id., 66. So, too, with law: Individual officials must act as if they endorse the law's claim that its use of force is justified, partly because they recognize that this claim is implicitly made by the legal system they administer.

[19] Kramer, *Legal Positivism*, 106. See also id., 73–7, where Kramer argues that legal rules may be based entirely on prudential, not moral, values – for both officials and subjects.

in the extreme case, a group of officials whose laws are openly admitted to serve only their own interest but who claim, citing Hobbes, that they are justified in enforcing any rules – including these – in order to prevent anarchy and collapse. Such a claim resembles the attempt mentioned in the last chapter of trying to collapse all laws into simple rules of the road (if it doesn't matter what rules we choose, we may as well choose those rules that favor our own interests). The claim is probably false and is not likely to be able to be defended in good faith in most societies; but if held in good faith, it presents a case of law making the critical minimum claim: that coercion on the basis of legal rules is morally justified, even if the values that underlie the rules being enforced are not themselves moral values. In short, the conceptual claim that legal systems must make a minimal claim to justice does not by itself require any particular content claim about the legal norm that is enforced: Only substantive arguments can show which kinds of content claims are necessary in order to make credible in particular cases and particular societies the claim that enforcement of such norms is believed in good faith to be justified. One thing *is*, however, ruled out by this account: Legal systems cannot respond to the victims of coercion who complain that coercion is unjustified by a shrug of the shoulders. Indifference to the morality of coercion or, worse, admitting that there is no justification for coercion turns the legal system into a coercive system. And this conclusion brings us to the most sustained recent attack on normative models of law.

COERCIVE SYSTEMS AND LEGAL SYSTEMS. That individual judges may have various attitudes toward the laws they enforce poses no problem for normative models of law. The situation changes dramatically, however, if one assumes that all or most of the officials in a legal system – all of those whose acceptance of the basic rules is necessary to establish the system in the first place – confess attitudes toward the system they enforce that are inconsistent with the minimal claim of justice. Matthew Kramer's recent defense of legal positivism, one of the clearest and most powerful analyses to appear in recent years, seems intent on supporting precisely this possibility: that all of the relevant officials in a legal system might have attitudes toward the system they enforce that involve no moral claims at all. Kramer explains how Mafia-like gangs can, in theory, come into power and exercise control over subjects for reasons based solely on each gang member's self-interest – and how even the relations among gang members themselves can be based on nothing stronger than prudence. He discusses how the range of nonmoral attitudes toward law, discussed in the preceding section as possibilities for individual judges, could also be adopted by all relevant officials. Thus officials might be indifferent to morality altogether and answer victims who complain that coercion is unjustified with a shrug and a "so what?" Or they might even adopt norms for strategic long-term reasons, even though the norms are conceded to be immoral and against the officials' own short-term prudential interests.[20] Finally, of course, it does not take a great leap of imagination to realize that officials who know their system is unjust might nevertheless hypocritically claim justice for their regime:

Slim is the likelihood, indeed, that every official will invariably forgo the ideological advantages of moral justifications. Much more likely is that at least some officials will explain at least some of their decisions in ways that serve to engender an appearance of fairness. Nevertheless, the pursuit of such an appearance is a matter of political shrewdness rather than of conceptual necessity.[21]

All of these variations on possible nonmoral attitudes of officials toward the system they enforce are variations on a common theme: All are coercive systems, if by that we mean exactly what Austin meant (and Hart originally criticized): systems in which it is conceded (or must be conceded if the hypocrisy in the last imagined example is penetrated) that legal "obligation" means nothing more than "being obliged." The question, then, is whether or not we should regard coercive systems as included within the category of legal systems; the subsidiary question is, what kind of answer does that question require?

To start with the latter question, note first that the question of whether coercive systems are legal systems has never been an empirical one. The question is not whether it is conceivable that coercive systems could develop and effectively gain control over definable territories. It may even be easy to point to existing examples from time to time of just such coercive systems, although many such examples, as in the case of military juntas that take control in a coup, will cloud the question of whether they are true examples by typically claiming they are justified, in an emergency for example, in temporarily suspending normal constitutional operations. Kramer adds to the empirical issue numerous creative and plausible arguments to show how such coercive systems might rationally develop, and he provides a few additional examples, both imaginary and real, to illustrate the possibility. All of this is, of course, beside the point if the question is conceptual, not empirical: Would we call these systems "legal," and why or why not?

Second, it is worth noting that Kramer himself never undertakes to answer the conceptual question. He indirectly suggests that the answer is obvious by accusing those who refuse to count systems as legal where good-faith belief in the justice of enforcement is absent as guilty of "natural-law dogmatism," apparently because "anyone who wishes to contest the thesis of an inherent claim-to-legitimacy is almost certain to focus on the posture of some wicked

---

[20] See Id., 62–71, 83–9, 94–8 (analogizing law to Mafia-like gangs or organized crime syndicates); 105 (suggesting that the "so what?" response is a possible response for officials indifferent to the morality of their regime); 107 (imagining an official choosing, for long-term strategic reasons, to adopt an unjust tax scheme that does not serve his or her own short-term self-interest).
[21] Id., 91.

legal systems. . . ."[22] "But wicked legal systems will not prove the point. Natural-law dogmatism is a charge commonly leveled by positivists against theories that attempt to incorporate substantive tests of justice as criteria for law along with formal tests. The air of dogmatism results from the clash between such theories and the ordinary use of the word "law". As Kelsen notes:

> If justice is assumed to be the criterion for a normative order to be designated as "law," then the capitalistic coercive order of the West is not law from the point of view of the Communist ideal of justice, nor the Communist coercive order of the Soviet Union from the point of view of the capitalist ideal of justice. A concept of law with such consequences is unacceptables. . . .[23]

It is these clear clashes with ordinary language that give these versions of classical natural law their dogmatic character. But no similar clash results between ordinary language and a theory insisting that legal systems make sincere claims-to-legitimacy for the simple, if unfortunate, reason that evil regimes all too often believe in and are willing to defend their ideologies, however wicked those ideologies might appear to others.[24] Even Nazi Germany, that notorious borderline example of a legal system in jurisprudence, might qualify as "legal" if the Nazis believed in the theories of Aryan superiority that underlay their evil laws.[25]

So the charge of dogmatism is unwarranted. But even if it were justified, the charge goes both ways. One cannot simply dogmatically assert that coercive systems are legal systems without confronting the problem of definition and the conceptual arguments for deciding whether to view law in the narrower way, which excludes the coercive system, or in the broader inclusive fashion. To that issue we now turn.

THE PROBLEM OF DEFINITION. We noted in Chapter 1 that claims about which features are essential to a concept are often thought to be arbitrary,

---

[22] Id., 104.

[23] Hans Kelsen, *Pure Theory of Law*, trans. Max Knight (Berkeley: Univ. of California Press, 1970), 49. Hart makes a similar point: "It is precisely on the ground that such a view would deny the title of 'law' and 'legal duty' to what are for many good reasons regarded as law and legal duties that this view cannot be correct." Hart, *Essays on Bentham*, 146.

[24] As Neil MacCormick notes: "When evil is done in the name of the law, the greatest evil is that whatever is done in the name of the law is also and inevitably done in the name of a public morality." Neil MacCormick, *H. L. A. Hart* (Stanford: Stanford Univ. Press, 1981), 161.

[25] See MacCormick, "A Moralistic Case," 1, 29 ("It is sometimes thought shocking that Nazis and their like can do evil in the name of the law. So it is. But it strikes me as yet more shocking that the evil they do is done in the name of moral duty and racial purity and such like supposed moral values"). The Nazi system might, however, fail to meet the test for law defended in this study, not on the grounds of insincerity but on the grounds that the Nazi belief could not be defended in good faith. The frequent use of secret laws, for example, is the kind of failure to qualify as legal that people like Lon Fuller cite to suggest at least a borderline case of law in Nazi Germany. The need for secrecy would support Fuller's suggestion by indicating that the Nazis knew that their beliefs were too far beyond what could defended in good faith in the modern world.

reflecting only the subjective values of their proponents. In response, we noted two ways in which arguments about the essence of a concept can be defended. First, conceptual claims are justified by showing that the feature is essential in order to avoid inconsistency with other existing concepts or practices. Second, these conceptual connections help reveal the purposes behind the classification scheme that explain how our concepts are used – purposes that reflect not the theorist's own values, but the values of those whose practices and concepts the theorist examines.

Arguments about the nature of law have, at different times, taken different features as the critical feature for revealing what might be essential to law. The connection between law and morality, of course, has always been a central inquiry; but Hart, in his critique of Austin, also made the connection between law and coercion a major focus.[26] That the latter relationship has now reemerged as a central issue in jurisprudence is due, in part, to Hart's own later retreat from the apparent implications of his original critique, as well as to the fact that these issues, like most fundamental issues in philosophy, have a way of reappearing, just when one thought the issue was settled, to galvanize new attempts at understanding. Retracing a bit of this history of how coercive systems have been viewed by major legal theorists will help us evaluate the recent Austinian revival.

Begin with Kelsen.[27] As insistent as any modern positivist about the normative nature of law, Kelsen nevertheless struggled to explain the difference between a "robber gang" and a legal system. After all, the gunman's order to hand over my money contains at least a prudential "ought": I ought to do as ordered if I value my life. Kelsen's explanation for the difference was that, though the orders of both the gunman and the legal system may have the same subjective meaning, the gunman, to use our terminology, does not also make the claim to justice of the sort that characterizes law.[28] But a robber gang *could* make such a claim – witness the terrorists who claim justice for their cause and the right to enforce their commands. Does this mean that the robber gang becomes a legal system if it makes the right kind of normative claim (presupposes the appropriate basic norm)? Kelsen's answer is problematic. The robber gang will not become a legal system as long as it remains insufficiently effective within a defined territory, "in short, if the coercive order regarded as the legal

---

[26] Recently, the connection between the concept of law and that of certainty has moved to center stage in the argument over whether moral standards that are inherently controversial can count as legal standards. I briefly consider this debate in the next chapter.

[27] For a useful overview of Kelsen's thought see J. W. Harris, *Legal Philosophies* (London: Butterworth, 1980), 59–75. For a collection of recent commentary see *Normativity and Norms: Critical Perspectives on Kelsenian Themes*, ed. Stanley L. Paulson (Oxford: Clarendon Press, 1998).

[28] To use Kelsen's terminology, although both the robber and the law might issue commands with the same "subjective" meaning, "we attribute only to the command of the legal organ, not to that of the robber, the objective meaning of a norm. . . ." Kelsen, *Pure Theory of Law*, 45.

order is more effective than the coercive order constituting the gang." But let the gang become dominant over a definable territory, and "then the coercive order may indeed be regarded as a legal order and the community constituted by it may be regarded as a 'state.'"[29]

The Austinian flavor in this answer is unmistakable: Apparently what counts in deciding whether a coercive gang is a legal system is exactly what mattered for Austin: The gang must be sufficiently independent to be a "sovereign" in a definable territory. What has happened to the necessary normative claim that characterizes legal systems? Kelsen *asserts* that having achieved effective independence, the "objective" validity of the gang's commands will now emerge as the basic norm presupposed by the gang. But this creates a problem: Either Kelsen's assertion amounts to "social science stabs at the psychology of the law abiding citizen"[30] or the assertion is arbitrary: There really is no difference between an effective robber gang and a legal system. The normative claims of law are not essential to the concept, and coercive systems that operate by "sheer imperatives" are still legal systems. This possibility, as we have seen, is the one defended recently by Kramer.

Hart's argument against the coercive model originally took a much more promising tack. Hart launched two distinct kinds of objections at Austin's model of orders backed by threats. The first is a set of technical objections – descriptive objections, aimed at showing that a sanction-based model of law does not fit many familiar features of legal systems. Power-conferring rules, for example, are ill suited to the "sanction as nullity" explanation that the coercive model requires. Similarly, a model that turns legal obligation into a prediction of possible sanctions could not explain why, for example, we continue to say that people have legal obligations, even though they have escaped the jurisdiction or bribed the judge and, hence, have no chance of incurring sanctions. But in addition to making these technical or descriptive objections, Hart mounted a conceptual objection – precisely the right kind of argument – in support of a normative model of law by noting that under the coercive model, legal obligation could only mean being obliged, and thus is inconsistent with the language of legal obligation reflected in current practice. For the model of orders backed by threats, Hart substituted a model of rules accepted by officials.

The retreat from the implications of Hart's normative model came in two stages. First, in the *Concept of Law* itself, Hart indicated that judges could accept the basic rules of the system for a variety of reasons, including "calculations of long-term interest . . . or the mere wish to do as others do."[31] Second, in the debates that followed with positivists, like Raz, who insisted that judges must endorse or pretend to endorse the rules as normatively acceptable, Hart

---

[29] Id., 48.
[30] Graham Hughes, "Validity and the Basic Norm, *Cal. L. Rev.* 59 (1971): 695, 702.
[31] Hart, *The Concept of Law*, 198.

reaffirmed the view that judges could accept rules for a variety of reasons, not necessarily moral ones. "Individual judges may explain or justify their acceptance of the legislator's enactments by . . . motives which have nothing to do with the belief in the moral legitimacy of the authority whose enactments they identify and apply as law."[32] What happens to obligation under such a view, and how is it different from simply being obliged? Hart's answer is cryptic but in line with the theory defended here:

I find little reason to accept . . . a cognitive interpretation of legal duty in terms of objective reasons or the identity of meaning of "obligation" in legal and moral contexts which this would secure. Far better adapted to the legal case is a different, non-cognitive theory of duty according to which committed statements asserting that others have a duty do not refer to actions which they have a categorical reason to do, but, as the etymology of "duty" and indeed "ought" suggests, such statements refer to actions which are due from or owed by the subjects having the duty, *in the sense that they may be properly demanded or exacted from them* [emphasis added].[33]

There are at least two ways to interpret Hart's retreat, as evidenced in these two passages, from the original conceptual argument about the meaning of legal obligation. First, one might suggest that Hart is making the mistake, described earlier, of failing to distinguish law from its agents. If the insistence that judges may have a variety of nonmoral attitudes toward the rules they enforce is meant as a claim about individual judges, the point is both true and irrelevant to the question of how the law presents itself. Second, one can interpret the last, longer quote from Hart as moving back to a view of the minimal claim of justice defended here: What law claims is not that citizens necessarily have an obligation to comply with legal norms, but only that enforcement of such norms is justified. The claim is not that there is a content-independent obligation to obey just because it is law; the claim is only that, even if the state is wrong about the content of the law, it is entitled to enforce its own views of the matter.

We can now more easily assess Kramer's recent defense of a coercive model of positivism. Kramer's interpretation of the variety of nonmoral attitudes judges may hold toward the rules they enforce makes it clear that he would apply Hart's suggestion in this respect to all officials, not just to individual judges. Regimes may operate with "sheer imperatives." Kramer claims that this

[32] Hart, *Essays on Bentham*, 265.

[33] Id., 160. Joseph Raz suggests that this passage from Hart displays a "Kelsenian twist to Hart's view of legal duties . . . [by implying] that duty-imposing laws are instructions . . . to courts to apply sanctions or remedies against people who are guilty of breach of duty." Raz, "Hart on Moral and Legal Rights," *Oxford J. Legal Studies* 4 (1984): 123, 131. But the virtue of Kelsen's "twist" in focusing on what a judge ought to do is that it helps emphasize the necessary minimal normative claim defended in this study, i.e., that the law (through its judges) is entitled to enforce the legal norm. As we shall see, this still leaves room to account for statements of legal duty in the sense of content-dependent claims about reasons for subjects to act, but it does not require a stronger content-independent claim of authority in the sense of reasons for subjects to defer to the state's judgment.

account is not simply an Austinian account, for, like Hart, he rejects many of the problems associated with a model of orders backed by threats. But the problems for Austin that Kramer avoids are the "technical" objections to Austin. Kramer purports to have defended a more sophisticated account of law than Austin by incorporating a role for rules and prescriptions in a model of law, but the role that these prescriptions play is simply that of a larger, more general club. Officials may use rules because they are more efficient ways of giving general directions to those they govern: The rules themselves need not be defended morally, even among the officials who accept them.[34] In short, the major conceptual objection to Austin, that under the coercive model obligation can only mean being obliged, applies as well to Kramer's version of positivism. We end where we began: looking for a conceptual argument for why the coercive system should or should not count as a legal system.

The conceptual argument for excluding coercive systems from the concept of law is essentially the argument Hart made initially: To reduce the concept of legal obligation to nothing more than the notion of being obliged is inconsistent with the practice and language of law. I have defended this conceptual explanation in previous work.[35] Raz, in a different context, makes the point vividly:

> We are to imagine courts imprisoning people without finding them guilty of any offense. Damages are ordered, but no one has a duty to pay them. The legislature never claims to impose duties of care or of contribution to common services. It merely pronounces that people who behave in certain ways will be made to suffer.[36]

Such a society, says Raz, never existed and, if it did, we would not regard it as exercising what we mean in our political institutions by legal authority.

Suppose now that the persistent defender of Austin's model of obligation concedes that existing practices and the use of the language of legal duty are inconsistent with the coercive model of law. Why not change existing practices? What purpose might be served by the current classification? This question seems to invite one to entertain the possibility of stipulating a wider or narrower use of the term "law," just as Hart imagined choosing between a concept of law that

---

[34] See Kramer, *In Defense of Legal Positivism*, 100–1.

[35] See Soper, *A Theory of Law*, 22–38, 172 n.21, 173 n.26. For similar arguments see Jeffrey D. Goldsworthy, "The Self-Destruction of Legal Positivism," *Oxford J. Legal Studies* 10 (1990): 449; Deryck Beyleveld and Roger Brownsword, "Normative Positivism: The Mirage of the Middle-Way," *Oxford J. Legal Studies* 9 (1989): 463; R. A. Duff, "Legal Obligation and the Moral Nature of Law," *Juridical Rev.* 25 (1980): 61.

[36] Raz, *The Morality of Freedom*, 27. The imagined example employed by Raz is actually used by him for a different purpose: to show that a theory that suggests that legal systems claim only coercive authority (a justification right to use coercion) are inconsistent with common practice and language. As I show later in this chapter, the quotation does *not* reveal an inconsistency with the minimal conception of a legal system that claims only a justification right of enforcement (coercive authority only); but it does show quite well what is wrong with counting as legal a purely coercive system that makes no claim to authority at all.

would or would not exclude immoral laws. The point, of course, is not actual stipulation,[37] but the discovery of the latent purposes that might be served by the current practice. Why not count effectively organized coercive regimes as legal? The most obvious answer is that the coercive regime, which makes no claim to either coercive or moral authority, doesn't meet even the necessary conditions for political obligation. By designating as legal only regimes that claim a certain kind of authority, we at least preserve the possibility of justifying obedience to law and defending the legitimacy of state coercion. To preserve that possibility, which underlies such a long history of theoretical inquiry and debate, is enough by itself to explain why coercive systems are distinguished in practice and language from legal systems.[38]

Defending the Claim to Justice

Enforcing Erroneous Laws

We have already suggested that the preceding account of law's minimal normative claim does not result in any significant divergence between the descriptive and evaluative branches of legal and moral theory. By claiming only the right to enforce, rather than an obligation to obey, the law does not take a position on a controversial issue within political theory. For some people, however, even the minimal claim of a right to enforce leads to a divergence between the law's claim and the method the law typically uses to justify that claim in particular cases. The dominant legal method is the method of formal appeal to preexisting legal standards, rather than direct justification by reference to the effect of illegal acts on the substantive purposes that underlie those standards. Because

---

[37] I have explained elsewhere why the attempt to choose between alternative accounts of law on pragmatic or moral grounds is unlikely to be helpful. See Philip Soper, "Choosing a Legal Theory on Moral Grounds," *Soc. Phil. & Policy* 4 (1986): 31.

[38] Note that this explanation – insisting that our current understanding of the concept of law is one that requires preserving the *possibility* of defending the legitimacy of the state and/or citizen obligation – does not beg the question. We are not saying that legal systems must be such as to ensure moral fidelity or state legitimacy (these are obviously different concepts). We are only preserving the possibility of showing legitimacy, thus making plausible the continued attempts to ground citizen obligation or state legitimacy. The coercive system, which dooms from the start any ability to establish moral legitimacy, is for that very reason worth differentiating from legal systems. Frederick Schauer, who, in contrast to Kramer, explicitly confronts the question of whether to call the coercive system a legal system, offers a different argument for the wider concept. He suggests that there are "instrumental moral reasons" for not including the normative claims in the concept of law because we thereby remove the possibility of taking "law's legitimate authority as a given." Frederick Schauer,. "Positivism Through Thick and Thin," in *Analyzing Law*, 76–8. I have previously expressed doubts about selecting one's legal theory on moral grounds – see Soper, "Choosing a Legal Theory." But the more basic problem with Schauer's argument is that it assumes that law's normative claims can only be accommodated by the view that law claims authority. If this study is correct in explaining how law makes normative claims, but not claims of authority, Schauer's worry disappears.

this formal method of justification raises the same problem in attempting to defend the law's normative claim that is raised in debates between act and rule utilitarians within moral theory, we might call this "the utilitarian critique."[39]

The utilitarian critique has two targets: The first is the posture of the law vis-à-vis the ordinary citizen; the second is the normative position of the judge or other official who imposes sanctions for legal violations. In the first case, the critique aims to establish that law does not have the authority over the citizen that is usually assumed – for example, that no duty to obey law qua law can be established on utilitarian grounds. In the second case, the target is the law's claim that it is justified in imposing sanctions just because the law is broken. My concern at this point is with the second issue: Since the law's minimal normative claim is that it is justified[40] in imposing sanctions for breaking laws as long as the content and procedures are believed to be correct (regardless of whether they are correct in fact), this issue – the justification of the sanction – becomes the critical one. The first question – whether citizens have a general obligation to obey – leads to the question that I consider later in asking whether the law makes any claim about citizens' obligation. Although these are distinct normative claims (one about the duty to obey and one about the right to impose sanctions), for many people there is an obvious connection between them: If utilitarian theory shows that citizens have no duty to obey the law (and may, perhaps, even have a duty in particular cases to disobey), how, then, can one justify punishing such citizens who, by hypothesis, have acted morally?[41]

I shall not recount here the familiar debate about why (and whether) legal rules, even if they are fashioned as carefully as possible, inevitably lead to cases where compliance with the rule is less desirable than disobedience.[42] I shall assume, for purposes of explaining how the law defends its claim to justice, what many others have concluded: that any rule, even if perfectly designed to

---

[39] The utilitarian critique has an obvious relationship to formalism and similar theories that purport to justify sanctions solely by reference to norms that can be identified through fairly straightforward empirical means. The problem discussed in the text does not assume that the law always justifies its actions by such formal methods; it is enough that the law typically (or at least sometimes) adopts the formal method. See generally Joseph Raz, "On the Autonomy of Legal Reasoning," *Ratio Juris* 6 (1993): 1, 5–10 (discussing the limits and implications of formalist views that see legal reasoning as autonomous and unrelated to moral reasoning). For a good recent discussion of the problem as it relates to rule application in law, see Frederick Schauer, *Playing by the Rules* (Oxford: Clarendon Press, 1991). For two of several illuminating discussions by a theorist who has explored the problem extensively as it applies to law, see Larry Alexander, "The Gap," *Harv. J. L. Pub. Policy* 14 (1991): 695; id., "With Me, It's All er Nuthin'": Formalism in Law and Morality," *Chi. L. Rev.* 66 (1999): 530, 548. See also Larry Alexander and Emily Sherwin, *The Rule of Rules* (Durham, N.C.: Duke Univ. Press, 20001), ch. 4.

[40] I am using "justified" here to mean simply "not culpable." See footnote 17.

[41] This puzzle is at the heart of Heidi Hurd's exploration in *Moral Combat*. It also forms the core of the illuminating recent study by Alexander and Sherwin, *The Rule of Rules*.

[42] For an earlier exploration of this issue see my discussion in "Law's Normative Claims" in *The Autonomy of Law*, 222–9. For an extensive treatment, see the sources cited in the previous footnote.

promote a particular purpose (e.g., speed limits that attempt to balance concerns for safety, fuel conservation, and quick transit), must inevitably be overbroad in application. Whether this inevitable overbreadth is a logical feature of rules (a rule that was guaranteed never to be overbroad would be so cluttered with exceptions for particular cases that it would no longer be a rule) or whether it is a contingent fact of human limitations in designing rules is unimportant in our present context. I shall also assume that an individual judge, enforcing a law that is overbroad, cannot always justify his action on utilitarian grounds. That is to say, I shall assume that, even though different consequences attend a judge's decision compared to a citizen's, those consequences cannot always guarantee that applying sanctions without allowing direct appeals to utility will prove to be the optimific action.[43] Even if one concedes all of this, the utilitarian critique misses the point: It fails as an attack on the ability of law to justify its claim to justice because it aims not at the posture of the law, but at the problems confronting an agent of the law (the judge), and that makes all the difference.

The utilitarian critique shows only that judges often are required to enforce laws that, as applied, are wrong – actions are condemned or punished that, in fact, were the best actions to take under the circumstances. But that legal norms can be wrong is obvious; it does not require an extended debate about whether and why rules are always overbroad to know that the law sometimes enforces norms that require or condemn the wrong behavior. Good-faith belief that one has enacted the correct norms is not a guarantee that the norms are correct. The utilitarian debate happens to focus on rules aimed at morally defensible goals and fashioned as carefully as possible to reach just those cases where these goals are implicated – presumably to show that in even the best of all worlds, perfect coincidence of legal norm and right action is impossible. But the failure of overbreadth in these cases is only a small part of the category of cases in which legal norms may in fact prescribe or forbid erroneously. Whether it is simply a case of misguided policy (a silly speed limit, based on errors in judgment about the effects on energy conservation) or serious injustice (evil laws), no

---

[43] The question of whether better consequences always result from following rules, even though they will be overbroad in particular cases, is not exactly settled among moral philosophers. Compare R. Sartorious, *Individual Conduct and Social Norms* (Encino, Calif.: Dickenson, 1975), ch. 5 (an act-utilitarian can consistently explain, using the legal system as an analogy, how rules might be enforced formally without allowing direct appeals to utility and without making such rules mere rules of thumb) with R. Brandt, *A Theory of the Good and the Right* (Oxford: Clarendon Press, 1979), 276 (endorsing Sartorius's attempt to rescue the role of rules by analogy to the legal system but commenting that "it is surprising that [Sartorius] thinks it consistent [with act-utilitarianism] to do so"). See also David Lyons, "Utility and Rights," in *Ethics, Economics, and Law*, eds. J. Roland Pennock and John W. Chapman (New York: New York Univ. Press, 1982) (Nomos XXIV), 107; (the practice of enforcing legal rights by the formal methods of the law is inconsistent with utilitarianism); R. M. Hare, "Utility and Rights: Comment on David Lyons's Essay," in id., 148 (defending the formal method by which law enforces rights according to rules that are "intuitively" sound without allowing direct "critical" appeals to the utility of the act).

utilitarian of any sort is likely to argue that blind enforcement of all such laws, without regard to their merits always leads to the best results.[44] For that matter, consider the judge with an antiutilitarian, deontological commitment who thinks that certain laws, say a state's liberal abortion laws, are seriously wrong. Like the utilitarian judge confronted with the need to blindly enforce rules, the deontological judge will have to decide whether the implicit promise to act as the law's agent justifies enforcing a law that the judge believes to be immoral. There is no reason to expect that the correct decision for such a judge will always lead to the conclusion that the judge must apply the law.[45] But even conceding that the judge may have a duty to resign or to subvert the law, the judge's situation is not the law's.

The Law and Its Agent (Again)

We noted in the previous section the significance of the distinction between the judge as agent and the law. That distinction is important not only in understanding whose motives or attitudes are essential in establishing the normative claims of law; it is also important in explaining how the law defends its claim to justice. In distinguishing the law from the judge, it is important to recognize that for all of the focus in recent legal theory on adjudication and the problems of legal reasoning, traditional inquiry into the nature of the law has focused instead on the lawgiver, or legislator, rather than the law applier. Political and legal theory alike have long considered the moral posture of the state by viewing it as a single actor – a sovereign, a leviathan, a ruler named Rex. The justification for this focus on the officials who are responsible for the creation and content of legal norms (not just their enforcement and implementation) is a reflection of the minimal normative claim we have already discussed: The claim to be acting justly often requires a defense in the first instance of the norms that have been chosen to govern society. It is the implicit attitude of those who create these norms that underlies the claim of justice.[46] Viewing the law from this perspective, it is easy to imagine the implicit response to the claim that the state's laws and rules are unjust either because they are overbroad or because of human

---

[44] The only argument to this effect would be one that claimed that the rule "Always obey the law" (a moral, not a legal, rule) is itself a rule that is likely to produce better consequences than any more limited rule. Few think this utilitarian defense of the obligation to obey is plausible.

[45] See, e.g., David O. Brink, "Legal Positivism and Natural Law Reconsidered," *The Monist* 68 (1985): 364, 376–84 (arguing that judges could *not* have a moral obligation to apply law that is too unjust).

[46] I do not see any morally relevant distinction between officials who accept basic rules and enforce them and officials who create the content of such rules: In both cases, as long as official acceptance is a necessary feature of a legal system, the officials are responsible in the relevant sense for the content (implicitly claiming that the content is just). As discussed earlier, individual officials, of course, may dissent from this official view, but when they do, they are dissenting from the implicit posture of the law.

error. The law, recall, claims only to act in good faith as respects both content and process. It believes the laws to be just, even though citizens and agents may not. When it enacts rules to be followed and requires judges to apply them without directly calculating the utility of doing so, it does so (implicitly) because it believes in good faith that this method, as an empirical matter, is the most likely way to produce the best consequences – even though it is logically possible to imagine cases where that judgment might prove false.[47] Its response in any of these cases to claims that the state's judgment was in error will be the same as its response in any case of error: The state has the right to decide these questions and, as long as it does so in good faith, error – even subsequent legal confession of past error – does not make the state culpable: The imposition of the sanction will remain morally defensible.[48]

From the law's viewpoint, in short, the problem of overbroad rules presents a different issue of justification than the problem of enforcement that the judge confronts. When the law (conceived of as legislator) faces the choice between enacting a formal rule (do not exceed 55 mph) or a flexible standard (drive at a reasonable speed), it faces the familiar problem of whether to formulate standards for conduct in fairly specific rulelike form or to provide more general, discretionary standards like "reasonableness" for courts to apply to particular situations. The issues that bear on the choice between these two methods have often been discussed, with Hart perhaps providing as succinct an account of the matter as any.[49] The more one incorporates into a rule vague standards like reasonableness or moral concepts like "due process" or "equality," the more one postpones decisions about the specific content of the law to the later point in time when judgment is made by the court. Though such postponement seems more consistent with the utilitarian critique, even the utilitarian presumably would not suggest that it is always better from the legislator's point of view to proceed through standards rather than through rules. The state's response, then, to the alleged overbreadth of rules will simply be that this is the state's best judgment in this particular field about the question of whether to regulate by

---

[47] It should be noted that in cases where the law provides judges with discretion to decide whether to impose the sanction, or where the law provides for defenses like the necessity defense, the problem of formal justification is lessened and may disappear: The judge will be empowered to entertain direct appeals to utility. But this escape from the problem will not always be possible: If it were, judges would become the legislators and creators of law, not the law's agents, and would find themselves in the different normative situation discussed in the next section.

[48] The only limitation on this claim will parallel the limitation on any individual's attempt to deny culpability. Persons who commit moral errors may not be culpable so long as they did their best to determine the moral facts and acted accordingly; but this excuse is limited by concepts of "gross negligence" or "good faith" that put into issue the degree of care that was taken before acting. Actions that are clearly immoral may thus be morally culpable, even though an individual did not know it at the time. I have suggested elsewhere that this same limitation on the state's posture may be evidenced in practice in the theoretical acceptance of the Nuremberg principles. See Soper, "Some Natural Confusions About Natural Law."

[49] See Hart, *The Concept of Law*, ch. 7.

rule or by case-by-case development of standards.[50] The implicit justification
of the law, in short, is based on the merits of deciding to enact rules rather
than more flexible standards; that justification cannot be attacked by pointing
out what the law already knows: That there will be cases, inevitably, where
overbreadth results. The posture of the law is that, though it is aware of the
possibility, even the inevitability, of overbreadth, it could not have done a better
job in designing the rule, consistent with the need for general social control and
regulation.

The apparent problem with formal rule justification thus turns out to be but a
subcategory of the more general problem of human error in the choice of norm.
Whether citizens (or judges) think that a rule's content is wrong, or whether
they think that the rule, though laudable, is overbroad in a particular case, the
state's normative posture is the same: It purports to have decided both sorts
of questions in good faith. That an individual or judge disagrees with either
decision is irrelevant – why should one think that the judge, after all, knows
better than the designated lawgiver what justice requires or whether rules are
better than standards? If one suggests that there are principles to use in deciding
when to allocate decisions to judges and when to legislatures, then the response
is: Of course there are, but on that matter, too, the law claims the right to decide.

The right to decide escapes the major thrust of both sorts of attacks on
the law's normative stance. From the large issues of political theory (should
the state be restricted to the role of night watchman, or may it redistribute
wealth and interfere in other ways with the private sector?) to the details of
lawmaking (should the law proceed by rule or by general delegation of standards
to courts or agencies?) to the midsize issues of constitutional arrangements
(which issues should courts decide and which legislatures?) the state's posture
is the same: Though all these questions are controversial and reasonable persons
can disagree about them, the state claims the right to make the ultimate decision
and act on it (impose sanctions accordingly). Such action is morally defensible
as long as the decision is reached in good faith.

Does the State Claim Authority?

The most serious suggestions that the law's normative claims are inconsistent
with prevailing moral philosophy do not make the mistake of collapsing the

---

[50] This implicit claim of the law that proceeding by rules, rather than delegated standards, is
justified in a particular case entails a variety of subsidiary claims, such as: (1) proceeding by
rules, rather than more flexible standards, is likely to produce the best results; (2) even though
it is foreseeable that the rule will apply to some cases that should be excepted, it is not possible
(would be counterproductive, etc.) to try to foresee and describe those excepted cases now;
(3) inviting judges to create exceptions by considering direct appeals to utility would be less
desirable than requiring recourse to the legislator to change the rule. Any of these claims can be
wrong; all that matters is that the state in good faith thought them to be true in a particular case
of rule enactment.

law's posture into that of its agents. These suggestions focus directly on the claims of the state in much the same way that one would on the claim of any individual (parent, military commander) who claims a certain kind of practical authority. "Authority" here means more than just "the right to legislate" or the "right to decide" or "the right to impose sanctions to enforce one's decisions." Authority, as used here, refers to the issue discussed at the beginning of this chapter that is typically raised in connection with the question of the obligation to obey, namely, the claim that citizens have duties to obey just because it is the law. One of the motivations of the current study, as explained earlier, is the odd position supported by much recent discussion of law's normative claims: Almost all of the recent discussion, as we saw when we began this chapter, seems to agree that law makes a claim to authority that is not justified.[51]

We have previously noted that the term "authority" can be used in a variety of ways. At the risk of some repetition, it is worthwhile to clarify again just how the additional claim of authority examined here differs from the minimal claim of justice described and defended in the previous section. Law *does* claim, in the terms developed here, coercive authority. That claim is a claim about the state's own actions – a claim that wielding coercive force to support legal norms is justified. The alleged claim of authority that we examine in the present section is a claim about subjects' actions: The question is whether the law necessarily claims that there are reasons (and, if so, what kind) for subjects to comply with legal norms. But there are two ways that a state might claim that subjects have reasons to comply with legal norms, only one of which involves the claim to authority that I investigate in this section. A state might claim that citizens have reasons to follow a legal norm because the content of the norm is correct. Earlier in this study, I called such a claim an ordinary moral claim. An ordinary claim is a claim about the content of the action required by the law – a claim that the content of the law is correct and rests on reasons that anyone should acknowledge, including subjects. In contrast to ordinary claims are strong moral claims. These claims implicitly include a claim that the content of the law is correct, but they also claim that one has reasons to follow the law even if the claim about the content is incorrect. Strong moral claims are content independent; ordinary moral claims are not.

The claim of authority that I examine here is a strong moral claim – a claim of moral authority, not just coercive authority, and not just a claim about the content of the law. In the terms of this study, the question is whether legal systems essentially claim that there is always some reason to defer to the judgments of the state even if those judgments are erroneous. This is the classical question of political theory, and it is this claim of moral authority that many recent theorists apparently attribute to law at the same time that they deny its validity as a matter of political theory. There are, of course, as we noted earlier,

---

[51] See footnote 4 and sources cited.

two ways to avoid the resulting conflict between legal and political theory. One might dispute the substantive question of political theory about whether a claim to moral authority is justified. Alternatively, one might challenge the descriptive claim in legal theory about whether the law does in fact claim moral authority.

This study, as already noted, undertakes both tasks. In Part II I defend an account that suggests that the law has moral authority. But I put this normative issue aside here to focus instead on the legal theory issue: What is the evidence for the assertion that law claims moral authority? In light of the widespread agreement that law makes such a claim, I confess to a certain tentativeness in offering a different view. But the current view is odd for two reasons. First, assertions in the literature about what the law claims are typically just that: assertions. The thesis is often presented as an empirical or descriptive one whose proof lies in simply "looking and seeing" to discover that this is the claim states typically make. In contrast, both the normative half of the question (is the claim to authority justified?) and the related conceptual issue (what does it mean to claim authority?) receive extensive discussion and are given all the care in constructing definitions and arguments that characterize the consideration of any difficult issue in moral philosophy. This difference, undoubtedly, is due in part to the difference between descriptive, conceptual, and normative claims; but it may still leave one who sees law as making a different kind of claim somewhat at a loss about how to continue to resolve the disagreement.[52]

The second reason the current view is odd reflects the point made at the beginning of this study. How could it be that the practice of law, in the claims it makes, is so out of step (and presumably has always been out of step as long as states have existed) with the conclusions of moral philosophy? Rather than simply conclude that law's normative stance is autonomous in this respect, shouldn't the discrepancy induce reconsideration of either the normative or the descriptive claim?

I shall express my tentative doubts about whether law claims authority in two ways. First, I shall consider, and reject as inconclusive, what I take to be the major positive argument for attributing such a claim to the state. Second, I shall advance a variety of arguments for why this attribution seems to be one that is, if not indefensible, at least incapable of being established as the simple empirical proposition it purports to be.

---

[52] I, too, have taken for granted in earlier work that the law makes the claim of a duty to obey that is at the center of political theory. See Soper, *A Theory of Law*; id., "Legal Theory and the Claim of Authority." I took that claim to be strong evidence that contemporary political theories – denying an obligation to obey – were wrong. I now think that the more interesting problem is the apparent discrepancy between the legal and moral points of view – a discrepancy that can be resolved without abandoning the claim that there is a general prima facie duty to obey the law. As the text explains, there may be an obligation to obey, but the state need only claim what is necessary to defend it's own actions (the right to coerce), with the question of its authority (and the duty to obey) to be resolved through moral and political theory.

The Positive Arguments

The suggestion that the "right to rule" can be logically separated from "the duty to obey" has often been made of late, usually as a conceptual or normative matter rather than as a suggestion about what states claim.[53] Since it is this latter question that I want to pursue, it may help first to clarify exactly what is at issue. Note first that the question is not whether certain concepts in our language – such as "command" – necessarily entail a claim of correlative duties. Sometimes the issue is put this way: The law, it is suggested, claims not only the right to decide what norms to enforce, but also a correlative duty to obey. I do not want to quarrel with the conceptual claim about our language. I will assume that the right to command is an example of a concept in our language that connotes a correlative duty to obey. Having made that concession, one simply poses the current question in a different way: Does the state claim the right to command (with a correlative duty to obey) as well as the right to enforce its norms?

TURNING PUNISHMENTS INTO PRICES. The most frequently encountered argument against the claim that the state claims only a right to enforce its decisions is that this posture would be tantamount to inviting each citizen to decide on his or her own whether to obey. The sanction cannot be avoided, but if the state makes no claim that citizens must obey just because the law says so, then the state in essence invites each citizen to view the sanction as the price to be paid for engaging in prohibited conduct. Such a view is inconsistent with the normative language of praise and blame that distinguishes, for example, taxes from fines and accompanies the judgment that the latter are punishments. Thus, it is concluded, entities that did not claim a duty to obey would not correspond to any of the actual entities we know as legal systems.[54]

Note that this argument is exactly the argument we considered in the previous section to establish law's minimal claim. The argument provides a conceptual defense for the conclusion that coercive systems must be distinguished from legal systems by at least claiming the right to enforce in order to avoid inconsistency with the current language and practice of law. The argument is also the right kind of argument for trying to decide whether law makes a stronger claim than the minimal claim: It looks for inconsistencies in our normative practices that would result if we took one description rather than another to be characteristic of the law's posture. In the present case, however, the argument

---

[53] See footnotes 5, 7.

[54] For an example of the argument, see Raz, *The Morality of Freedom* 27 (quoted at p. 70). See also MacCormick, "A Moralistic Case," 21 ("The very imposition of a "punishment" as such always involves some element of moral stigma (whether deservedly or not); . . . . Utilitarians may think this is a mistake. Punishment, perhaps, in their eyes is just a price charged for rule-breaking, set at a level which tries to price breaches out of the market").

fails. It overlooks the fact that the minimal normative claim of the state typically involves two claims: the claimed right to enforce and the claim that the norms being enforced are believed to be just – the content is believed to be correct. The latter aspect of the claim ensures that the language that accompanies the imposition of sanctions will continue to be the moral language of blame and praise; the law will still distinguish between taxes, which citizens are invited to view as the price for engaging in designated conduct, and fines, which entail *claimed moral duties* to refrain from the conduct. All that the state needs to do in order to continue coherently using the familiar moral language in its legal practice is to maintain its moral posture with respect to the content; it does not need to add a content-independent moral judgment about the duty to obey the law qua law.

CONTENT AND CONTENT-INDEPENDENT CLAIMS. Understanding how claims about content support the language of praise and blame and legal duty is the key to understanding why it is not essential that law make any stronger claim of authority. Content claims, as we have seen, are typically of two sorts. Substantive claims point to the reasons the legislator believes justified enacting a norm – reasons that are held out as reasons that subjects should also acknowledge, independently of the law. The law against murder or theft, or any law, for that matter, that proscribes acts that are *mala in se* will typically be based on reasons that are claimed by the state to apply to subjects even if the law had not been enacted: These acts are wrong, regardless of the law, though without the legal norm, no legal sanction would be threatened. The same is true even if the underlying reasons are controversial; laws on abortion, for example, purport to represent the state's best judgment about the issue and thus claim to be based on reasons that apply to subjects as well. Coordination claims, in contrast, are not based on reasons that exist apart from the law. Rules of the road, laws that in general are *mala prohibita,* may be justified only because the law has made a choice rather than because of preexisting reasons that apply to subjects. In these cases, the law will appear to present itself as claiming that subjects should obey just because it is the law. But note how different even this claim, in the case of coordination cases, is from the claim of moral authority. Coordination cases, as we have seen, are classical examples of the exercise of authority under the restrictive account. This kind of authority claims only that subjects are more likely to engage in correct action by following the state's lead *instead of* making their own judgment. The claim of moral authority, in contrast, is a claim that subjects have reasons to defer to the state's judgment even after they have made their own, different judgment about what action is (prima facie) correct. In coordination cases, the difference between these two kinds of authority becomes elusive but still exists. The state might, after all, be wrong about whether coordination is necessary; or, as we have seen, even perfectly appropriate coordinating rules will often be overbroad and not apply in particular cases. In these cases, it may appear that law claims a degree of restrictive authority that is broader than is actually justified. But the state will not claim moral authority: It will not claim, for example, that subjects who disagree with the state's judgment about whether coordination is necessary, or that subjects for whom the law is overbroad (the "expert pharmacologist who . . . may not be subject to the authority of the government in matters of the safety of drugs"), have reasons nonetheless to defer to the state's contrary judgment.[55] In short, content claims of either the substantive or coordinating kind will always support claims about subjects having content-dependent reasons to comply with the law. To avoid inconsistency, one does not need to add the additional claim that subjects also have content-independent reasons to defer to the state's judgment when that judgment is wrong.

The Negative Arguments

The arguments for denying that the state claims authority build on the preceding explanation for why no inconsistency results if one fails to ascribe to the law any stronger claim than the minimal claim of a right to enforce. To make the point vivid, consider this: What exactly could a state do to make clear that it either was or was not claiming that citizens had a content-independent duty to obey? My hypothesis is this: Nothing in the practice of law as we now know it would change if the state, convinced by arguments that there is no duty to obey law qua law, openly announced that it was abandoning any such claim.[56] If this hypothesis is correct, then I do not see how the posture of legal systems today can be assumed to be one that claims authority in the sense of a content-independent duty to obey as well as the right to coerce.

---

[55] See the discussion in the previous chapter at 41–2. Note that if the thesis about law's claiming more authority than it has were limited to apply only to claims of restrictive authority, the thesis might be defensible. Law does, sometimes, base its norms on apparent claims of restrictive authority (coordination-based claims about the content of the law). And these claims are inevitably overbroad. Thus the assertion that "law inevitably claims more restrictive authority than it has" could be true (and would not be inconsistent with political theory) – but only if the assertion is qualified by admitting that law makes no claim about subjects' reasons for following a legal rule when they believe the rule is overbroad. But the thesis thus qualified is of limited interest, partly because it leaves out of its account all of the laws that are based not simply on coordination claims, but also on substantive claims about the law's content. It is also a much more modest thesis about law's claim of authority than seems to be intended by those who support the thesis. Indeed, it does not seem to be a claim of authority at all, but only a claim about the coordinating reasons that underlie the legal rule.

[56] When I say that the practice of law would not change, I mean the normative practice: No inconsistency would arise, comparable to the inconsistency that would be presented if law imposed serious sanctions on others without purporting to justify such actions. Whether *behavior* would change (whether fewer people, for example, would obey the law if officials claimed no duty to obey law qua law) is a separate question.

In evaluating this hypothesis, the following factors seem to me relevant:

(1) The duty to obey the law is not itself typically a *legal* norm. The speeding defendant, for example, does not get two fines – one for speeding and one for failing to obey the norm that laws are to be obeyed just because they are the law. Lawbreaking, in short, is not worse just because it is *law* breaking; lawbreaking is bad because the act is thought, on the merits, to be wrong.[57]

(2) Abandoning the view that the state claims that citizens have a duty to obey does not mean that the state must abandon its own moral view about the underlying act that led to the legal rule and sanction. That moral judgment will continue to be reflected in the institutional process by which offenders are identified and sanctioned, and punishments will thus not become prices *from the state's point of view*. (Nothing, of course, will prevent a citizen from adopting the economic or bad man's point of view, but that is not what is at issue.)

(3) A corollary of the preceding suggestion is that a state *could*, without contradiction, openly adopt the bad man's point of view; but that *would* be tantamount to declaring that all sanctions are taxes on conduct, with the implication that the state takes no view about the morality of the conduct. That is a possible position; it just happens not to be the position that most states take about most laws (and we might not even think of such a society as a legal system); most important, it is not the position that would be entailed if the state made no claim about a duty to obey.

(4) Any suggestion that the state makes a claim to authority because that claim helps ensure the state's survival must confront the frequent observation that legal systems can survive well enough, thank you, with coercion alone. States design sanctions to ensure compliance by those who don't share the underlying moral judgment about content; in any healthy state, most citizens will share that judgment (or at least they will share the judgment about the processes by which undesirable norms are recognized as such and so changed). The suggestion that the state's survival requires a claimed duty to obey in addition to this shared moral

---

[57] A similar argument has been made by M. B. E. Smith in suggesting that any moral obligation to obey the law would be trivial because it could not add significant moral weight to the existing moral evaluation of the content of the act. See Smith, "Is There a *Prima Facie* Obligation to Obey the Law?" *Yale L. J.* 82 (1973): 950, 970. I have criticized this argument elsewhere as it applies to the question of moral obligation. See Soper, *A Theory of Law*, 86–7. But the parallel argument in trying to decide whether there is a distinct *legal* obligation to obey the law qua law seems to me to have some force, as long as one assumes that legal norms are typically identified, in part, by the existence of sanctions. Sometimes, as in the case of penalties for scofflaws or punitive damages for willful disobedience, the law *does* impose a separate sanction to reflect the wrong involved in the fact that one broke the law (in addition to the sanction for the wrong involved in engaging in the proscribed conduct).

judgment about the content of its norms (plus, of course, the sanction) seems empirically untenable.

Objections

So many theorists have suggested that the state makes a claim to moral authority that the previous conclusion, questioning that assumption, would be stronger if we could explain the source of the mistake. Here are some possibilities.

EXPANSIVE AND RESTRICTIVE AUTHORITY. We have already noted that one source of possible confusion arises from cases involving coordination where the only content-dependent reason supporting the legal norm is the fact that it is against the law. Where the justification for a law just is the fact that it is a law – like rules of the road, or conduct that is *mala prohibitum* – the state does appear to claim that subjects should obey the law just because it is the law. But this claim, which resembles a claim of restrictive authority, can also be right or wrong (the law may be mistaken about whether coordinating activity is needed, for example, or whether the legal rule may be appropriate but overbroad). For reasons explained in the previous section,[58] if this is what is meant by law claiming more authority than it has, it may be conceded: But as long as law makes no claim that citizens have reasons to comply when the rules are overbroad (though the state still claims the right to enforce them even then), it hardly seems to be making any claim of authority.[59]

OFFICIALS VERSUS THE LAW. It is also important again to distinguish what the law claims from what particular individuals, including officials, might claim. That particular judges or even legislators often claim that citizens have a duty to obey – as a matter of their personal judgment about the issue within political theory – is a commonplace fact and easy to understand. (There is little to lose, and perhaps something to gain, by adding a claim of citizen duty to other reminders of why one should obey. Besides, it might be true.) Once again, though, it is important to distinguish the law from any of these persons acting in an individual capacity. The best way to do that is to recall the method by which we began in explaining how the law makes claims and what the minimal normative claim must be. When one asks whether the practice of law would change if the law were seen as making no claim about a duty to obey, one is asking whether any normative inconsistency would arise within the practice.

---

[58] See 80–1.

[59] One could represent coordinating rules as reflecting, for example, the claim that subjects should "follow them when you think they are not overbroad; otherwise, do as you wish, risking, of course, the sanction that we are entitled to impose (because we cannot tell in advance when they are overbroad) – and also risking being wrong in thinking that they *are* overbroad."

My suggestion is that no inconsistency would arise comparable to the inconsistency that would be presented if law imposed serious sanctions on others without purporting to justify such actions.

AUTHORITY IN OTHER CONTEXTS. It might be objected that my test – what would be different if the claim to authority were abandoned – is the wrong test. By that test, could one not also question whether parents or even military officers claim authority? After all, the parent only needs the right to enforce his or her decision (a consequence of the parent's right to decide); any other additional normative claim that the child should obey could be explained as an implicit judgment about the content of the act that is prescribed, not a claim about the parent's right to be obeyed just because he or she is a parent. I confess that I am no longer sure whether even these classical paradigms of authority ought still to be regarded as paradigms of the concept. If this conclusion is too radical, one might distinguish the parent's position (and the military officer's) in the following way. Perhaps the normative argument for parental authority is uncontroversial (and true) in a way that does not apply to law. If so, it may be that the parent's claim (you should obey) automatically conveys in practice both reasons – the content-based reason as well as the content-independent one. My own view is that parents probably do not think in these terms: They do not stop to consider whether the child has a duty to obey just because the parent said so. The force of the "just because" is conveyed by the right to enforce the parents' decision; the force of the "duty" is exhausted by the belief that the content is correct. To claim an additional duty to obey just because the parent said so requires a level of sophistication that only philosophers typically display. So, yes, parents *could* abandon any such claim and nothing would change. On the other hand, having abandoned the claim only means that it is left open – to be decided by moral philosophy, and if moral philosophy concludes that parents have such authority, it will automatically attach to the parent's directive whether the parent thinks about it or not. Finally, note again that many parents might claim a duty to obey as a matter of their own opinion on the issue within moral philosophy. Just as one must distinguish personal views of officials from what the concept of law entails, so too one might suggest that the concept of parenthood does not entail the claim that children have a content-independent duty to obey, even though many parents, for understandable reasons (including the possibility that they are correct), may make such a claim as a personal matter.

As for military commands, one could say much the same thing: Probably nothing in the practice would change if soldiers were thought to have no duty to obey just because of the command, sanctions would be effective enough. It might be thought that the military is different because of the empirical question of survival mentioned earlier: Military commands, one might suggest, are so invasive of personal interest that only a moral duty to obey, as well as the sanction, can guarantee the required level of effectiveness. But this, too, seems farfetched. Soldiers reluctant to risk their lives in the face of threatened sanctions for disobedience are hardly likely to reconsider because of an additional *claimed* moral duty to obey. (If there actually is a moral duty to obey, conscientious soldiers presumably will have additional incentives to obey; whether this is the case is independent of any claimed duties made by commanding officers.) Nobody is suggesting that abandoning the claim of authority, even in the military context, means that soldiers are being invited to sit around and decide for themselves what orders to obey. The order will still be to act *now* (you may deliberate or not as you like, just as long as you do it), and the sanctions will be correspondingly severe to reflect the extent to which the order requires overcoming self-interest or contrary moral judgments.

All of these cases – military orders, parental directives, and legal norms – share one common feature that casts doubt on the assumption that any of these are cases involving an essential claim to authority in the sense we are considering. That feature is the difference in approach to practical reasoning between ordinary individuals, on the one hand, and moral philosophers, on the other. Consider again the case of law. There is something odd about the suggestion that law claims that citizens have a moral duty to obey the law, just because it is the law. Legal systems are not in the business of making pronouncements on fundamental questions of moral philosophy; they are, rather, in the business simply of making judgments about the norms to be enforced in society. The idea that law would simply assert a duty to obey without defense, without bothering to consider whether the claim is true, is odd, to say the least. The oddity is illustrated by imagining the dialogue that might ensue if one could explicitly discuss the question with the law (or, an easier case to imagine, with a parent). The law insists that its legal norm is just, and that it has the right to create and enforce such norms for the community. Because the law believes the norm is just, it also believes citizens should comply for that reason – the content-based reason. If one asks whether the law also expects obedience, even if the norm turns out to be wrong, the response is likely to reflect the odd hypothetical nature of this counterfactual. Since the law thinks the norm is correct, it is difficult to know what to say about the hypothetical counterfactual:

CITIZEN: "What if it turns out that you are wrong in your moral judgment about the norm's content. Do you still expect me to obey then?"
LAW: "I'm not sure what you're asking. Since I think the norm is just and am entitled to act on my own judgment, what difference does it make that my judgment might be wrong (but not culpably wrong)? I still expect you to *comply*, if that's what you're asking, and, of course, the imposition of the sanction (if I've acted in good faith) will be morally defensible even if the judgment about content is later proved to be wrong. Isn't that enough? If you want to know whether you also have moral reasons to comply apart

from the content of the norm, I'm interested in that question too – as a matter of moral philosophy (we can debate that question if you like at our leisure, after you've complied); but whatever the answer moral philosophy reveals about that question doesn't seem to affect what I'm asking you to do. You have a prudential reason to comply because of the sanction (which *is* independent of content), and you have a moral reason as well if I am right about the content. If moral philosophers prove that you also have a content-independent moral reason to comply, so much the better. Actually, I don't spend much time thinking about that question."[60]

HAVING AUTHORITY AND CLAIMING AUTHORITY. The preceding discussion suggests a distinction between persons who might actually have authority and those who have it but who need not be seen as claiming authority. Is that distinction plausible? As I suggested earlier, this distinction seems plausible enough in the case, for example, of theoretical authorities. One might offer an opinion about a factual matter without claiming to be an authority – perhaps because one is uncertain about one's relative standing among so-called experts; yet it may be clear that the opinion *is* authoritative and advisees would be wrong not to regard it as such. Whether one has theoretical authority, in short, is a matter of the facts about the expertise of the person providing advise or information; the person giving such information may be ignorant of, or unconcerned about, the facts that establish him or her as an authority.

There does not seem to be any obvious reason why practical authority should be different in this respect from theoretical authority. The preceding discussion explains why: The explanation for what makes one a practical authority is a complex matter of moral theory; that people might convey their desires or demands to others, without thinking about whether moral theory gives their desires or demands the special weight that they would carry if they actually have authority, seems just as plausible as in the case of scientists who might have authority but do not know or care about the facts that establish their authority. One can have authority (or be an authority), in short, without knowing it and thus, a fortiori, without claiming it.

CLAIMING AUTHORITY AND EXPECTING COMPLIANCE. A final distinction worth considering is whether it makes sense to distinguish an expectation of voluntary compliance with one's wishes or desires from a claimed duty to comply. In ordinary contexts, this distinction also seems plausible. A colleague, friend,

---

[60] Note, again, that this imagined dialogue is between the law and the subject, not between subjects and particular officials who may, as individuals, be just as interested in the question of a duty to obey as any political theorist. The point, once again, is that we are looking for a conceptual argument, pinning law to claims of moral authority in order to avoid inconsistencies with current practices. The dialogue is meant to show that no such inconsistency results when the law, qua law, remains agnostic about the question of its moral authority.

or spouse may ask one to perform an important task and expect compliance without suggesting that failure to comply would be morally wrong. Requests are commonly thought of in this manner. But one should not assume that mere requests, so conceived, never result in a duty to comply. There may be some requests that, though the person making them does not claim a duty to comply (for the reasons just discussed), nevertheless create such a duty. Whether that is the case will depend on the relationship and the kind of respect that is due to someone who expects my compliance. In the case of law, this distinction is important for two reasons. First, it will help account for another common descriptive thesis about law, which may be confused with the claimed duty to obey. It is often noted that the law's posture toward the sanction is that the legal sanction is not intended to be the primary motive for compliance; voluntary compliance with legal norms (regardless of content) is expected. The point is that even if this expectation of compliance attaches to legal directives, it is distinct from a claimed duty to comply. Second, if the law did not at least expect voluntary compliance, it is probably unlikely that it could have moral authority. If the duty to obey exists, it is probably the result of a theory that is based on the respect that is owed the state, which seems to require at least the expectation of voluntary compliance (without such an expectation, the failure to comply would show no disrespect).[61]

The Claim of Authority versus the Aspiration to Authority

The distinction just made, between an expectation of compliance and a claimed duty to obey, points toward a different description of the law's attitude to its own authority and the possibility of a (moral) obligation to obey the law. It is possible that the phenomenon moral philosophers think they have detected in describing law as claiming authority is not a "claim" – a bald assertion that citizens have a content-independent duty to obey; rather, it may be just a "hope" that it will turn out that political theory will demonstrate that there are content-independent moral reasons to obey. I said earlier that the law's survival does not depend on an actual duty to obey, much less on a (false) belief in such a duty. But that does not mean a state may not hope that such a duty does exist – simply because one would rather have those who disagree about the content of legal norms obey because of moral duty rather than out of fear of the sanction. One could say the same of parents: Parents do not, I suspect, think about the question of whether children have a moral duty to obey even if parents' directives are badly misguided or unjust; they rely, like the law, on the right to have their

---

[61] See Kent Greenawalt, *Conflicts of Law and Morality* (Oxford: Clavendon Press, 1987), 49 ("If a good government adopts valid laws whose scope is much broader than any expected compliance, a conclusion that the government is legitimate presumably would not acknowledge a duty to obey that reaches further than official hopes about obedience").

moral judgment become the norm that is enforced within the family. But if they did think about the question, there is reason to suspect that they would hope that moral theory is rich enough to show that the motivation for children's complying even with wrongheaded directives stems as much from a true moral theory about the respect that is owed parents as it does from the fear of the sanction.

At the risk of repetition, the latter comments will, I hope, forestall any misunderstanding that to "demote" the claims of the state by abandoning the view that law necessarily or even typically claims authority does not entail giving up on the question of whether the law does in fact have such authority. Quite the contrary: The argument I make here simply restores that question to the position it has always occupied – a matter of concern primarily for moral philosophy (not for bald assertion by the law) and, of course, a matter of concern for any conscientious citizen.

4

The Nature of Law

Before proceeding to the normative half of this study to examine whether law actually has moral authority, this chapter briefly summarizes the conclusions of Part I by indicating how they bear on certain familiar issues in legal theory. Three distinct but related questions dominate discussions about the nature of law. Two of these questions have long-standing pedigrees as critical paths to a better understanding of the concept; the third question, a more recent arrival on the scene, is a close cousin of the first two and shows signs of becoming equally central to the current debate. The three questions are: (1) what do we mean by legal "obligation"?; (2) what is the connection between law and morality?; and (3) what is the connection between law and certainty?

The Meaning of "Legal Obligation"

Moral philosophers usually distinguish between what one ought to do and what one is obligated to do. Obligations, it is usually said, are more important or more serious than mere oughts. Though there is disagreement about exactly how to model this difference in force, the suggestion that obligation is more serious has nothing to do with the fact that oughts can be used in nonmoral contexts as well as moral ones. For even when moral oughts are the focus, it is usually thought that to say one ought to do something falls short in terms of significance from saying that one has an obligation to do the same. Thus, that one ought to contribute to charities may be conceded without conceding that one has a moral obligation to do so.[1] Oughts, even moral oughts, we might say, point to reasons for action that must often be weighed against other reasons in deciding what to do; in contrast, obligation or duty suggests a bond between

---

[1] See Ronald Dworkin, *Taking Rights Seriously* (Cambridge, Mass.: Harvard Univ. Press, 1977), 48 ("it is one thing, for example, simply to say that someone ought to give to a particular charity and quite another to say that he has a duty to do so. . . .").

the subject of the obligation and the person to whom it is owed that preempts ordinary reasons for action.[2]

Legal theorists, at least since Hart, have posed the question examined in the preceding chapter by asking how statements of legal obligation resemble and differ from statements of moral obligation. Why does law use the same language that one finds in morality to describe subjects' duties? Modern positivists who support a strong conception of law's normative claims conclude that both statements have the same meaning.[3] In contrast, Austin, as we have seen, implied that the overlap with moral language was a coincidence at best, and that legal obligation really meant no more than that one was obliged by law to heed its commands. Austin preserved the bond that characterizes obligation but turned it into the bond of pure coercion; modern positivists preserved both the bond of obligation and the sense that the bond was identical in meaning with that of moral obligation.

This study supports a position between these two extremes. Statements of legal obligation are at most only statements about what one ought to do, not statements about the obligations that subjects have. Why then use the language of obligation to make such statements? Why doesn't the law simply declare what people ought to do rather than what they have a duty to do?[4] This study helps provide an answer to that question. In law, the ought statements that underlie legal norms are not ordinary judgments about what others ought to do; they are judgments by the state, which gives them the peculiar additional quality of being backed by the claimed right to enforce, whether or not the content of the legal norm is correct. The image of the bond that cannot be escaped is found in the coercive nature of legal authority, and in that sense, Austin was correct. But the claim that such coercion is justified and the related claim that the state believes in good faith that its norms ought to be followed (because they are based on reasons thought to apply to subjects) give the statement of a legal duty more than just the meaning of being obliged. Legal obligation shares with moral obligation the sense that prescribed actions have a moral justification; but it is *legal* obligation, rather than *moral* because the lack of option in the case of law stems from the state's claim of coercive authority, not from any claim of moral authority. The fact that the right to enforce is content-independent makes the legal statement that one ought to act in accordance with the legal norm appear to be nonoptional in a way that explains why one uses the language of obligation rather than that of mere ought.

---

[2] See H. L. A. Hart, *The Concept of Law* (Oxford: Clarendon Press, 1961), 87 (buried in the word "obligation" is "the figure of a *bond* binding the person obligated ...").

[3] See Joseph Raz, *The Authority of Law* (Oxford: Clarendon Press, 1979), 158 ("normative terms like 'a right', 'a duty', 'ought' are used in the same sense in legal, moral, and other normative statements").

[4] See Dworkin, *Taking Rights Seriously*, 48 ("The law does not simply state what private citizens ought or ought not to do; it provides what they have a duty to do or no right to do").

Law, Morality, and Certainty

The analysis of the preceding chapters also has implications for the familiar debate between positivism and natural law about the connection between law and morality. Even the strongest form of positivism must concede at least one respect in which the natural law theorist's claim about a necessary connection between law and morality is correct. The strongest form of positivism, as indicated earlier, is probably the conceptual argument from law's function in guiding conduct. If we assume that this function requires determinative standards, and if we further assume that only factual standards grounded in social sources are capable of providing sufficiently ascertainable standards, we have a case for claiming that law is exclusively determined by social sources – human fiat or will.[5] But even if we accept this positivist view of law, there will still be at least one necessary connection between law and morality – necessary if the positivist also agrees (as most contemporary positivists do) that law is a normative system rather than a purely coercive system. In this section I sketch the argument for this conclusion, which might be called the "classical" version of natural law. It is classical in two senses. First, the claim is that there is a necessary connection between the *concepts* of law and morality: It is not a claim that depends on a theory of adjudication, like Dworkin's, about the role of morality in determining what the law is in any particular case. Second, the claim corresponds roughly to the classical suggestion that if law is too unjust, it "is no law at all."[6] Contemporary commentators on this classical version of natural law often note that this way of putting the claim about the connection between law and morality can be interpreted as simply a statement of political theory: Law that is too unjust does not create an obligation to obey – a conclusion fully consistent with a positivist theory about how to *identify* law.[7] I shall suggest, however, that this classical natural law thesis is also defensible as a claim about how to identify law, and thus affects legal theory and positivism as much as it does political theory. In the remainder of this section, I develop this argument by considering

---

[5] This "social source" version of positivism, most notably associated with the work of Joseph Raz, seems to entail the conclusion that moral standards cannot count as part of the law – an issue briefly discussed in the next section. Thus, where courts appear to invoke moral considerations in reaching decisions, the standards they invoke are not legal; what counts as law in the end is the court's decision. It is in this sense that social sources such as fiat – human will or decision – serve as the ultimate source of law. Note, too, that there does not seem to be any relevant distinction here, as respects the claimed lack of connection between law and morality, between the will of the sovereign, under classical theories of positivism such as Austin's, and the acceptance of a rule of recognition under a theory such as Hart's; both are the products of human decision or will.

[6] 2 Thomas Aquinas, *Summa Theologica* ques. 96, art. 4 (Fathers of the English Dominican Province trans., 1952).

[7] See, e.g., John M. Finnis, *Natural Law and Natural Rights* (Oxford: Clarendon Press, 1980). For a general discussion, see Philip Soper, "Some Natural Confusions about Natural Law," *Mich. L. Rev.* 90 (1992): 2392, 2396.

two possible connections, one contingent and one necessary, between morality and law.

Contingent Connections with Morality

The debate over whether law can incorporate moral standards contingently while still remaining a positivist account of law has been the focus of considerable recent discussion.[8] The strongest versions of positivism (exclusive positivism) mount three major objections to counting such standards as legal; none of them are convincing. The first objection is that if moral standards are indeterminate, they cannot fulfill law's function of providing guidance for subjects and hence cannot count as law. This objection assumes that guidance is not only a sufficient test for law but also a necessary one. That legal systems must provide a fair degree of guidance can be conceded (else we would have no system at all), but there is little reason to deny the possibility that law might serve other functions as well. By inviting judges and citizens to view moral standards as legal, states serve the "educative" function of encouraging judges and litigants to think and argue in moral terms.[9] If the positivist responds that such educative purposes are not essential in the way that providing guidance is, we might begin to share the doubts of those who disparage the utility or possibility of settling disputes about the purpose of law through descriptive or conceptual analysis. The response, however, misses the point. The question is not whether the educative function is *essential*, but only whether it is a contingently possible use to which legal systems might be put. Legal systems can be used for all sorts of things in addition to guiding conduct. Furthermore, one can even make a case that this particular contingent use of the legal system to reinforce cultural beliefs in the viability of moral argument is important: Because legal systems must themselves make the claim to justice that we described earlier if they are to remain distinct from coercive systems, there is good reason for law to foster the belief in the meaningfulness of such claims. In this manner, we can use the essential normative claims of law to help resolve the incorporation debate about the contingent connection with morality.

A second objection against including moral standards in law has recently been formulated by Scott Shapiro.[10] Shapiro's argument is based not directly on

---

[8] Many of the contributions to volume 4 of *Legal Theory* (1998) (a symposium on the postscript to Hart's *Concept of Law*) discuss this issue, which also receives book-length treatment in W. J. Waluchow, *Inclusive Legal Positivism* (Oxford: Clarendon Press, 1994).

[9] See Waluchow, id., 121–2, 134–5.

[10] See Scott Shapiro, "The Difference That Rules Make," in *Analyzing Law,* ed. Brian Bix (Oxford: Clarendon Press, 1998), 33; Shapiro, "On Hart's Way Out," *Legal Theory* 4 (1998): 469. See also Coleman, "Incorporationism, Conventionality, and the Practical Difference Thesis," *Legal Theory* 4 (1998): 381, 386 (suggesting that the strongest argument against viewing incorporated moral standards as legal standards is Scott Shapiro's Practical Difference Thesis). Most of the articles in *Legal Theory* volume 6, no. 1 (2000) also discuss Shapiro's thesis.

the uncertainty of such standards, but on the fact that such standards can do no *independent* work in legal decisions. If the Rule of Recognition, for example, requires judges to decide "as fairness requires," all apparent moral principles or standards adopted in particular cases will be "heuristic" only, adding nothing to what is already specified in the Rule of Recognition. At most, this argument seems to show not that moral standards couldn't be incorporated in a Rule of Recognition, but that they can only be incorporated once, as it were: Subsequent principles derived from the incorporated rule will have no force of their own; one can always ignore any such derived principles if one believes the derivation was improper. But the argument also seems to overlook how much morality itself makes derived decisions critical (because of litigants' expectations, for example), thus giving them considerable independent force.[11] Kramer, in a forceful critique of Shapiro's argument, suggests (correctly, in my view) that the issue one must confront in deciding whether one could make morality a *sufficient* condition for law is whether the resulting regime would have enough regularity and predictability to count as a legal system.[12] Kramer argues that the

[11] Shapiro's argument means that any Supreme Court decision applying, for example, the morality clauses of the Constitution cannot itself count as law. An equal protection decision, for example, has no force (beyond its heuristic force), because any subsequent court must ultimately apply the equal protection clause for itself. See Scott Shapiro, "Law, Morality, and the Guidance of Conduct," *Legal Theory* 6 (2000): 127, 161–2 (if judges can apply a legal rule only if it does not violate fundamental rights, they cannot be guided by any purported rule without deliberating about its merits; so the rule is not a rule). Presumably, the same might also be said of nonmoral rules. If the Rule of Recognition declares "no vehicles in the park," a judicial decision applying that rule to motorized skateboards would not be law: Any later court should be guided by the "no vehicles" standard, not by any particular derivation. See Kenneth Einar Himma, "Hart and the Practical Difference Thesis," *Legal Theory* 6 (2000): 1, 22 (explaining how Shapiro's general argument "has nothing to do with morality"). Thus interpreted, the argument represents an unusual view of precedent, and seems directed mostly at a particular conception of what a rule is (rules must preempt deliberation about the merits to count as rules). See W. J. Waluchow, "Authority and the Practical Difference Thesis: A Defense of Inclusive Legal Positivism," *Legal Theory* 6 (2000): 45. If one believes that the preemptive account of rules is not a necessary feature of authority or of what we are entitled to call a "legal rule," as I have argued, Shapiro's argument at best is a reminder that a theory of law also requires a theory of precedent and an explanation of how the limits on overruling prior decisions can make prior decisions "authoritative" in the relevant sense. See Larry Alexander and Emily Sherwin, *The Rule of Rules* (Durham, N.C.: Duke Univ. Press, 2001), ch. 6 ("Reasoning in Light of Precedent"). Undoubtedly, much more needs to be said than this, which I cannot do here. Though I continue to think that the main issue arising from the incorporation of moral standards in law is the problem of uncertainty, Shapiro's argument is an original and useful demonstration of how this issue is inevitably connected to the whole idea of what a rule is and what it is to be guided or motivated by a rule.

[12] See Matthew Kramer, "How Moral Principles Can Enter Into the Law," *Legal Theory* 6 (2000): 83, 95–9. Shapiro claims that this argument confuses the question of whether such a system could count as legal with the empirical question of whether it is likely to come into existence. See J. Shapiro, "Law . . . and the Guidance of Conduct," 156–8. But the advantage of Kramer's focus on the practical consequences of incoporating moral standards is that it connects the issue of certainty with law's central function of guidance, rather than worrying about whether we would call such a system "law" or not. (Compare the problem discussed in the preceding note: whether we call a derived moral principle or judicial precedent "law" or not seems less important than accounting for the way that it influences subsequent judicial and citizen behavior.) I also agree

expectations of litigants in such a regime will not ensure sufficient regularity partly because, knowing that judges are deciding by direct reference to what is fair, no legitimate expectations can form.[13] Once again, though, this argument overlooks the fact that people will hope for consistency, even when they know they aren't entitled to it; that hope will surely figure into any good judge's decision about what fairness requires. Moreover, most litigated cases are likely to be "hard cases," where the closeness of the argument about what is fair ensures that once a decision is made, the expectation and hope for consistency that are formed after the decision will be morally more important than whether it was correct.[14]

A third objection to including moral standards as law arises out of the same concern about the uncertainty of such standards that underlies each of the preceding objections. Even if one admits that moral standards might be used by legal systems for a particular educative function, the question in deciding whether to count them as legal standards is whether they can be said to constrain adjudication in the way that we normally require in order to count something as preexisting law.[15] In essence, this objection *does* amount to making the guiding function a necessary condition for counting a *standard* as legal, at least when we are talking about courts deciding "according to law." Though legal systems may have other functions that permit reference to moral standards, the only standards that could count as law for the purpose of deciding cases must be relatively certain or determinable standards and hence cannot include

---

with Kramer that Shapiro's thesis, even under his own conception of rules, fails when applied to standards that make conformity to morality a *necessary* condition of legality. Thus, a rule that invalidates any law that is "too unjust" gives plenty of room for particular laws to provide guidance so long as they fall below the level of gross injustice. See "Moral Principles," 88–92.

[13] See Kramer, id., 98–9 ("Insofar as officials adhere to such a Rule of Recognition, they focus primarily on matters of substantive justice, and they regard content-independent matters of consistency as secondary considerations. . . . Consequently, the expectations held by citizens will not weigh in favor of the achievement of settledness and predictability in . . . decisional patterns").

[14] Thus, for example, it may be arguable whether it was fair for the common law to enforce promises only if they had consideration. See Charles Fried, *Contract as Promise* (Cambridge: Harvard Univ. Press, 1981), ch. 3 (criticizing the contract doctrine of consideration). But once that decision is made, the precedent assumes force of its own that trumps attempts to revisit the issue on each new occasion. For the very reasons that Kramer emphasizes (the need for stability and regularity), what "fairness requires" quickly becomes a matter of honoring past decisions rather than starting over. See Philip Soper, "Legal Theory and the Obligation of a Judge: The Hart/Dworkin Dispute," *Mich. L. Rev.* 75 (1977): 473, 512n. 129 ("'doing justice' includes taking account of settled expectations under [prior] cases, even if it is thought that some of them had initially been decided erroneously"). Kramer's argument would succeed only if one assumed that the Rule of Recognition incorporated a moral standard that explicitly relegated consistency to a secondary role (as suggested in the passage quoted in the preceding note). But that does not sound like a defensible moral standard. See also Alexander and Sherwin, *The Rule of Rules*, ch. 6 ("Reasoning in Light of Precedent").

[15] See Kramer, "Moral Principles," 107 (where hard cases do not permit a unique answer from applicable moral principles, the moral norms invoked by judges to decide the case "cannot accurately be presented as the pre-existent law thereon"). Note that the focus now is not on principles derived from an incorporated moral principle (and the question of whether they can make a difference) but on the incorporated basic principle itself.

moral standards. The force of this objection is most evident when one considers that courts reaching decisions on the basis of controversial moral standards will appear, for all practical purposes, indistinguishable from legislatures. If moral standards are too uncertain or indeterminate to guide conduct, it seems to follow that such standards are also too uncertain to be used to predict or control judicial decisions. In that case, we cannot distinguish judging from legislating: The standards judges use when they refer to morality must belong to the same category of "background morality" that underlies a legislative decision, not to the category of legal standards that control a court.

I have suggested elsewhere one possible response to this objection, a response that indicates how one might justify viewing standards as legal, even though indeterminable, when used by courts in reaching decisions[16] The objection, as we have just restated it, assumes that there is a conceptual difference between courts and legislatures: to count as a court engaged in judging requires that an institution be bound by standards capable of being interpreted and applied with some degree of certainty. Where the institution is not so bound, it can only be acting as a legislature – an institution that is free to draw on controversial background morality because it is not legally bound to reach any particular decision when it legislates. What this conceptual argument overlooks, however, is the reason we normally want a court to be bound. One prominent reason is that if the court is not applying reasonably ascertainable standards, its decisions will appear to be instances of ex post facto legislation, punishing litigants for transgressing laws that were not in existence at the time they acted. If, however, litigants *believe* that the standards being used are objective and meaningful, however indeterminate, and if they *believe* that courts are particularly good at discovering and applying these incorporated moral standards as part of the law, then the sense of unfairness is reduced and may evaporate altogether. In short, what counts in deciding whether an institution is fairly judging or unfairly enacting ex post facto legislation may be what is believed to be the case. It may be that in deciding whether an institution is a court or an official is a judge, the attitudes of litigants and courts toward moral standards and whether they are meaningful is more important than the philosophical or metaphysical facts about the objectivity of moral norms.[17] Furthermore, we can once again use the discussion of law's normative claims in the preceding chapter to show why this attitude that moral claims are meaningful might arise in a legal system: Because the state must claim that coercion is justified in order to distinguish its own use of force from that of a purely coercive system, it is in the state's own interest to foster an attitude toward moral norms that sees them as meaningful standards.

---

[16] See Philip Soper, "Two Puzzles from the Postscript," *Legal Theory* 4 (1998): 359, 369–72.

[17] For a different kind of attempt to show that what counts as "judging" need not depend on whether legal standards are determinative, see Steven J. Burton, *Judging in Good Faith* (Cambridge: Cambridge Univ. Press, 1992), xii ("The good faith thesis abandons the determinacy condition completely. . . . It understands the legitimacy of adjudication to depend on respect for the reasons, not agreement with the results, in cases").

Necessary Connections with Morality

Whether legal systems include *particular* moral standards as legal standards is a contingent question. But there is one sense in which any legal system, including one that purports to limit law to social sources, must admit a connection with morality that makes the conclusion that a legal directive is law dependent on the moral conclusion that the directive is not too unjust. The argument for this classical version of natural law is a straightforward application of the normative claims of law discussed earlier. The state must claim that its actions in setting and enforcing norms are morally defensible. To do so means that it must claim (1) that it has right to exist (because someone must decide, we must have a state) and (2) that as long as the authorized official makes the decision about which norms to enforce in good faith, the resulting action is justified (no moral wrong is done), even if one later discovers that the decision was wrong. We have already noted that the first claim is contested only by the anarchist. That somebody must decide is, in short, the quick defense of fiat.[18] The second claim, that the state does no wrong so long as its decisions are based on its own best judgment about what justice requires, is a familiar feature of legal systems. Think how often process (good faith attempts to get at the truth) trumps substance in any legal system. Innocent persons may be imprisoned for years, only to discover that a factual error was made and no crime was committed. For the most part, such persons seldom have a claim for reparation as of right, rather than being dependent on legislative grace for redress. In short, we justify mistakes *in applying the law* on the ground that we did our best. It should hardly surprise us, then, that we also justify on the same ground enforcing laws that we thought at the time were just but that we now believe were unjust. Here, too, the defense that we did our best at the time to act as we thought justice required is all that is required to avoid moral culpability.[19]

The state's claim to be acting justly, in short, is not a claim that it is infallible but only a claim that it is not culpable. That claim is all that is needed to distinguish the normative legal system from that of the gunman writ large. But even this claim has its own limitations. The state's ability to deny moral culpability, and thus to distinguish itself from a coercive system, reaches a limit when the

---

[18] See Soper, "Some Natural Confusions About Natural Law," 2420.

[19] *Korematsu v. United States*, 323 U.S. 214 (1944), which held that the internment of Japanese American citizens during World War II was consistent with constitutional guarantees, may serve as an example. Even if it is thought today that the case was wrongly decided, that conclusion does not entail that the state was culpable so long as it reached the decision it did in good faith. The recent decision overturning aspects of the case on procedural grounds (without reconsidering the constitutional questions) confirms this conclusion. See *Korematsu v. United States*, 584 f. Supp. 1406 (N.D. Cal. 1984) (vacating the conviction because of prosecutorial misconduct). On the definition of "culpability," see Heidi M. Hurd, "Justification and Excuse, Wrongdoing and Culpability," *Notre Dame L. Rev.* 74 (1999): 1551, 1558 ("Moral culpability consists in intending to do an action that is wrongful, knowing that one will do an action that is wrongful, or failing to infer from available evidence that one will do an action that is wrongful").

law that is enforced is so unjust as to override the excuse that "we acted, in good faith as we thought best." The instances in which this limit is reached in practice are likely to be rare for two reasons: (1) it is only serious moral error (which no reasonable person could in good faith fail to acknowledge) that limit's law's ability to make the normative claim of justice; (2) the decision that even this extreme limit has been reached will itself have to be made by a potentially fallible institution (either a different tribunal or a later tribunal, but in either case a fallible human institution).

Legal systems, if they are not to collapse into coercive systems, must in short admit that all standards tentatively identified as law by a positivist pedigree will count as valid law only if they are not too unjust and thus remain capable of supporting a good-faith claim that using coercion to enforce the law is morally permissible. Several points are worth emphasizing. First, the argument for this classical natural law view has both descriptive and conceptual support. Descriptive support for the claim that the concept of law includes this built-in moral limitation on what can count as law is found in the increasing international recognition of the Nuremberg principle, according to which domestic law provides no defense when one commits crimes against humanity. Conceptual support for the claim is found when one asks, "Why not still call a directive 'law,' however wicked, so long as it has the proper pedigree?" The answer is that if it is so wicked that no practical consequence attaches (other than coercion) – no defense for those who obey or enforce the law and are later prosecuted, no justification for state enforcement, no obligation for citizens to obey – then to continue to call the directive law, as Dworkin notes, puts us "suddenly in the peculiar world of legal essentialism."[20] Second, the concern that natural law leads to anarchy by inviting subjects to second-guess the state and decide for themselves whether particular laws are unjust is misplaced: Only in extreme cases of wicked law, not ordinary cases of injustice, will the law lose its ability to claim that coercion is morally justified. The extreme cases are sufficiently rare that the spectacle of anarchy is unreal. Moreover, the increasing willingness to create Nuremberg tribunals and prosecute crimes against humanity provides evidence that we are quite able to tolerate, at least in international law, the principle that domestic law can always be trumped where grave injustice is committed. There is, in short, no concept of "finality" in applying the concept of law where extreme injustice occurs. Third, the fact that pedigree and fiat will normally suffice to identify the applicable law helps explain why one might

---

[20] Ronald Dworkin, "A Reply," in *Ronald Dworkin and Contemporary Jurisprudence*, ed. Marshall Cohen (Totowa, NJ: Rowman & Allenheld, 1983), 247, 259. Lon Fuller made a similar point much earlier and quite forcefully in his famous debate with Hart. See Fuller, "Positivism and Fidelity to Law – A Reply to Professor Hart," *Harvard L. Rev.* 71 (1958): 630, 655 ("So far as the courts are concerned, matters certainly would not have been helped if, instead of saying, 'This is not law,' they had said, 'This is law but it is so evil we will refuse to apply it.' Surely moral confusion reaches its height when a court refuses to apply something it admits to be law . . .").

adopt the positivist's test for law as a "presumptive" test *in the evidentiary* sense: That is, in most cases, pedigree alone *is* a sufficient test for law, even where the law is unjust (but not too unjust). But it is a mistake to turn this evidentiary presumption into a presumption that positivism as a legal theory is correct.

It is worth emphasizing this last distinction between presuming that positivism is a correct legal theory and presuming that, most of the time, the positivist's test for law will identify the legal standard that governs a decision. In this respect, the argument developed here contrasts with Schauer's argument in defense of what he calls "presumptive positivism."[21] Schauer's defense of positivism is a "descriptive claim about the status of a set of pedigreed norms within the universe of reasons for decision employed by the decision-makers within some legal system."[22] Schauer suggests that whenever judges call on nonlegal norms to reach a decision different from that required by the pedigreed (positivist) set, as they arguably did in cases like *Riggs v. Palmer*[23] and *Henningsen v. Bloomfield Motors, Inc.,*[24] they show only that in that particular legal system, positivism as a descriptive thesis about how legal decisions are made is flawed. How often legal systems actually depart from the pedigreed norms in deciding cases, however, is an empirical question that will vary from one society to another. If the departure is frequent, as Dworkin's arguments suggest it is in the United States, it casts doubt on the usefulness of positivism as a description of our own legal system. But in most cases, the departure is probably sufficiently infrequent, Schauer seems to argue, to justify the presumption that the positivist's pedigreed norm will be the controlling factor in a legal case. The argument developed here differs from Schauer's in two respects. First, the claim I defend here is a conceptual one, not a descriptive one. It is not an empirical question of whether some legal systems might decide to trump the pedigreed norm in a particular case because the norm is too unjust to enforce or otherwise be given practical effect. It is, instead, a consequence of what we mean by law that decision-makers must always in theory be prepared to judge the pedigreed norm against the suggested moral standard; it is a consequence, in short, of our insistence that the concept of law refers to a normative rather than a coercive system.[25] Second, unlike Schauer, who is willing to restrict legal standards to

---

[21] See Frederick Schauer, *Playing by the Rules* (Oxford: Clarendon Press, 1991), 196.

[22] Id., 203.

[23] 115 N.Y. 506, 22 N.E. 188 (1889)

[24] 32 N.J. 358, 161 A.2d 69 (1960)

[25] Schauer offers a normative (as well as a descriptive) defense of presumptive positivism by stressing (1) the importance of enforcing the pedigreed set of rules in most cases in order to avoid constantly calculating the best result in each case ("the virtues associated with rules" [p. 202]) and (2) the need to preserve respect for the system by overriding the rules when the reasons for doing so are particularly strong. (For a similar "ethical" defense of positivism, see Tom Campbell, *The Legal Theory of Ethical Positivism* [Aldershot: Dartmouth, 1996].) Indirectly, these normative arguments reinforce the argument of this study. Whereas Schauer invites courts to avoid disrespect for the system when particularly strong arguments exist for ignoring the rules,

the set of pedigreed norms, suggesting that judges are using nonlegal standards whenever they rely on moral or other principles to justify departure from the pedigreed norms, the argument developed here is that we have already included as a conceptual matter certain minimum moral standards within the pedigreed core, along with the more easily determinable social sources.

Schauer's case for presumptive positivism has considerable force when presented as an evidentiary argument: In most cases, a social facts test for law probably is reliable and conclusive on the question of legal validity because in most cases the pedigreed norm probably cannot be said to be too unjust to be called law. But to say that such identifications of law remain only presumptive is to say that, as a conceptual matter, the pedigreed norm must always in theory be subject to rebuttal as a ground for justifying a *legal* decision. That this theoretical rebuttal of the presumption may not happen often is irrelevant to the conceptual issue. To the contrary, just the opposite is the case. Natural law is the only legal theory that can presumptively accommodate the view of law as a normative system. The alternative is to return to Austin's coercive model and the coherence problems that result when law presents itself as no different from the gunman writ large.[26]

this study argues that when the rules reach a level of gross injustice (undermining the claim of justice), then the concept of law itself requires ignoring the rules. Schauer wants to let in many Dworkinian principles as extralegal sources of decision in cases like *Henningsen*. My claim is that in Nuremberg-like cases of gross injustice, our concept of law already embraces enough of a commitment to morality to make moral principles in the extreme case *legally* determinative.

[26] Schauer suggests that whether one calls the moral principles used to invalidate otherwise legal action law or not threatens to become a terminological dispute. See *playing by the rules*, 205. (For a similar suggestion, see Richard A. Posner, *The Problems of Jurisprudence* [Cambridge: Harvard Univ. Press, 1990], 238–9.) As regards that dispute, Schauer argues that there is little to be gained by adding moral tests to the criteria of legal validity, because those tests must in the end be applied to some preevaluative facts (the "pedigreed facts" that count as law under the positivist's test). We "would only replicate positivism at a different remove, thus providing essentially no advantages." Frederick Schauer, "Positivism as Pariah," in *The Autonomy of Law*, ed. Robert George (Oxford: Clarendon Press, 1996), 31, 42. The response to this argument is the same as that given in the text. Schauer's argument that whether or not we call these preevaluative facts law before applying moral tests doesn't entail *practical* consequences may be true in the wide range of cases. But, once again, the willingness of the international community to proceed against those guilty of genocide or other crimes against humanity without recognizing excuses based on domestic law is indirect evidence for the claim made here about what we mean by law, as well as for some limited practical consequence of maintaining this much of a connection between law and morality (it may have some deterrent effect on cruel state actors or dictators who might otherwise think they could rely on the defense that their actions were consistent with domestic law). In any event, the claim in the text is based on a conceptual argument, not an argument about practical consequences. We cannot make the "preanalytic" facts independent of all moral evaluation and still consistently make the other claims about law that we do (the right to enforce, etc.). It is consistency and coherence, not practical consequences, that support the argument for classical natural law. See Philip Soper, "Choosing a Legal Theory on Moral Grounds," *Social Phil. & Policy* 4 (1986): 32, 48 ("The question for legal theory is not whether it would be a good or a bad thing for [the claimed connection between law and morality] to be accepted as true, but whether it *is* true").

PART II

THE ETHICS OF DEFERENCE

5

The Puzzle of Promise

Introduction

Thus far, I have argued that law does not claim that subjects have reasons to defer to its judgments. But a central question for political theory has always been whether subjects do in fact have such reasons – a question typically posed by asking whether there is a prima facie obligation to obey the law. In Part II, I defend an affirmative answer to the question but do so indirectly. Instead of beginning with the question of political obligation, the next two chapters examine in turn two standard paradigms of obligation – promises and fair play – in order to show how these paradigms are themselves better understood when re-presented as examples of deference. The analysis of these two chapters will then be extended to the question of political obligation.

Two reasons justify starting with the problem of promissory obligation. First, political theory often assumes that political obligation could be established if only one could demonstrate actual or implied consent to the state. Most consent theorists, accordingly, focus on the kinds of actions that can plausibly be said to show consent. In this chapter, I argue that the implicit priority thus accorded to consent or promise is unwarranted because the difficulties of explaining why and how promises obligate are almost exact analogues of the difficulties that attend attempts to defend political obligation.[1] Two consequences, one negative and one positive, result. The negative consequence is that even where consent to the state can be found, the problem of political obligation is not so much solved as shifted to other grounds. The positive consequence is that by shifting the focus to the basis for promissory obligation, one may actually discover a better justification for political obligation than one finds in standard arguments.

---

[1] For a similar comparison of promissory and political obligation that also emphasizes the structural similarity of these concepts, see Hanna Pitkin, "Obligation and Consent," in *Philosophy, Politics, and Society*, 4th ser., eds. P. Laslett, W. Runciman, and Q. Skinner (Oxford: Blackwell, 1972), 45, 73–80.

A second reason for starting with promissory obligation is that it is a particularly good vehicle for illustrating how the ethics of deference contrasts with standard ethical theories. In the preface to this study, I suggested that a change in focus from the language of "obligation to obey" to "reasons to defer" does not essentially change the problem of political obligation and may actually avoid misleading inferences. The same is true of promissory obligation. We are not used to thinking about the question of how much and why promises obligate in terms of whether the promisor has reasons to defer to the promisee. Standard explanations of the basis for and extent of promissory obligation fall into two basic categories, reflecting the general distinction between consequentialist and deontological approaches to ethics. I argue in this chapter that these two standard explanations have created a puzzle that can best be understood, and arguably solved, by the ethics of deference. The puzzle is that neither consequentialist nor deontological explanations for the force of promise capture convincingly the dimensions of the practice. Consequentialist accounts focus on the harms caused by the breach of a promise – primarily the impact of the breach on (1) the promissee's reliance interests; (2) the expectations of the promissee; and (3) the prospects for future promissory transactions. For many people, this account falls short of capturing our intuitions about promissory obligations: Even if one assumes that the advantages of breaking a promise in a particular case outweigh all relevant harms, many people share the intuition that promises must still be kept. Deontologists begin with this intuition and attempt to account for it. But the accounts often have the air of a tautology: Promises must be kept, regardless of consequences, because that's what a promise requires. The deontologist's account suffers from not being able to give plausible reasons to explain why promises should have such seemingly absolute force. In short, consequentialist accounts have the advantage of employing a very plausible "instrumentalist" conception of reasons for actions, but those reasons cannot account for the intuition that promissory obligations persist even when breaking the promise would have the best consequences. Deontological accounts try to account for this intuition, but lack a convincing conception of the kinds of reasons that could justify keeping a promise when all instrumental reasons point toward breach.[2]

One possible reaction to this state of affairs, of course, would be to give up the intuition about the absolute force of promises and accept the consequentialist

---

[2] It may be of interest to note that some theorists seem sympathetic to the deontological explanation of promises while remaining consequentialists when it comes to explaining the obligation of law. This combination of views appears, for example, to be implicit in some of the work of Joseph Raz. Compare Raz, "Promises and Obligations," in *Law, Morality and Society*, eds. P. M. S. Hacker and J. Raz (Oxford: Clarendon Press, 1977), 210, 226–8 (expressing sympathy for the possibility of justifying promissory obligation as a form of categorical obligation), with Raz, "The Obligation to Obey: Revision and Tradition," *Notre Dame J. L. & Pub. Policy* 1 (1984): 139, reprinted in *The Duty to Obey the Law*, ed. W. Edmundson (Oxford: Rowman & Littlefield, 1999), 159 (suggesting that noninstrumental arguments for the duty to obey law fail, though they may justify a voluntary choice to respect the state through obedience).

account. This chapter opts for a different reaction. In the pages that follow, I show how the ethics of deference functions as an intermediate step in the debate between these two more general ethical theories. By explaining why one might have reasons to defer to the views of the promisee, we can explain, without the deontologist's air of tautology, the intuition that more is involved in deciding whether to keep a promise than comparing the harms and benefits that result from breach.

The chapter proceeds in two parts. The first part, which is primarily conceptual or descriptive, explores the structural similarities between promises and laws. Just as I asked in Chapter 2 what it would mean to have practical authority, here I shall ask what it would mean to have promissory authority. The second part offers a substantive justification of promissory obligation, explaining how the obligation to keep a promise can be explained, at least in part, in terms of the ethics of deference.

Promises and Laws: Structural Similarities

Promisors as Legislators

Assume that Henry and Jane own adjacent cabins on a small island. Both are also members of the three-person Resort Association, a governing body for the island that has power under state law to enact local ordinances by majority vote. Last spring, Henry and Jane voted in favor of a proposal to require owners to remove snow and ice during the winter months from the pathways that border their property. Because many owners are not in residence in the winter, and because the Resort Association lacks enforcement personnel, the proposal included a provision assessing homeowners a fee that would be returned to those who complied with the ordinance, but that would otherwise be used to pay for snow removal. Six months later, as winter approaches, the fate of this ordinance is uncertain. The number of owners living on the island has dwindled to the point where the state has decided to strip the Resort Association of its legislative powers, effective at the beginning of the new calendar year; it is not clear whether the existing snow-removal ordinance can be enforced after that date. Henry and Jane discuss the situation and decide that the potential demise of the ordinance will make no difference to them: They both still think the ordinance is a good idea, and, accordingly, both agree that they will continue to share the expense of snow removal from the pathway that runs between their cabins in the new year. How do the rights and duties of Henry and Jane differ under the ordinance they passed in the spring compared to the promises they made in the fall?

The suggestion that promises are analogous to laws is hardly new. Standard contracts textbooks invite one to think of promises as the creation of a norm by a "two-person legislature" that will govern the conduct of the parties to the contract[3] Indeed, determining whether there is "mutual assent" to a contract is much like deciding whether a bill has become a law: Have both parties to the contract "voted" for the same proposal within the time allowed? The hypothetical ordinance agreed to by both Henry and Jane is meant to underscore this similarity between the norms created by law and by promise: In both cases, precisely the same standard of conduct has been agreed to, first in the understanding that the norm will become law, then in the understanding that a promise is being made. To see how the normative situation that results in both cases is similar, we should first consider some of the possible differences.

The Relevance of Voluntariness

No argument about the essential similarity of promise and law is likely to be convincing without some explanation for the fact that people *think* there is a difference. The most apparent difference is that the conflict with another person that results when I make a promise that I now don't want to keep stems from choices I made earlier; I freely promised and now don't want to perform. It might be thought that our hypothetical snow removal ordinance obscures this difference because both Henry and Jane voluntarily agreed to (voted for) the ordinance. Thus it may seem that their situation more closely resembles that of parties to a promise because they chose and presumably approve of the norm they have created. In contrast, the typical confrontation with law is involuntary: Many citizens neither consent to the government nor have anything to say about the content of the laws they confront. This difference in the history leading up to the clash of interests does make a difference, but not, I shall suggest, in the way that promises and laws operate to create obligations. The difference represents at most a contingent feature of promises rather than an essential difference between promises and laws.

UNJUST LAWS AND UNJUST PROMISES. To see how voluntariness is less critical than is commonly thought, consider first the sense in which both the ordinance and the promise do not represent expressions of consent. Henry and Jane, though they both agreed to the ordinance, did not necessarily agree to obey the law. Certainly there is no *express* consent to comply, even though there is apparent agreement about the content of the law. But is there even implicit consent? Political theorists who find implicit consent in such acts as voting or even continuing to reside in the country may think it is obvious that Henry and Jane implicitly consent to obey the law they have enacted. But that conclusion

---

[3] See, e.g., L. Fuller and M. Eisenberg, *Basic Contract Law*, 6th ed. (St. Paul, MN: West, 1996), 90 ("parties to a contract exercise a kind of legislative function . . . [t]heir agreement stands as a kind of private statute regulating their affairs"). See also id., 349 (comparing the problem of determining the intent of parties to a contract to the problem of determining legislative intent when interpreting a statute).

is not logically required, and in fact, our earlier discussion helps show that even legislators voting for a law are not necessarily implicitly consenting to obey the law. We saw in Chapter 3 that legislators make no essential claim that those subject to law have content-independent reasons to obey. The same holds for the legislators themselves. Inferences of tacit consent are justified only where the facts support the interpretation that a promise is made through conduct, if not through express language. Thus arguments from tacit consent can always be rebutted by expressly denying that one is consenting. Imagine, for example, that Henry and Jane, while discussing the ordinance, also raise the question of political theory considered in this study. Henry and Jane wonder whether people in general have content-independent reasons to obey the law just because it is the law. After a brief discussion that reveals what a complicated issue this is, both Henry and Jane proceed to the business at hand and pass the snow-removal ordinance. Both explicitly announce in doing so that they are still uncertain about the question of whether there are content-independent reasons to obey the law. Both also expressly deny that they are agreeing to obey the law for such content-independent reasons: After all, since they think the content of the ordinance is justified, they have no need to consider whether they also have an obligation to obey just because it is the law. Thus, if Jane changes her mind and decides that the ordinance is a bad idea, arguments to explain why she should nevertheless comply with the law must be drawn from considerations outside of consent theory. The same is true for the promise. When Henry and Jane exchange promises, they do not promise to keep their promises: Whatever explanation underlies the duty to keep promises must also, to avoid circularity, be drawn from considerations apart from the promise itself.

But agreement to the *content* of the law does make a difference, and it is a difference that helps explain why promises often *appear* to create problems different from those created by laws. Political obligation becomes problematic when laws to which one did not consent appear to be unjust or unwise. When one believes that the content of the law is correct, the question of whether one has an independent duty to obey is less likely to arise: The reasons to comply presumably are the same as those that led one to endorse the law in the first place. It is for this reason that promissory obligation appears to raise questions distinct from those raised by political obligation. In the typical case of promise, the promisor does not think the act he promises to do is immoral because he has the choice over content that is typically denied the citizen in a state. (Even democracies don't pretend that the content of law is actually selected by citizens, though we do sometimes think of legislators as agents acting for the citizen as principal.) Thus it is rare that promises will lead to obligations that diverge from the promisor's own estimate of what he thinks he ought to do. It is easy to see, however, that this is not a necessary distinction between promises and laws. At least two situations can be imagined where divergence can occur between what one ought to do and what is required by the norms created by both promise and law.

PROMISES KNOWN TO BE UNJUST. Consider first the case of promises that are known or believed from the start to be unjust. Most philosophers conclude that one cannot misuse promise in this way to create even a weak prima facie obligation to do wrong just because one promised to do wrong.[4] So if Jane believes from the outset that it is wrong to remove snow and ice from the pathways (because, for example, the salt that is necessary for ice removal damages the environment and harms others), her promise to Henry cannot trump her obligation to leave the path uncleared. This does not mean that the promise in such a case is meaningless. It is not a contradiction for Jane to say, "I promise to remove the ice, even though I believe it is morally wrong to do so."[5] Presumably such a promise indicates that some kind of commitment has been made – just not a moral commitment. In the same way that one can physically bind oneself (say, to a mast) even though one ought not to, so, we might say, one can also bind oneself to another person through a promise that creates a nonmoral obligation. In what sense would Jane be bound (nonmorally) by such a promise? For the answer to that question, consider the parallel case of law.

The parallel with legal obligation is striking. Assume that Jane and Henry vote for the snow-removal ordinance even though they believe it is wrong to require snow removal. They vote for the ordinance, for example, only because they own the snow removal company that is likely to profit from the fees assessed for snow removal, and they defend the ordinance as law on only those grounds. Assume also that no claim about a right to enforce such a law, enacted for these self-interested reasons, is advanced. In this case, the implicit claim to justice that we said distinguishes legal from coercive systems is missing.[6] Those subject to the ordinance may not be able to prevent enforcement or avoid sanctions, but if the Resort Association no longer makes any moral claim about the right to impose sanctions, legal obligation here simply means being obliged. The

---

[4] See Jan Narveson, "Promising, Expecting, and Utility," *Can. J. Phil.* 1 (1971): 207, 211 ("we regard promises to do what is wrong as simply invalid from the start"). David Lyons relies on a similar point to deny that judges could have a duty to apply immoral laws simply because they promised when they took office to apply the law. See Lyons, "Justification and Judicial Responsibility," *Cal. L. Rev.* 72 (1984): 178.

[5] For an example of this argument, see Pall Ardal, "And That's a Promise," *Phil. Quarterly* 18 (1968): 225, 230. Ardal's example is of a girl who promises her boyfriend that she will sneak out and meet him after her parents have gone to bed, even though she believes she ought not to do so. Ardal, unlike Narveson, suggests that by making the promise she may actually have a moral duty to keep the promise that conflicts with her duty to obey her parents. It seems more plausible, however, to think that if she has created any sort of obligation through her promise, it is a nonmoral commitment.

[6] I do not mean to suggest that the claimed "right to enforce" that distinguishes legal from coercive systems cannot arise if laws are justified solely because they serve the interests of particular groups. If a state sincerely advances the Hobbesian-like claim that it is entitled to enforce whatever laws are enacted (see the discussion in Chapter 3, 63–4), or if it justifies laws as involving trade-offs between the interests of competing political groups, it will still be making the minimal claim necessary to count as a legal system. The example in the text assumes no claim of a moral right to enforce is made.

result is the same failure to correspond to our normal concept of law that we explored in the previous chapter. In this case, it is easy to see what a nonmoral sense of legal obligation might mean because there is an enforcement apparatus that conveys the sense of being obliged. In the case of promise, the absence of such an apparatus makes it harder to see what could be meant by a nonmoral promissory obligation. By analogy to the legal case, however, an explanation can be constructed. If Jane promises Henry to remove the ice and gives him a deposit as security (which Henry may demand, particularly because he knows she thinks it is wrong to make this promise and thus she is more likely to change her mind), the analogy with the ordinance is maintained. Henry now has the power to enforce the promise, even though he may have no moral right to do so and even though it was wrong for Jane to make this promise in the first place. Thus we have an example of a promise that may be said to be nonmorally binding.[7]

PROMISES THAT SUBSEQUENTLY BECOME UNJUST. I said earlier that questions about the duty to obey the law are typically raised when the law's prescriptions deviate from what one believes correct action requires. This deviation may seem less likely to arise in the case of promisors for the same reason it is less likely to occur in the case of our hypothetical snow-removal ordinance: The act promised presumably already reflects the promisor's views about what constitutes correct action. But of course, one can be wrong and change one's mind about the morality of the promised act. Or new facts can make a promised act that was originally morally neutral now morally suspect: The classic example is the promise to return a weapon to someone who, the promisor now thinks, plans to use it to commit suicide in a temporary state of depression. But these possibilities for discovering a mistake can also occur in the case of the snow-removal ordinance. After voting for the ordinance, Jane may come to believe that the ordinance is seriously mistaken or unprincipled. She believes, for example, as we imagined before, that snow removal unjustifiably harms the environment or, perhaps, that the government has no business interfering with private landowners' decisions about what to do about the snow. In like manner, after promising Henry in the fall to remove the snow, Jane may have a similar conversion and now believe that snow removal is a grave mistake. In both cases, she faces the question of whether she has an obligation to obey the law or to keep her promise.

These reflections show that promises and laws can both lead to similar problems of explaining how it can be right to take an action that would otherwise

---

[7] For an alternative account of promissory obligation as a nonmoral obligation, see R. Sartorius, *Individual Conduct and Social Norms* (Encino, Calif.: Dickenson, 1975), ch. 5. Sartorius's explanation, which applies to all promises, not just those thought to be immoral from the start, uses the nonmoral sense of obligation to explain how an act-utilitarian can acknowledge obligations based on past actions (the promise), consistent with a theory that considers only future consequences in deciding what one ought to do.

be wrong apart from the law or the promise. In both cases, the conflict comes about despite an initial belief that the action is correct; indeed, there would be little need to worry about promissory obligation if promisors never changed their minds. So the fact that most citizens don't have the chance to determine the content of laws they think unjust does not essentially distinguish them from promisors who have changed their minds about the wisdom of their promised acts. It should not surprise us, then, that the arguments one encounters in attempting to justify promissory obligation will turn out to resemble arguments about how to justify law's authority. We shall compare the structure of these arguments after first considering a second respect in which voluntariness might be thought to distinguish promises from laws.

ENTERING VOLUNTARILY INTO THE PROMISSORY STATE. So far, we have been considering voluntariness as if its relevance lies mainly in the choice it gives the promisor over the content of the promised act. But those who think that the obligation to keep a promise is on sounder theoretical ground than the obligation to obey the law usually insist that voluntariness is critical for another reason: It is not simply that one has control over content; one also has control over whether to get into the situation in the first place. Law doesn't give many people direct control over content, but neither does it give them control over which government they shall have or whether they shall live in any state. That difference, it might be thought, is what the consent tradition in political theory was all about, and that is why promise seems to start off in a better position than law.

This intuition about the difference that voluntary entry into the situation makes is important and, in one sense, is an intuition that also underlies the argument of this chapter. But it is a difference not in the general theory that explains the obligations of promise or law, but only in the factors that justify applying the general theory to each case. The voluntary decision to make the promise in the first place helps explain why the promisee now has a right to deference in a way he or she otherwise would not have. In the case of law, the justification for deferring to the state depends on recognizing that the state is necessary: Except for anarchists, political theorists mostly agree that the enterprise of subjecting conduct to the governance of rules is the only alternative to the much worse situation described in state-of-nature theories. By "necessary" here I do not mean that it is logically impossible to imagine living without a state or that states *must* exist in some modally necessary sense. "Necessary" here means only what "hypothetical consent" theories usually aim to demonstrate: namely, that the point of having a state is so well grounded in general human interests that any rational person presumably would agree to its establishment. It is the *rationality* of the enterprise, and the implications of conceding this point about the value and functions of the state, that underlie arguments for political obligation, not actual consent. And the same is true for promise. The fact that one has voluntarily made a promise shows only that in that particular case, the commitment entailed by the promise appeared more desirable than the alternative. The explanation for why that commitment is binding must depend on explaining the point of the practice of promising and the implications of recognizing that point. It does not depend on consent, which, presumably, is withdrawn when the promisor changes his or her mind and wants to know why he or she is obligated to keep the promise. In short, there is no essential difference here between the promisor and the ordinary legal subject. Both confront norms that prescribe conduct they do not now believe to be justified. Whether they once believed the norms were correct and have since changed their minds or whether they never had a chance to express their views is not an essential difference. One does not need, of course, to make any particular promise in the same way that one needs to live in a state – and it is in that respect that voluntariness makes a difference in the case of promise. Choosing to make a promise is like choosing to enter and become a citizen of a particular state. The choice evidences actual acknowledgment of the value of this particular promise, whereas most citizens can only be charged with hypothetical acknowledgment of the value of the state. But as long as the argument for both political and promissory obligation, as I shall argue later in this chapter, stems from the values implicit in the practice – the point of having a legal system and the point of having the institution of promise – the manner in which one comes to acknowledge the value of the practice is irrelevant.

This point, about the tangential nature of voluntariness in explaining promissory obligation, can be made in another way by considering what one might conclude about those who actually do disagree about the value of the state or the value of promises. Political anarchists cannot escape the state even if they would prefer to do so. "Promissory anarchists," on the other hand, who do not think any promises are desirable, can avoid entering the promissory state by simply refusing to make promises. Promises for such people would be replaced by statements of future intent, qualified as such, and clearly assigning the risk of change of mind to those who rely on the statement. Thus people can opt out of promising in a way that they cannot opt out of the state. That is why the justification for letting the state impose its will must be stronger – a case of being necessary, not just desirable. Promising is desirable but not necessary. That is why I can't be forced into mutually beneficial exchanges without my consent. Voluntary choice is required in order to give the promisee the ascendancy over my will that he or she claims. Voluntariness, in short, is a less stringent condition than necessity. In fact, there are few enterprises apart from the state (families come to mind) in which one could justify deference on the ground that those subject to the enterprise must implicitly acknowledge that the enterprise is necessary in order to achieve certain basic values in the same way that actual consent evidences the value of a particular promise.

Voluntariness is the only way to show that a particular promise has (or had) value to the promisor; consent to the state, on the other hand, is in a sense superfluous: One can already show that any person would consent to (admit the value of) the state rather than live in the alternative state of nature. It is possible, of course, that voluntary consent to a *particular* state will add to the reasons for political obligation – by demonstrating the special value of this state over states in general. In this respect, we need not deny that consent can have some impact on arguments for political obligation (just as Hume should have conceded that promises can affect arguments for political obligation, even if the ultimate explanation for why they do so is the more basic utilitarian explanation that underlies both kinds of duty[8]). But this concession still results in assigning consent theory to a tangential, supplementing role, reinforcing obligations to particular states, rather than the central role it has typically been assigned in grounding political obligation in general.

Voluntariness, then, as an explanation of the foundation of promissory obligation, plays a role parallel to that of necessity in a general theory that seeks to explain why and when some persons have power to require greater deference to their views than they normally would.[9] But it is difficult to be more precise about the relative strength of these two ideas (voluntariness and necessity) in conferring such privileged status on others without talking substantively about why promises bind. Before moving to that issue, I first consider other respects in which arguments about promises and laws share similar structural features.

Promissory Obligation and Practical Authority

The preceding discussion, comparing promises to laws, reveals one feature that both promises and laws share that is seldom discussed in the literature. One standard set of arguments about the duty to keep a promise, as mentioned earlier, focuses on the harm that the promisor causes if the promise is not kept. The rights of the promisee under this view are derived primarily from the promisor's duty not to cause harm by breaking a promise. By re-presenting promise as a norm created by a two-person legislature, we can recast the problem of explaining the promisor's duty as a problem of explaining why the promisor should accept the norm he or she has created as authoritative. Legal systems, we said, do not claim authority, but they do expect voluntary compliance. So, too, with promises. The conflict that requires me to explain why I do no wrong

---

[8] This point is elegantly made by Leslie Green in his analysis of Hume's argument. See Green, *The Authority of the State* (Oxford: Clarendon Press, 1990), 180.

[9] The argument developed here concerning the *subject's* recognition that the state is necessary should not be confused with arguments that base the obligation to obey on the *state's* need for subject compliance. See Tony Honoré, "Must We Obey? Necessity as a Ground of Obligation," *Va. L. Rev.* 67 (1981): 39. For criticisms of the latter argument see Kent Greenawalt, *Conflicts of Law and Morality* (Oxford: Clarendon Press, 1987), 168–70.

if I break my promise would not arise if my promisee, having no objection to my changing my mind, releases me. So too with law: If no one cares about my apparent legal transgression (such as the neighbor who doesn't mind if I commit a technical trespass by taking a shortcut through his yard[10]), then I commit neither a legal nor a moral wrong. Thus the question of the obligation of both promise and law always assumes a dispute: The will of one person, or group of persons, is opposed to mine, and the question is what theory might support deference to the wishes of the other, even if the action expected would otherwise be wrong. Earlier we asked what it would mean to claim that someone has or is a practical authority. Similarly, we may now ask what it would mean to claim that a promise is binding – how similar are the conceptual features that characterize promises and practical authorities?

PREEMPTION. In Chapter 2, I suggested that to acknowledge practical authority is to acknowledge reasons to defer to another's views even if those views are wrong. The major dispute in the literature over this issue concerned the degree of deference (or preemption) required: Is complete deference required, or is it sufficient that some weight be given the authority's views? Similar observations and questions arise in the case of promises. To say that a promise binds is to say, in part, that one's ordinary calculations about what best serves one's own interests must be deferred to some extent to the promisee's interest. Disagreement about the degree of deference required reflects, in part, disagreement about why and how much promises bind. Deontological and rule utilitarian accounts of promise often insist that deference in favor of the promisee is absolute, or nearly so.[11] Utilitarians respond that, although the interests of the promisee do have a special claim,[12] the degree of deference required is consistent with weighing the additional reliance and/or expectation interests of the promisee against one's own interests, and then acting in whatever manner will produce the best consequences.

CONTENT INDEPENDENCE. The reasons for deferring to practical authority, we have seen, are distinct from the reasons that normally bear on the action in question. To be an authority is to provide new reasons, independent of content, for deference to the authority. Indeed, it is these reasons that resolve the air of paradox in suggesting that it is sometimes right to do the wrong thing. What we are really saying is that the new reasons supplied by the authority outweigh the reasons that normally counsel against the action in question. Debates about

---

[10] See Kent Greenawalt, "Comment, the Obligation to Obey the Law," in *Issues in Contemporary Legal Philosophy*, ed. R. Gavison (Oxford: Oxford Univ. Press, 1987), 157 (even if one concedes that the trespass law is just, there may be no moral duty to avoid walking across someone's land when one will not be seen and will not cause damage).

[11] See, e.g., John Rawls, "Two Concepts of Rules," *Phil. Rev.* 64 (1955): 17.

[12] See Ardal, "And That's a Promise," 235.

practical authority in the case of law center on whether any such new reasons actually exist. The restrictive account of authority, which requires that authority be justified in essentially the same manner as theoretical authority, has difficulty explaining how legal authority can make a difference in the sense of providing new reasons for action, as opposed to simply serving as a salient point that facilitates coordination. One stops for red lights not because the law gives one new content-independent reasons to do so, but because the law's presence alters the balance of existing reasons.[13]

This debate finds a perfect reflection in arguments about promises. It is often suggested that promises bind because they provide content-independent reasons for action. But this claim is subject to the same doubts raised in connection with practical authority. In particular, one needs to distinguish two kinds of reasons for acting that might be generated by promises and laws: (1) those that arise only because of the promise or law but are nevertheless context-dependent and (2) those that are truly content-independent.

To illustrate, consider again our snow-removal example. Suppose that the action in question is whether Jane should remove the snow from the path that borders her property and Henry's. The reasons bearing on whether she should do so will include prudential ones (her own convenience and safety), as well as possibly moral ones (the property rights of her neighbors or the risks she imposes on any passerby who must use the path), balanced against the expense of snow removal and other possible harms (e.g., environmental damage). Now add the assumption that Jane has promised Henry to shovel the path or the assumption that an ordinance requires her to do so. Jane now has additional reasons bearing on the decision about snow removal that are distinct from the ones already mentioned: reasons that can be used to explain how promises and laws can create new reasons for action that are not, however, necessarily content-independent. In the case of promise, Jane may have created expectations in Henry that will now be disappointed or Henry may have relied on her promise (by planning a party, for example, on the assumption that his guests will not risk a slippery walk). In the case of law, Jane may now suppose that the sanction will induce other homeowners to clear their walks, which may affect her own willingness to do so; or she may worry about the effect of her example on others if she flouts the law; and so on. Note that these are the ordinary consequentialist kinds of explanations about the differences that promises and laws often make. These new reasons, however, are not content-independent reasons. They are, instead, what might be considered context-dependent reasons: They alter the balance of reasons that bear on the content of the act by placing the act in a wider context that requires recognizing new potential consequences. Indeed, one could probably collapse all content-independent reasons into reasons bearing directly on content by a suitable redescription of the act in question. The act in question

---

[13] See Chapter 2, 40–1 and footnote 14.

is no longer simply "shoveling the walk." Rather, the act is "shoveling the walk after having promised my neighbor to do so" or "shoveling the walk after having been legally required to do so."

As is clear from these examples, any good utilitarian can readily admit and take account of the difference that *context* makes in explaining why a promise or a law affects the reasons that must be considered in deciding what ought to be done. Indeed, it seems almost to be a defining feature of the utilitarian account (some would view it as a virtuous feature) that a utilitarian never needs to go beyond such context-dependent reasons in order to explain the difference that promises and laws make.

One way to explain the distinction between context-dependent and content-independent reasons in the case of promises is to recall the debate about restrictive and expansive concepts of authority. If we ask how Jane's promise, re-presented as a norm created by her and Henry, can have authority over her, we will receive different answers from these two accounts of authority. The restrictive account requires that the justification show that keeping the promise is the best way to realize Jane's own interests. This account easily accommodates the utilitarian focus on context-dependent reasons. All of the additional consequences that attach to and arise out of the context created by a promise become reasons for achieving Jane's own ends – ends that include her own desire to foster trust and reliability in the future, as well as to avoid causing disappointment now. This is the "service" conception of promise. The alternative conception, the "leader" conception of authority, points to a different answer. The leader conception invites one to see a promise as a delegation of authority to the promisee to *lead* in the sense of allowing the promisee's own opinion about whether the promise should be kept to dominate the promisor's. To distinguish the two conceptions, we have to imagine that Jane has carefully evaluated all of the reasons that arise from the context of promise and has *correctly* concluded that, in this case, breaking the promise is the correct course of action. The leader conception invites us to explain why one might, even in this case, have reasons to defer to the contrary judgment of the promisee that the promise should be kept.

Thus far, the conclusion we have reached is a limited one. We have not yet shown that the reasons for keeping promises and obeying laws *must* include content-independent as well as context-dependent reasons. Indeed, since the major thesis in this part of the chapter is simply that promises and laws are essentially alike, it is enough at this point to note only that whichever view one takes, it leads to similar conclusions about the obligations created by both promise and law. Thus the utilitarian who thinks there can only be, at most, context-dependent reasons for keeping promises and obeying law will often conclude that there is no obligation to keep a promise or obey law because, even after taking context into account, utility is maximized by breach or disobedience. One who accepts the content-independent view of promise and law, on the other hand, and the expansive concept of authority on which it is based presumably endorses something like the view suggested in the previous chapter: There are intrinsic reasons for deferring to the views of others, legislatures in the case of law, promisees in the case of promise, that cannot be captured by an account that recognizes only context-dependent (instrumental) reasons.

Promissory Obligation – A Substantive Theory

The Puzzles of Promise

Although the remainder of this chapter continues the general exploration of the similarity between promise and law, it is no longer easy to do so without talking directly about the substantive issues involved in explaining why and to what extent promises obligate. Accordingly, I review here three standard puzzles about promises that dominate the literature. Two of these seem to me rather minor puzzles that are fairly easily resolved. My only excuse for retreading what is by now well-traveled ground is that the review of these two puzzles provides background for the third puzzle – one that is not so easily resolved. The third puzzle lies at the heart of moral theory and often serves as a dividing line between utilitarians and Kantians. I call it "the" puzzle of promise. It is this puzzle that I am primarily interested in and that I think can be illuminated by the comparison with political obligation.

The three puzzles are these. The first is whether promissory obligation depends on a preexisting convention or societal rule about the effect that promises shall have. The second puzzle is primarily about meaning: What does it mean to promise and how is a promise different from, say, a statement of intent? The third puzzle, connected to the second, concerns the explanation for why – and to what extent – a promise obligates. This explanation partly depends on one's conclusion about what it means to promise. Or one could put it the other way around: Different explanations of the force and grounds for promissory obligation will result in different claims about what it means to promise (which is why some utilitarian accounts of the force of promise often end by suggesting that promises are in effect nothing more than statements of intent).

Promises and Conventions

The first puzzle can be stated in various ways. One variation of the puzzle suggests that there is a logical impasse involved in explaining why promises obligate.[14] If the obligation of promise results from the promisee's reliance

---

[14] For a discussion of this argument, see P. S. Atiyah, *Promises, Morals, and Law* (Oxford: Clarendon Press, 1981), 63. Atiyah includes Prichard, Warnock, Robins, and Hodgson among the "many writers who have made this point." *Id.*, note 43.

on the promise, why is such reliance justified? Doesn't the recognition of the promisee's right to rely on the promise presuppose a societal rule or convention that recognizes such reliance as legitimate? If so, if the force of promise depends on a convention or societal rule that declares that reliance on promises is justified, why is one justified in relying on the convention? Doesn't the existence of the convention itself also rest ultimately on the acceptance of rules – a kind of consent – so that relying on the convention to justify relying on the promise is ultimately circular.

This story will remind some of the puzzles common law courts encountered in developing the theory of promissory estoppel – the right recognized in contract law to recover for breach of a gratuitous promise where the promise results in detrimental reliance by the promisee. Since donative promises prior to the development of promissory estoppel were not enforced, why was the reliance of the promisee on such a promise justified? Couldn't the promisee be presumed to know the law and to know that only promises supported by consideration would be enforced? If so, any change of position in reliance on the donative promise ought to be at the promisee's own risk. The implicit answer the courts reached is indirectly a confirmation of the answer that now appears widely accepted in the philosophical literature as a solution to the parallel question of whether promises depend on preexisting conventions: The force of promise arises simply from what appears to be an entirely reasonable response on the part of the promisee to the message communicated. The promisee, having been explicitly invited to rely on the promisor, does exactly that; he or she need not know anything about conventions or rules or contract law in coming to the conclusion that it is reasonable for him or her to do so. It is simply "linguistically appropriate"[15] for the promisee to do so.

It appears, then, that the appropriate communication of an invitation to rely, coupled with general arguments about causation and responsibility for preventable, foreseeable harm, can explain how one becomes obligated to keep a promise even in the absence of a societal convention about promise-keeping. But can promissory obligation also survive in the face of a contrary convention? It is easy to understand that the existence of a convention can help reinforce the promissory obligation by making it even more likely that the promisee will rely. Is the opposite also the case? If there is a convention that positively declares reliance on a promise to be illegitimate – that is, the risk of change of mind is on the promisee – does that prevent promises from creating obligations?

Imagine that we are in a society of risk-loving people who like to be able to change their minds with impunity and who prefer the uncertainties that result over the ability to tie down the future with enforceable promises. Imagine further

---

[15] Narveson, "Promising, Expecting, and Utility," 215. The point is also made, inter alia, by Neil MacCormick, "Voluntary Obligations and Normative Powers," *Proc. Arist. Soc.*, Suppl. 46 (1972): 59, 63.

that this society, as a means of trying to make good risk-loving citizens out of cowards whose natural inclination might be to control uncertainty, passes legislation declaring that anyone who relies on a promise does so at his or her own risk: That is, a promisor may with impunity change his or her mind (compare consumer protection statutes that provide for "cooling-off" periods, in which buyers may change their minds with impunity). For that matter, if it really was thought to be a serious character flaw to make promises, one could even imagine the society declaring that any attempt to make a promise is a crime, subject to fines or other penalties. (Compare antitrust law, which makes criminal some kinds of promises in restraint of trade, and consider legislative proposals – and existing laws in some states – that forbid surrogacy contracts.)

Now I think one has to concede that the law in the society I have imagined – "All promises are illegal" – is an empirical possibility, however unlikely a picture of human nature it suggests. Moreover, as we shall see in examining the meaning of promise, this law in essence forbids the practice that we know as promising. It declares that all promissory language shall henceforth be treated as mere statements of intent, with the risk of change of mind on the addressee. Is it true now that the obligation of promise could not arise? If promise does not require a reinforcing convention, does it at least require that no inhibiting convention exist?

A negative answer to this question follows from the same general argument just made about the irrelevance of a preexisting convention on promises. Promising only takes two people who each know that the message communicated is the honest intent to invite reliance in the relevant sense. Suppose you live in this brave new society of "Free Mind Changers" but you think it is a silly policy – for the very reasons that make promise a staple of most societies. You want to be able to rely on the word of the person you do business with rather than incur the expense of stockpiling goods, and so on. All you have to do is discover that the person you are dealing with is equally able to see the advantage of promise and begin to exchange "real" promises with that person. You may not be able to use the normal language of promise.[16] If promise has, in effect, been redefined by this society, you may need some other way to signal that what you mean is the old-fashioned kind of promise where you cannot freely change your mind, so perhaps you cross and uncross your fingers, or raise your hand and swear, or engage in some other ritual – like affixing a seal – to make clear your intent.

Thus, far from requiring a supporting convention, promises can arise and thrive in the face of contrary conventions. In our imagined society, arguments

---

[16] See Joseph Raz, "Voluntary Obligations and Normative Powers II," *Proc. Arist. Soc.* Supp. 46 (1972): 96, 100. Raz shares MacCormick's view that social convention is not necessary for promissory obligation, but he notes that social convention may determine the acts (including language) necessary to communicate a promise. Raz's disagreement with MacCormick about the meaning of promise (claiming that promises convey an intent to incur an obligation) will be examined later.

of estoppel will still arise when one's "partner in crime" relies on one's honest communication of intent, making the promisor responsible for the harm caused in breaking a real (but illegal) promise. The only doubt about this conclusion is that if the society really does detest this practice and makes it a crime to engage in it, you, as the promisor, will have committed an illegal act. You have not promised to do something illegal, because the act you promised to do wasn't illegal: It is the fact that you made a promise at all that is the illegal act in this society, so the issues that arise are rather different from promises known from the start to involve unjust or illegal actions. The issues that arise are similar to those presented when coconspirators in a crime nevertheless try to hold each other to promises made (honor among thieves). My imagined society will give no relief if the promise is broken, but that does not settle the question of whether there is a moral obligation to keep one's promise.[17]

I shall leave this issue in this state, noting that while there are still interesting questions in explaining all the ways that conventions might interact with promises to either reinforce them or inhibit them, at least the basic claim seems correct: The obligation of promise does not depend on a preexisting rule or convention, but only on the ability to communicate honestly with another and to be aware of the likely consequences of that communication.

The Meaning of Promise

If promises do not depend on existing conventions, they do depend on being able to communicate a message about one's intent to perform a certain action. Characterizing the message communicated – determining the meaning of promise – is the second puzzle of promise, one not quite so easily handled as the first. The increased difficulty in establishing the meaning of promise arises because, as indicated previously, the meaning of promise often seems connected to the major puzzle of the grounds for promissory obligation. In what follows, I attempt to separate these two questions of meaning and grounds by simply listing a range of possible "translations" of promissory language into somewhat cruder elements. This list will be in order of increasing apparent commitment to do the act in question. We have already considered one standard argument about what a promise means, namely, that it is the communication of an intention to act in a way that knowingly invites the promisee's reliance. That translation is the third one on the list of five that follows. It is preceded by two translations that are weaker in terms of the commitment that is made and by two that appear to be

---

[17] Suppose that two competitors enter a price-fixing agreement that is forbidden – the very act of agreeing is forbidden – by the antitrust laws. Is there no moral duty between the coconspirators based on the promise? In law, courts sometimes invoke the doctrine of *in pari delicto* to prevent recovery under such contracts. But they do not always do so, which suggests that even a societal norm forbidding agreements could, without contradiction, recognize that some obligation attaches to such agreements even though they are made in violation of the law.

stronger commitments.[18] To keep the discussion from becoming too abstract, I shall use the same concrete example used by Neil MacCormick in a somewhat different context.[19] You have invited me to attend dinner next Tuesday night, explaining that your nephew, who wishes to meet me, will also be asked. Here are five possible responses with corresponding comments on what I take to be the meaning that is communicated:

FIVE DEGREES OF COMMITMENT. (1) "At the moment I think I'll be there, but I don't know how I'll feel on Tuesday."

No commitment has been given at all, only an expression of present inclination; no responsibility for failing to attend arises. It is unreasonable to view my statement as affecting very much the probability that I will go (though, no doubt, there is a greater chance of my going than if I had said I had no present plans to attend at all). You should decide what to do just as you would if I had said nothing

(2) "I intend to go (and you may count on it), though I'm not making a promise."

Again, no commitment has been made, and there is no responsibility for failing to go. Now, however, it is reasonable to interpret my statement as increasing the probability that I will go. Indeed, it would be unreasonable *not* to view the probability as greater now than before the statement was made. But all of this goes only to the rationality of your own decision about what to do; the explicit disclaimer that I am not promising indicates that you still take the risk that I might not show up and you have no legitimate complaint if I don't attend (though you may have a right to be warned in time if I can easily do so).

(3) "I promise to attend (i.e., you may count on it, and I knowingly understand that you may rely on it and that you know I am inviting you to so rely)."

This is MacCormick's explanation of what a promise is, tying the obligation that results to the negative utilitarian obligation not to cause preventable harm. The obligation of promise becomes a species of estoppel.[20]

(4) "I promise to attend (i.e., you may count on it, and I understand that you may both rely on my promise and develop expectations that will be disappointed if I break my promise)."

This appears to have much the same force as (3), but it extends the scope of the foreseeable harms to include actually formed expectations as well as reliance losses. This interpretation of what a promise is approximates a standard utilitarian account.[21]

---

[18] My list of the range of possible meanings of language expressing one's intent about a future act follows a similar listing of possible meanings in Don Locke, "The Object of Morality and the Obligation to Keep a Promise," *Can. L. J.* 2 (1972): 136.

[19] See MacCormick, "Voluntary Obligations – I," 69–70.

[20] Id.

[21] See Narveson, "Promising, Expecting, and Utility."

(5) "I promise to attend (you may count on it, and I assume responsibility to do what I say whether or not you have relied on it or formed any special hopes or expectations)."

This represents promise as making the strongest possible commitment: Promise is more than a statement of intent coupled with an invitation to rely; it is a statement made with the intent to incur an obligation to do the thing promised.[22]

Each of these translations represents a linguistically distinct and coherent possibility. Each conveys a somewhat different message. The first two statements do not represent promises at all and thus do not lead to questions about how to justify promissory obligation. The third and fourth explanations track, roughly, utilitarian accounts of what it means to make a promise and indirectly point to a standard utilitarian explanation for how promises obligate: Promises create new (context-dependent) reasons for acting based on the reliance and/or the expectations of the promisee. The fifth translation is the prelude to what I have called *the* puzzle of promise: It seems to suggest that promisors undertake to perform without regard to whether harm is caused to the promisee's reliance or expectations interests, indeed without regard to any reasons at all apart from the voluntary assumption of the obligation. Attempting to explain what sorts of reasons might support such an interpretation of promise is the goal of much of the rest of this chapter. First, however, it is important to clarify one final dispute about the meaning of promise suggested by the preceding formulations.

DO PROMISORS INTEND TO INCUR OBLIGATIONS? There is one difference in the preceding formulations that points to a controversy about the meaning of promise not yet discussed. Are promises statements of intent only – intent to act and to induce reliance on that intent – or do promisors, by the very act of promising, intend to incur an obligation to act?[23] This dispute parallels once again the dispute in legal theory about whether law claims authority. Is it the case, from the viewpoint of the legal system, that when a legislature creates a new law it necessarily claims that citizens have an obligation to obey the law? When Henry and Jane vote for the snow-removal ordinance, must we assume that they intend by that very act to impose an obligation on citizens (including themselves) to comply? As we have already seen, the answer to that question is a qualified no: Henry and Jane make no claims about whether citizens should obey *just because it is the law*. (They do not, in other words, claim moral authority.) But they do claim that citizens *ought* to comply with the law (because they

---

[22] See Raz, "Voluntary Obligations – II". Raz's view is more fully developed in Joseph Raz, "Promises and Obligations," in *Law, Morality, and Society: Essays in Honour of H. L. A. Hart*, eds. P. M. S. Hacker and Joseph Raz (Oxford: Clarendon Press, 1977), 210.

[23] This dispute is the focus of the exchange between Raz and MacCormick in the articles cited previously (see footnotes 15, 16, 19, 22).

believe the content is justified), and they claim that they are morally entitled to enforce the law, even if they are wrong in their judgment about the content. Why can we not say the same of the norm that is created through the promise? When Jane promises Henry to clear the walks, she need take no position on whether she is incurring an obligation *just because she promised.* She does not, in other words, necessarily take a stand on the issue of promissory obligation that is in question any more than the state takes a stand on the controversial question of political theory when it enacts laws. But does Jane at least imply that she intends to incur an obligation to do the act in question (shovel the walk)? She certainly makes it clear that she thinks this action is correct and intends to do it. Furthermore, in order to distinguish a mere statement of intent from a promise, doesn't the "intent to induce or invite reliance" require one to explain what it means to induce or invite reliance? And won't that explanation turn out to be something like an expressed willingness *to assume responsibility* for harm caused if reliance occurs and the promise is broken? And isn't an expression of willingness to assume responsibility an expression of an intent to incur an obligation?

These questions give some force to the claim that a promise is the communication of an intent to incur an obligation. But difficulties remain. The problem in choosing between the intent conception and the obligation conception of promise results in part from the difficulty of distinguishing foreseeable consequences from intended consequences. The intent-based conception of promise, which is all that the utilitarian apparently needs, will admit that Jane can *foresee* that she will incur an obligation, whether she intends to or not, by communicating an intention to induce reliance. But must she necessarily *intend* to incur the obligation? If Jane leaves her walks in an icy and dangerous condition, she can foresee that she will incur an obligation to redress harms caused to those who slip and fall – but she can deny that she left the walks in an icy condition *with the intention* of incurring such an obligation. (She hopes, to the contrary, that nobody *will* slip and fall.) Why is Jane's situation different if she promises to clear the walks? Why should we assume that the promise communicates an intent to incur an obligation rather than just an invitation to rely, knowing that an obligation may result?

One possible argument for the obligation conception of promise might rely on a difference we noted earlier between promises and laws. The content of a promise, unlike the content of a law, is typically within the control of the promisor. Jane may leave her walks icy hoping that she won't (and thus not *intending* to) incur an obligation, though she can foresee that she *will* incur obligations to those who do slip and fall. Her negligence may be the cause of a fall, but she does not directly desire it and thus can plausibly be seen as not intending it. In contrast, it might be argued, she cannot similarly invite reliance on her promise to clear the walk, hoping the promisee won't be hurt by relying, since it is her own conscious decision to break the promise that causes the harm.

Knowing this, she must be communicating, by the very act of promising, an intention to incur an obligation.

There are several reasons why the preceding argument for the obligation conception of promise remains open to doubt. First, we could still say, parallel to the negligence case, that Jane hopes she won't break her promise but realizes that if she does, she will incur an obligation to compensate the promisee who relied – an obligation that she didn't intend to incur but that arises (whether or not she consents or intends it) for precisely the same reasons that obligations arise when people slip and fall on icy walks that should have been cleared. It is not obvious, in other words, why control over the promised act necessarily means that promises communicate an intended, as opposed to a foreseeable, obligation. In addition, we have already seen that it is not a contradiction to say, "I promise to do x, but I know I ought not to."[24] In this case, we said, the promissory obligation is probably not a moral obligation, which means that "promise" can sometimes be used in ways that do not commit one to an intent to incur a *moral* obligation. Finally, Jane might be uncertain (having read too much of the literature on promise-keeping) whether promises create binding obligations; so perhaps she could say, "I promise, but I hope that when I've finally figured out whether promises obligate, it will turn out that I don't have an obligation to keep the promise (though I understand I'll be responsible for harm caused through reliance on the promise, though I hope that doesn't happen)." If this possibility is a real one, it restores promise to the same position as law: One can create norms through law or promise while remaining aloof from the ultimate question of whether such norm-creating acts imply that legislators or promisors are taking implicit positions on controversial issues in moral and political theory.

It should be noted that choosing between the intent and obligation conceptions does not affect the puzzle of promise we have been considering. If one believes that it is unclear why a promisee is justified in holding the promisor responsible for his or her reliance, that logical impasse is not avoided by the obligation conception. Merely stating that I intend to incur an obligation doesn't mean that I do, and doesn't avoid the question of why the promisee is entitled to hold me responsible for his or her loss. Whatever answer we give to the question of assigning responsibility for harm caused when the promise is broken will be similar under both conceptions. Similarly, the problem of explaining how extensive promissory obligation is, and how it arises, is unaffected by the choice between the intent and obligation conceptions of what is meant by promise. Thus, even if one thinks that a promise expresses an intent to incur an obligation, it is possible that the only obligation one intends is a limited one – to reimburse reliance losses, for example, not to perform in the absence of reliance by the promisee. Thus the more limited expressions of commitment stated in the

---

[24] See 108–9, and footnotes 5, 7.

preceding list (the third and fourth) remain unaffected by the choice between these two conceptions of promise.

CHOOSING WHAT PROMISE SHALL MEAN. The result of the preceding discussion is this: Linguistic analysis alone seems unlikely to be able to resolve the question of what is meant by a promise. But there is a reason for this result that helps explain the peculiarity of promise and sheds additional light on some of the puzzles we have been considering. The reason it is difficult to undertake a conceptual analysis of what promise means is that what one means by this term may depend on what the promisor chooses to express. We suggested earlier that no one is required to enter the promissory state by making promises; by the same token, one may choose to promise only under conditions of limited liability. As the preceding formulations indicate, with appropriate qualifications one can always express varying degrees of commitment: One can make clear, for example, that one reserves the right to change one's mind with all attendant risks on the promisee. In that case, perhaps, linguistic analysis can show that one has not really made a promise. But what if one makes it clear that one will be responsible only for reliance losses, or reliance together with dashed expectations. Now, it seems, one has incurred some obligation, limited in the way that a utilitarian analysis limits obligation under promises. Thus, one cannot rule out this limited commitment as not amounting to a promise without begging the issue that is in dispute between consequentialists and deontologists. Indeed, presumably even those who think that promises involve greater commitments than the commitment to be responsible only for reliance and expectation interests will admit that one can always qualify one's undertaking down to the more limited level. One way, then, to rephrase the issue posed by the deontologist's challenge to a simple consequentialist account of promise is to ask whether it makes sense to imagine commitments that are even stronger than the promise that only assumes responsibility for losses caused? If one can limit the scope of the undertaking expressed by promise, can one also escalate the commitment? Is there, for example, an even stronger expression of commitment than the one that appears as number (5) in our list? Children, after all, sometimes engage in rituals involving "double swearing" or "crossing one's heart," as if to suggest that ordinary promises are not strong enough to express the requisite degree of commitment. What could these extra expressions of commitment mean? One possibility is that by "double swearing" or by adding to the promise escalating expressions such as "I *really* mean it," one intends to limit the kinds of defenses or excuses that might ordinarily permit one a way out of the promise.[25] Apart from this possibility, it seems hard to imagine how a promise can be stronger than the undertaking implied in the fifth formulation: an undertaking to do precisely as promised, without regard to any reasons that might otherwise counsel

---

[25] I am indebted to Don Herzog for this suggestion.

against performance – even if no harm of any sort will occur to the promisee from breaking the promise. Of course, if this is the ordinary meaning of promise, we have selected the most difficult interpretation to justify. If it turns out to be difficult to defend a commitment that seems to disregard all reasons that might justify such an extensive undertaking, perhaps the normal meaning of promise is the lesser expression of commitment listed earlier – one more consistent with standard utilitarian justifications.

The ability of the promisor to qualify the commitment he or she is making helps put into perspective another peculiar feature of promises that will be important in the next section in explaining how to justify obligation under even the strongest form of commitment. In a famous article, Searle once suggested that promises are examples of how one can derive an "ought" from an "is."[26] Searle's argument, paraphrased, is this: (1) The claim that a person made a promise is a factual claim, requiring only knowledge that certain language was used under certain conditions. (2) From the fact that a promise was made, one can derive the conclusion that the promise ought to be kept. (3) Therefore, conventions like promise-keeping are exceptions to the normal view that one cannot derive an ought from an is. Almost no one, apparently, has been persuaded by Searle's argument, though there is some disagreement about why the argument fails.[27] The major objection to the argument, as illustrated in an article by Narveson,[28] is that the ought that is derived here is not a moral ought at all: It is exactly like the ought that is derived when one concludes from the fact that a ball player has been thrown out that he ought to leave the field. This game analogy, which Searle himself uses, reveals a common equivocation in the meaning of ought. Sometimes the term is used simply as a way of describing a rule of a game – for example, in the statement that "one ought to move the bishop diagonally when playing chess": a descriptive use of "ought," not a normative one. In the case of the ballplayer, the conclusion that he ought to leave the field when thrown out is a moral ought only if we take account of nonlinguistic explanations that show why games are valuable and why people who begin to play a game implicitly consent to play by the rules and thus should not harm the interests of others by interjecting new rules in the midst of play. Russian roulette or dueling, on the other hand, to use the standard counterexamples to Searle's argument,[29] could probably never be defended as desirable in the first place, so that the ought will remain nonmoral at best. In this sense, one can always opt out of

---

26 John R. Searle, "How to Derive 'Ought' from 'Is'," *Phil. Rev.* 73 (1964): 43, reprinted in *Theories of Ethics*, ed. Philippa Foot (Oxford: Oxford Univ. Press, 1967), 101.

27 For a useful review of the literature and critique of Searle's argument, see Atiyah, *Promises, Morals, and Law*, 109–22.

28 See Narveson, "Promising, Expecting, and Utility," 228–31. A similar argument was advanced earlier by R. M. Hare; see his "The Promising Game," *Rev. Int. Phil.* 18 (1964): 398, reprinted in *Theories of Ethics*, 15.

29 See Narveson, "Promising, Expecting, and Utility," 228–32 (Russian roulette as a counterexample); Foot, "Introduction," in *Theories of Ethics*, 11–12 (dueling as a counterexample).

a conventionally accepted institution without committing a moral wrong even though, according to the convention, one ought to abide by the convention.

Try now to apply this conclusion about the ability to opt out of immoral conventions to the case of promising. Suppose that you have views about promissory obligation different from those that are conventionally accepted in your particular society. You think, for example, that promises never obligate: that one can always break a promise if, all things considered, that is the best thing to do. The society you live in thinks that promises bind absolutely – regardless of the consequences, one must always do as one promised. Unlike a dueling convention, you need never find yourself in conflict with an alternative societal convention about promising that you reject. As long as you make clear what your theory of promising is, you will be qualifying your commitment and thus will not really be making a promise, as understood by the society in which you find yourself. When you say, "I promise to ϕ, but in doing so I understand myself to be committed to ϕ only if, all things considered, it is the best thing to do," the promisee will understand that you are making a qualified commitment (and maybe no promise at all). But this option is open to everyone in the society. Anyone can expressly limit the commitment he or she is making (or choose not to make promises at all) for all the usual reasons that prompt one to limit liability; it just so happens that your reason for limiting the commitment reflects a disagreement about the theory of promissory obligation that is conventionally accepted by everyone else.

This peculiarity of promise does not affect the general conclusion that conventional views about the force of promise will only yield conventional or institutional oughts; the society we have imagined may, after all, simply be wrong in its view that absolute promissory obligations can be justified. But it does suggest that the potential for conflicting normative judgments about the force of promise tends to disappear in practice: People who hold different theories about whether promises obligate will, if the theories are openly confessed, simply find themselves making promises with different degrees of commitment.[30] The importance of this possibility – that promisors may have a choice, not only over the degree of commitment they express, but also over the theory of promissory obligation they accept – will become apparent in the next section.

Why and How Much Do Promises Obligate?

TAKING THE UTILITARIAN CHALLENGE SERIOUSLY. In the preceding section, I said that the third and fourth translations of promise on my list correspond

---

[30] Someone who did not accept the society's theory of absolute promissory obligation could conceal that fact and make promises. But then we would have a case of deception – knowingly making a stronger assertion of commitment than one intends – whose immorality can be explained on the basis of principles of veracity rather than promise.

roughly to a standard utilitarian view of what promises are and why they obligate.[31] That account, like the parallel account of the obligation to obey, leads to the conclusion that many promises, like many laws, may yield no obligation: Even taking into consideration the additional consequences that result from the context of promise or law, sometimes breaking the promise and disobeying the law will be the optimific act.

As mentioned in the introduction to this chapter, this conclusion conflicts with the intuition of many people that a promise gives the promisee some special right or places the promisor under a particularly weighty obligation that persists even if, by hypothesis, better consequences obtain from breaking than from keeping the promise.[32]

There are at least two respects in which the utilitarian account seems to fall short of what promises require. First, the implication of the utilitarian analysis is that in the absence of harm to the promisee, there is no obligation to perform.[33] Second, connected with this possibility of no harm is the possibility that, under the utilitarian account, one could discharge one's obligation by compensating for the harm or by otherwise restoring the promisee to his or her original position. If Henry regrets having promised Jane that he will remove snow from his half of the common walk, he can avoid his obligation by notifying her that he has changed his mind before she relies on it by, for example, inviting guests to use the walk. If he informs her in time (before she relies), she is no worse off than before the promise was made. If Jane complains that she has still been harmed because, for example, she was once relieved to know that the snow removal problem was resolved but is now distressed about Henry's change of mind, Henry can pay for a few therapy sessions to restore her peace of mind. In either case, he has not kept his promise but, it seems, neither has he caused any harm to Jane.

The difference between these two views of the force of promise can be summarized as follows: What might be called the strong account of promise,

---

[31] For an example of the standard utilitarian explanation, see Narveson, "Promising, Expecting, and Utility." A good review of utilitarian and non-utilitarian theories, and an appraisal of their relative strengths and weaknesses may be found in Atiyah, *Promises, Morals, and Law.*

[32] Some utilitarian accounts attempt to explain away this sense that promises create "special rights" in the promisee while remaining more or less consistent with a utilitarian account. MacCormick, for example, does not allow the promisor simply to weigh his gains from breaching against the promisee's loss: Rather, the promisee's loss will be a harm caused by the breach that is inconsistent with the negative utilitarian principle not to cause preventable harm to others. See MacCormick, "Voluntary Obligations – I." This restores the intuition about the promisee's special rights while remaining largely a utilitarian account. It seems to allow one to escape the moral obligation of promise only where there has in fact been no loss, though if we charge the promisor with responsibility even for dashed expectations, however slight they may be, it may be hard to find any case in which there is not some loss and thus some obligation generated by the promise.

[33] I suggested in the preceding footnote that it is possible to define harm in a way that would make its existence almost always empirically likely; but in theory, it is possible that there might not be harm. Certainly if actual reliance is the main concern (rather than dashed hopes), there will be many cases where a promise can be retracted before actual change of position.

in contrast to the utilitarian account, does two things: (1) it commits one to do the very act promised and (2) the obligation to do so is independent of the harm caused to the promisee. This is the sense, apparently, in which a promise is sometimes defined as a voluntary obligation:[34] I undertake to obligate myself to do this very act simply by promising to do it; my obligation does not derive from some other principle, such as not harming others or maximizing utility; it derives simply from my voluntary decision to assume this obligation.

Now I hope it is clear why this is such a puzzling idea. Of course, it will seem incomprehensible to the utilitarian who thinks that all questions of moral obligation are determined by assessing the consequences of contemplated action in terms of some axiology, some ascription of value, which normally means a description in terms of human interests that can be harmed or advanced. The challenge presented by the utilitarian account is to explain what human interests or moral theory could possibly justify this strong view of promissory obligation.

On the other hand, there must be some intuitive basis for the strong position to keep it flourishing so persistently, and I think it is clear what that is: The language used in making a promise supports the stronger deontological account of obligation. Even utilitarians, I think, concede this: When one promises, one says one will do the act promised; one does not qualify it with expressions such as "if harm would otherwise result" or "as long as I don't change my mind before you've relied" or "if I can't otherwise make you whole." That is why one finds in the Kantian literature so much talk about one's honor, "keeping one's word," and so on. The word *is* on the side of those who think the obligation is strong: *By reference to what one has said*, strict performance *is* required without regard to consequences. But this insistence on taking one's word at face value gets us nowhere: That one *claims* to be assuming an obligation may have as little connection with reality as claiming that the moon is made of green cheese.[35] The utilitarian's challenge is to make sense of this idea in some way that shows that it is more than just superstition. That challenge requires an answer. One must be able to show some point to the practice, some connection with human interests that justifies making this a true moral obligation. In the next part of this chapter, I try to do that.

A STATE-OF-NATURE THEORY FOR PROMISES. Anyone who thinks that promises and laws function similarly to create obligations might wonder why

---

[34] See Raz, "Promises and Obligations."

[35] Narveson makes this point forcefully by inviting one to imagine someone announcing that "whenever I throw a cup of cold water over my left shoulder in the dark of the moon, I am thereby obligated to eat beans for three days." Narveson, "Promising, Expecting, and Utility," 229. The point is that deliberate attempts to create voluntary obligations do not succeed by themselves: One does not create obligations just by saying that one does (any more than one does by throwing cold water over one's shoulder).

the puzzle of promise hasn't led to a similar state-of-nature literature to explain why promises obligate. The history of political theory is, after all, filled with examples of speculations about a world without law, and current discussions continue to use the same device.[36] These speculations typically invite one, after contemplating a lawless state, to acknowledge the force of an argument designed to explain both what law (the state) is (the legal theory question of meaning) and why law is justified (the political theory question). Why isn't there a similar literature for promising? Why don't more theorists imagine a world without promises and then, in explaining why the practice of promise would arise, discover the true meaning of promise as well as the justifiable scope of promissory obligation?

One answer to this question is implied by our earlier discussion of the relationship of promise to a societal convention. It takes only two people to discover the advantage of promise and implement the practice. Thus, comparing a world without promise to one with promise seems to have little advantage over a simple direct discussion of the advantages and the point of promise – between any two people. In contrast, legal rules, unlike promises, exist only where many people – an entire society – are effectively governed by them. Legal rules are necessarily conventional in the sense of requiring the acceptance or acquiescence of many as a condition of their existence.

Nevertheless, one could imagine a state-of-nature inquiry into the basis for promissory obligation, just as one could develop political theory without resorting to state-of-nature arguments by directly assessing the value of the state. In any event, that is what I propose to do: conduct a state-of-nature inquiry into the point of promising in order to try to answer the utilitarian challenge I have just described. In light of the observation that it takes only two to promise, let us imagine a society of two people trying to decide which of the alternative meanings of promise described in the previous section should be the accepted meaning of promissory language as between them.

Now there is no difficulty, if these people have so far been living without the device of promise, in understanding why they might want to accept at least the utilitarian account of promising. I will not repeat here the obvious reasons why promises are advantageous and why the obligation created by a promise should at least extend as far as the utilitarian account: No Kantian need deny that causing preventable harm is wrong and that promises at least obligate one not to pull the rug out from someone who has accepted one's invitation to stand on it. The critical question is what more one could think is accomplished by having a linguistic form of the sort that seems so puzzling: a device for undertaking an obligation to perform the act, just because you said you would, without regard to questions of harm if you don't. Here are some possibilities:

---

[36] See Robert Nozick, *Anarchy, State, and Utopia* (New York: Basic Books, 1974).

(1) "Strict Performance" as Necessary to Protect Reliance. One suggestion that might be made for moving beyond the utilitarian conception to the stronger conception of promise is that it will be even easier to rely on a promise if it's clear that there will be no excuses based on lack of harm, and so on. Now that, of course, is true: Reliance will be safer if actual performance is always required – particularly if there is doubt, as there often might be, about the question of the extent of the reliance that has occurred. But this is not a reason that would justify the strong sense of promise described earlier. If the reason for keeping the promise relates to the need to protect reliance, it will not support the strong conception that insists that reliance has nothing to do with whether one has the obligation. One can't, in short, support moving to the strong conception on the grounds that it lessens difficulties in determining how much harm is caused because considerations of harm, under this conception, are irrelevant (excluded).[37]

(2) "Strict Performance" as a Test of Honor. A second possible reason for moving to the strong promise convention is suggested in some of the Kantian-oriented literature, much of which, I confess, seems to me quite unhelpful. It is unhelpful because it uses words like "trust" and "honor" and "autonomy" and "respect for one's own will" as if it were somehow self-evident that these concepts remain untarnished only in the presence of the strong conception of promise.[38] But that assumption begs the inquiry rather than advancing it. If trust within a relationship is at stake, for example, why is that concept tarnished so long as I take care not to harm the other party? Why isn't the only trust that is needed that which is afforded by this assurance of not getting hurt? The argument for strict performance in order to foster trust, in short, seems just a variation of the one just considered for giving extra protection to reliance.[39]

---

[37] See Raz, "Promises and Obligations," 227 ("the increased reliability is excessive. The needs of reliability were admitted as reasons for [the utilitarian account.] Allowing them extra force as exclusionary reasons as well would be to tip the balance unduly in favor of this consideration at the expense of conflicting considerations and would not be justified").

[38] See, e.g., Charles Fried, *Contract as Promise* (Cambridge, Mass.: Harvard Univ. Press, 1981), 16. For an insightful critique of Fried's argument, see Stephen A. Smith, "Towards a Theory of Contract," in *Oxford Essays in Jurisprudence*, 4th ser., ed. Jeremy Horder (Oxford: Oxford Univ. Press, 2000), 107, 115 ("Stripped to its essentials, [Fried's] argument is that promises create obligations to perform because they are conventionally understood to create such obligations. This argument does not just have a bootstrap 'quality' to it, it is a pure bootstrap argument").

[39] For a recent attempt to explain the obligation of promise in terms of "the value of assurance," see Thomas Scanlon, "Promises and Practices," *Phil. & Pub. Affairs* 19 (1990): 199. For the reasons indicated in the text, Scanlon's argument seems to assume what is at issue: Why is it necessary to go beyond protecting harm caused to reliance and/or expectation interests in order to foster trust? For a similar critique of Scanlon's argument, see Dennis M. Patterson, "The Value of a Promise," *Law & Phil.* 11 (1992): 385.

A second idea may be conveyed by the talk of honor and respecting one's own will. It may be that the point of strict performance without regard to harm is simply a test of oneself. The examples that come to mind are vows to oneself – New Year's resolutions, for example. Could one think that the point of strict performance is a kind of test of strength, an ability to carry out one's pledge regardless of whether changing one's mind would cause harm?

Now I suppose this *is* a reason that could support the strict performance conception, but it does not seem to be a very good one, particularly if we are imagining Jane and Henry trying to decide whether this should be part of the general convention in their two-person society. It is not a very good one precisely because its value, if any, seems oriented solely to one's own interests in seeing whether one can stick to a decision. If I *do* change my mind about my New Year's resolution, I probably do not think I have committed a moral error (though there is some speculation about this in the literature). But even if I do think there is some moral responsibility *to myself* in making such a vow, why would I want to assume the same responsibility in connection with a promise made to someone else? Why would I want to use a device that is supposed to give me a reason to perform willy-nilly, based on my interest in testing my willpower, as a way of making a commitment to someone else? What is it to Jane if Henry changes his mind and decides he's had enough testing? Why should she be able to hold him to his promise on the ground that its point lies in testing Henry's strength of character? I hope no one will say that Jane and Henry might want to hold each other to these little exercises of will-testing as a way of strengthening general moral character and thus making each other better (more reliable again?) people, because that response in this context clearly begs the issue. What's moral about this? Why is this an aspect of moral character rather than simply a test of stubbornness?

(3) "Strict Performance" as a Gift of Self. Sometimes defenders of a strong conception of promise allude to another reason, or set of reasons, that is also often found in the Kantian-oriented literature. The point of the practice under investigation, it is suggested, has to do with a special bond often found between persons in close relationships.[40] The bond is the one created by deliberately deciding to give the promisee a special power or right over the promisor. The special power is precisely that defined by the strict performance conception, that is, the right to demand performance without regard to harm or consequences. Now the question is, how does this foster something valuable in human relationships, and

---

[40] See Raz, "Promises and Obligations," 227–8.

why might Jane and Henry, for example, think it was something to want to incorporate in their dictionary for the meaning and point of promise?

To see what kind of point is now being claimed for the strong conception of promise, compare promise with an actual transfer of property. If I give someone a valuable gift, I usually cannot change my mind and demand it back as of right even though the donee has not yet changed position or raised his or her expectations. Actual transfers of property, in short, are typically governed by a rule that has the same strong force that we are considering as a possible rule for promise. Why might we accept so easily such an absolute "no-taking-it-back" rule in the case of property but find it puzzling to accept a similar "no-change-of-mind" rule in the case of promise?

I do not intend to explore here the fascinating literature discussing this question.[41] Why the property rule is more easily viewed as absolute, while the promissory rule is not, is part of the puzzle of promise. Answers to the question usually point to a far greater societal interest in having firm, if arbitrary, lines to determine ownership than to determine when promises "vest." I mention the analogy with property to help underscore what is being suggested under this new conception of promise as important for particular kinds of relationships. The advocate of the strong conception of promise who invokes the property analogy is urging that we treat promises like actual transfers of property.[42] But what is being transferred here is the promisor's autonomy. The promisor is giving, as in the case of an irrevocable proxy vote, a limited right to the promisee to exercise the promisor's will – at least as respects the promised act. Without the need to show any harm to his own interests, the promisee may make the decision that the promisor would otherwise retain – that of whether to go through with the act. Normally the only person entitled to make that decision is the promisor. Only his interests

---

[41] For a particularly insightful discussion see Daniel Friedmann, "The Efficient Breach Fallacy," *J. Legal Studies* 18 (1989): 1. For the suggestion that promises should be analogized to the "widely recognized and simple model of completed gifts and exchanges," see P. Benson, "The Idea of a Public Basis of Justification for Contract," *Osgoode Hall L. J.* 33 (1995): 273, 319. See also R. Barnett, "A Consent Theory of Contract," *Columbia L. Rev.* 86 (1986): 269. For a critique of these "transfer theories" of promise see Smith, "Towards a Theory of Contract," 118–20.

[42] This invitation, expressed in terms of the creation, rather than the transfer, of rights, is explicitly made and defended in id., Smith, 120–9. Smith's suggestion is that contract law can be viewed, like property law, as a means of creating rights to performance, which is "valuable because of the intrinsic value of such obligations in creating special relationships and thus in achieving valuable lives." Id., 129. It is not altogether clear that Smith's argument avoids the charge of "bootstrapping" that he levels at Fried (see footnote 38). Though I am obviously sympathetic with the focus on the value of the promissory relationship as the key to promissory obligation, the explanation I offer here for the point of the practice is meant to fill in the abstract hint that something of value is at stake.

are affected (since we are assuming that breaking the promise does not harm the promisee) and he ought to be able, in the exercise of his autonomy, to undo a commitment just as surely as he was earlier able to make the commitment.

This property-based explanation for the strong promise conception might be called the "gift of self" explanation. It will probably be clear why those who have alluded to this possible rationale for the strong conception of promise remain tentative about whether the effect such gifts have on a relationship are desirable or not.[43] On the one hand, such gifts can be seen as particularly potent expressions of love and trust – witness the emotional power of self-sacrifice in both religion and fiction. Or consider not the private vow made to one self, but the exchange of vows at a marriage. On the other hand, there has always been something suspect about the idea of giving away one's autonomy – witness the concern about whether one can promise oneself into slavery. Of course, the gift here is of a far smaller portion of one's autonomy than in the case of slavery, but still: By hypothesis, I presumably either would prefer to change my mind (but can't because I gave my mind to you to exercise for me), or I don't want to bother to decide what it is in my interest to do: you decide for me. Either of these two explanations has a flavor of self-denial that can also appear debasing. Finally, even under the virtuous "love-enhancing" interpretation, there seems something odd about thinking that you, to whom I am offering this gift of myself, wouldn't – also out of love – give it right back: Release me from my promise when it becomes clear, as per the hypothesis, that you won't be hurt and I now want to change my mind. To use the proxy analogy again, why wouldn't you give the proxy back if in fact it no longer is going to matter to you (your candidate will win anyway), and I now explain that I have changed my mind about whom to support and want, symbolically at least, to express my true preference. Why, for that matter, does one need the promise at all if its point is simply to reinforce a bond as close as that between friends or lovers? As Narveson puts it, "it begins to be rather philistine to speak of the *obligation* to do what one has, out of love, agreed to do...."[44]

I think, however, that one could leave unresolved the ultimate question about the value of this interpretation of promise in fostering certain relationships and still deny that it is a very plausible explanation for why Jane and Henry should emerge from their state of nature with this as the standard meaning of promise. Indeed, it seems plausible that this

---

[43] See Raz, "Promises and Obligations," 228 ("It is not my purpose to argue that the special relationships . . . are indeed desirable").

[44] See Narveson, "Promising, Expecting, and Utility," 227.

gift-of-self explanation for the strong conception has a very limited use, hardly the standard one at all. It is surely unlikely that the normal contract between strangers (or even the accepted dinner invitation between friends) has this kind of reason as its justification. If one agrees that this explanation is implausible in most cases involving promises, one possibility might be just to recognize a different scope of obligation for promise in different contexts and leave it at that (certainly the idea that the obligation of contracts might rest on a somewhat different justification than promises generally is fairly widespread). But this gives up too easily. There is another possible explanation for the point of a strong conception of promise that is hinted at in the explanation about relationships I have just been considering but is obscured by focusing on the most personal kind of relationship. And it is this explanation that reveals how the ethics of deference can solve the puzzle of promise without waiting for the dispute between consequentialists and deontologists to be resolved.

(4) "Strict Performance" as Respect for the Promisee's Opinion. Consider again Jane and Henry, deciding in a promissory state of nature whether they need anything more than the utilitarian conception of promise to govern their promissory relationships. Suppose that Henry recalls a point we made earlier: The problem of explaining why one should keep a promise or obey a law arises only because there is a dispute. In the case of promise, presumably the promisor and promisee disagree about whether breaching would be morally acceptable. (If they agreed, settlement and release should be possible.) Reflecting on this (and having spent too much time reading the extensive literature in moral philosophy on whether and why promises obligate), Henry makes a suggestion. Suppose that we move to a conception of promise according to which, where there is disagreement about whether the promise should be kept, the party who insists on performance (the promisee) has the right to decide the dispute – at least as long as he or she decides in good faith. That is, the promisor can't simply act on his own assessment of the situation; he must give weight to the promisee's opinion that performance is required and weigh the promisee's interest in performance equally with his own interest in not performing – even if the promisor believes (and is right) that the promisee's arguments about why performance is required are wrong.

What kinds of reasons might support this conception, and is this in fact the strict-performance account we have been seeking? Take the second question first. Henry's proposal does seem to have the feature of showing how a promise can give one content-independent reasons for deference that preempt or outweigh one's own views about the rationality or permissibility of breaking a promise. In this respect, it comes closer to the strict conception of promise than does the utilitarian account. The reasons for deference do not make the obligation of promise absolute: It is still only a prima facie obligation, to be weighed against other conflicting obligations – including the promisor's own assessment of what he thinks is *really* the right thing to do. But that is consistent with the strict-performance model, which is not meant to resolve conflicts with other duties, but only to establish a moral duty based on reasons that are independent of the considerations that otherwise bear on deciding how to act. Henry's conception has this peremptory character because it purports to give a promisor an automatic reason to do the very act promised, in part just because the other side has not released him; that reason applies without regard to the balance of reasons that otherwise apply to the action.

What, then, is the point of this particular conception? Henry might explain that the point is to resolve doubts about whether harm will in fact be caused by breaking the promise – doubts, for example, about whether and how much the promisee has relied. That would collapse this conception once again into a super-cautious reliance conception. But Henry might think that the point is not simply to resolve uncertainty about potential harm. After all, there might be other reasons why people would disagree about whether a promise should be kept. Wholly apart from disagreement about whether there is harm, they might disagree about the moral theory that explains why promises obligate – not too unrealistic a hypothesis. Henry might become a Kantian, and even though Jane might think Henry is terribly misguided, surely she could not accuse Henry of thereby demonstrating bad faith. Or Henry, having read too many economic analyses of contracts, might worry that there will be disagreement over how to divide the spoils of an efficient breach.[45] Henry, in short, might want the right to impose his views on Jane in the event of good-faith disagreement for reasons that have nothing to do with the kind of harm or reliance that underlies the utilitarian account. It may have far more to do with the uncertainty of value judgments and the diversity of plausible moral theories – value disagreements that, for political theorists like Locke, is one of the major explanations for the emergence of the state.

Second, Henry might emphasize as a reason for this conception not the problem of uncertainty in establishing values, but the idea that maybe a promisee's views deserve respect of a special sort. True, absent the promise, Henry (as promisee) would have no right to insist that his views be given a special hearing or special weight, and certainly Henry could not normally expect Jane to accede to his views if Jane thought they were wrong. So Henry will have to explain why, being the promisee, he should have a special right to

---

[45] See Friedmann, "The Efficient Breach Fallacy." Compare Richard A. Posner, *Economic Analysis of Law* (Boston: Little, Brown, 1973), 57, with Posner, *Economic Analysis of law* (Boston: Little, Brown, 1998), 130–1.

have his views heeded, or at least weighed, along with the views of Jane. Now, I think, it is plausible that Henry could give a plausible explanation for such special rights by pointing to the importance of relationships, stressing this time, however, not the strong personal bonds of love or friendship but the weaker bonds of community and good faith even among strangers. Somebody's going to have to get his way; promise is a temporary two-person community governed by a law we've both passed but that one of us now wants unilaterally to undo. How shall we decide whether either party to this promise-created norm should have a special privilege, particularly if it is unclear whether harm will result if the norm is violated? In the case of law, the answer was that there was no alternative: The state has to have a relative monopoly on power and cannot be expected to do more than exercise that power in good faith as it thinks justice requires. We can't say the same of promise: It isn't inevitable that someone impose his or her view on the other. We could just flip a coin or take turns: Henry and Jane each gets to decide on alternate occasions whether breaking a promise is justified.

But Henry does have some reasons for suggesting that it is the promisee who deserves the respect that is shown by being given the right to arbitrate this dispute. First, we can now understand the role that is played by the language of promise. Though we said earlier that the language of promise cannot prove that persons are obligated just because they say they are, we can at least note that the language of promise helps support the more modest proposal that, as between promisor and promisee, it is the promisee who should be given the right to decide in the case of disputes. The promisor did, after all, say he would perform strictly; if the only problem is giving a reason why he should, that reason can lie in the respect shown for the opinion of the other, as well as in the respect shown for the harm that might be caused. Second, requiring one to seek release (persuade or obey)[46] furthers the chance for dialogue and continuation of the temporary two-person community, whereas giving the party who wants to breach a free way out encourages unilateral action. Finally, the good-faith limitation on the promisee's right to demand performance (coupled with the fact that entrance into the arrangement in the first place is voluntary) reduces considerably the potential threat to the promisor's autonomy.

PROMISING AND THE ETHICS OF DEFERENCE. We can now explain how the ethics of deference provides a solution to the puzzle of promise. In Chapter 1, I provided an outline of the kinds of reasons one might have to defer to the opinions of others. Broadly speaking, these reasons are either instrumental or intrinsic. Intrinsic reasons, in turn, are either objective or subjective. Objective reasons arise from the value of respect that is required by a relationship that is in fact objectively valuable and enhanced through deference. Subjective reasons are based on one's own values: They are reasons that arise from the need for

---

[46] See Philip Soper, "Another Look at the Crito," *Am. J, Jurisp,* 41 (1996): 103, 124–5.

self-respect and for acting consistently with one's own understanding of the point or value of a practice, regardless of whether the practice is objectively valuable. In the case of promises, one often has instrumental reasons to defer to the views of the promisee about whether a promise should be kept. These instrumental reasons are plausibly captured by the context-dependent reasons that allow the utilitarian to account for the difference that a promise makes in affecting decisions designed to produce the best consequences. But instrumental reasons will not always justify deference. In some cases, it will be clear that more is to be gained by breaking the promise than by deferring to the views of the promisee. That leads to the puzzle of trying to make sense of a practice that many believe includes commitments greater than what is entailed only by the limited commitment of a utilitarian account. Deontological explanations that insist one keep one's word, regardless of consequences, remain hollow or tautological in the absence of some reason or rationale for such a strict conception of promise.

The ethics of deference supplies the missing rationale for the Kantian instinct in two steps. First, one must discover and defend a "point" to the practice of promising that makes sense of the apparently stronger commitment entailed by the Kantian conception. In this case, that point is seen to lie in a conception of promise as a device not simply for undertaking an obligation to do a specified act, but also for allocating the right to decide about the extent and basis of that obligation in cases of disagreement. Second, having recognized and defended the point of such a conception, one now has two possible kinds of intrinsic reasons for deference that favor keeping a promise even when instrumental reasons do not. One has objectively intrinsic reasons to defer when the two-person relationship constituted by the promise is sufficiently intimate or close to make deference a sign of respect for the other's views under this conception of promise. Intrinsic reasons for deference show respect for one's promissory partner in a relationship that requires one party to have the right to decide in the case of disagreement. But intrinsic reasons for deference are harder to establish in this objective sense in the case of promise than in the case of close personal relationships because the promissory relationship is typically far less intimate. A promise between two strangers who may never meet again is not a particularly good example of a valuable relationship that requires showing respect for the promisee who (erroneously) believes a promise should be kept. Long-term, repeat relationships involving promises may be better examples of contexts in which one has objective reasons to defer. Between these extremes are a wide variety of contexts in which promises might be made, not all of which can be defended as involving objectively valuable "promissory relationships" that require deference to erroneous views. So objectively intrinsic reasons alone cannot establish a prima facie obligation to keep all promises. That leaves subjectively intrinsic reasons. Even if the promissory relationship is too temporary and casual to justify deference as a way of showing respect for a valuable good, one will always have a subjective reason to defer based on one's own recognition of the point of the promising conception we have described – a conception that recognizes that the promisee has a right to decide in cases of disagreement.

Several points in this explanation deserve emphasizing. First, I am not suggesting that one *must* concede the point of promise described here as involving an allocation of the right to decide as well as the undertaking of an obligation. If one does not share the view that this conception is a valuable one, one will not have subjective reasons for deference: There will be no inconsistency with one's own values when one fails to defer to the promisee. But this only means that one should not make the kind of promise that entails the stronger commitment in the first place. As noted earlier in this chapter, promises do not come in a single variety or size. One can always explicitly limit the commitment one is making and make clear that no obligation beyond, for example, what is consistent with a utilitarian account is being undertaken. The aim of this chapter has been simply to see whether a stronger conception of promise is plausible and defensible. The ethics of deference makes sense of the stronger conception for those who want to continue a practice in which such promises are made.

Second, the subjective argument for intrinsic reasons for deference is not tautological in the way that some Kantian accounts of the duty to keep a promise appear to be. We are not saying that those who recognize that a "promise must be kept regardless of the consequences" are being inconsistent with their own values if they do not keep the promise. That way of putting the argument does make it tautological. The advantage of the ethics of deference is that it begins by defending, not simply assuming, the value of a conception of promise as involving allocation of decision-making rights in cases of disagreement. We do not beg the question by ascribing such a role to promises; we simply recognize that promises are another example (like law) of a case in which the possibility of disagreement and the inability to resolve that disagreement before taking action might warrant some mediating decision-making device. Having established this point of the practice by such independent arguments, one then appeals to those who accept the argument to act consistently with their own values when they make promises under such a conception.

Third, the explanation given here shows how the ethics of deference straddles the larger, more general traditions of consequentialists and Kantians by suggesting that sometimes there are moral reasons to guide conduct despite – in fact, because of – continued failure to resolve once and for all the dispute about which of these larger ethical theories (if either) is correct. The ethics of deference is a theory about the need to act before ultimate truth is revealed; it relies on a small bit of truth about the human condition – namely, that sometimes action must precede enlightenment – in order to establish a small domain for ethics in practice.

Conclusion

I have said enough, I hope, to justify the claims made at the outset of this chapter. First, promises and laws operate in essentially similar fashion. Second, that operation in the case of promise can result in a general obligation to perform the promised act, in the sense of having reasons to defer to the opinion of the promisee, even though better consequences would result from breach. Third, the explanation for this obligation in the case of promise lies closer to explanations typically found in political theory for the legitimacy of the state than in the literature on consent and voluntariness. As in the case of political theory, the explanation in the case of promise depends on explaining why another person deserves the right to make his good-faith views about whether to perform a reason for me to act as desired. In the case of law, as I shall argue more fully later in this study, this special position is the result of necessity and my acknowledgment that I would expect no less if I were in charge. In the case of promise, the special position is justified either because one's own understanding of promise acknowledges that this is a desirable means of resolving uncertainty about value disputes or because it helps foster a small bit of community even among strangers.

6

The Problem of Fair Play

Introduction

Mary and Jim are roommates. They share an apartment with separate bedrooms and common living and eating areas. Both suffer during the winter from dry air – a problem that can be solved by installing a humidifier that will add moist air to the entire apartment. The cost of a humidifier is significant for both Mary and Jim. One day, Mary installs a humidifier and asks Jim to pay half the cost. Does Jim have an obligation to pay?

The literature on the duty of fair play is filled with variations on this simple example. In fact, the inventiveness of theorists in creating hypothetical cases to test intuitions about the duty of fair play is matched only by – and is probably a reflection of – the inability to reach a consensus about the underlying theory that grounds such a duty. It is as if, to borrow from Rawls's concepts of reflective equilibrium and considered judgments, explanations of the duty of fair play are so confused or lacking in consensus at the level of general theory that most of the work continues to be done at the level of intuition. Examples and counterexamples parade for inspection in the hope that judgments about whether a duty exists in a particular case can be connected to a general theory, thus making the judgments more secure and considered. But intuitions about particular cases often differ, and thus, instead of leading to confidence that a considered judgment has been reached, the opposite occurs: Judgments about particular examples remain contested, so that the examples themselves, instead of providing evidence for a particular theory of obligation, become tautological illustrations of a preconceived and contestable theory.

In this respect, the literature on fair play contrasts instructively with the literature on promise-keeping. Roughly speaking, philosophers agree that promises create obligations. That is to say, the general consensus at the intuitive level is sufficiently widespread that there is little need to search frantically for yet another example of a promise that might support the intuition that an obligation exists. Disagreement in the promissory literature occurs, instead, at the level of general theory as philosophers argue about why these apparent promissory obligations arise and how extensive they are. All this seems reversed in the case of fair play: The focus is mostly on examples, and it is difficult to get beyond the intuitive level to a general theory that will ground or dispel the intuitions.

This reliance on intuitions and particular examples would not by itself warrant skepticism about the possibility of understanding how fair play works except for one thing – it is not always clear why *new* examples are constantly needed. Instead of focusing on a paradigm case of a fair play obligation (like a paradigm case of a promise), theorists tend to develop new and different examples, ranging from the farfetched to the mundane. Some of the examples are ingenious and many are clever, but the sheer variety tends to underscore the basic difference between fair play and promise: It is less clear in the case of fair play that one can produce any example that all will agree serves as a paradigm of the duty of fair play. Furthermore, the contexts in which people can find themselves the recipients of unsolicited benefits are infinitely varied, and examples used to explore fair play arguments are also infinitely varied and easy to invent. As a result, the examples produced in the literature often seem so different from each other that one is never sure which similarities and differences are relevant. Does it matter, for instance, that Jim and Mary are roommates rather than partners in a business relationship? Would one's intuition about Jim's obligation change if Mary had shoveled a common sidewalk that she and Jim share as neighbors?[1] What if Mary, a stranger, simply shows up and shovels Jim's walk, presenting him with an invoice for her services?[2] What if the context expands to include an entire group – a neighborhood engaged in a beautification project, or a community that voluntarily installs pollution control devices, or an entire society that provides everyone in its jurisdiction with security from domestic assault or foreign invasion? In all of these cases, one can point to people benefiting without cost to themselves from the efforts of others without being quite sure whether there are significant differences in the cases due simply to the number of people involved, or the nature of the preexisting relationship, or the kinds of goods provided, or any of a variety of other potentially relevant factors.

My excuse for inventing in this chapter yet another example, this time of two roommates, is related to this problem of trying to find as simple a paradigm as possible for exploring fair play arguments. I have deliberately chosen an example somewhere between that of two people in a close relationship (where duties of friendship might confuse the issue) and wider contexts involving

---

[1] See George Klosko, *The Principle of Fairness and Political Obligation* (Lanham, Md.: Rowman & Littlefield, 1992), 44–5.

[2] See Robert Nozick, *Anarchy, State, and Utopia* (New York: Basic Books, 1974), 93–5 (strangers thrusting books into others' hands: an example now widely recognized as easily distinguishable because of the excludability condition discussed in the text).

neighborhoods, communities, or whole societies. My hope is that understanding how fair play works in a simple case will ease the task of applying the theory to broader contexts – in particular, the context that motivates most of these investigations in the first place, namely, that of political obligation.

To understand how a duty of fair play might arise, it will be helpful first to review recent discussions of the problem that attempt to move beyond the level of intuitions about particular examples to a general theory – a set of critical elements, or necessary and sufficient conditions, for the existence of a duty of fair play. Accordingly, this chapter begins with a quick review of this emerging theory, using the roommate example to illustrate the essential conditions that create obligations of fair play, according to writers who have recently defended such obligations.[3] In cases where disagreement exists about how to interpret or apply a particular condition, I shall make the assumption that is most favorable to the existence of the obligation. My goal, in other words, is to make the strongest possible case I can for the claim that Jim has a duty to pay Mary his share of the expense of the humidifier. The claim I shall defend is that even where every condition is construed in a way that most favors finding such an obligation, doubts can still be raised about whether Jim has any duty to pay. Those doubts arise not because, as some claim, there can be no obligation in the absence of consent; to the contrary, obligations of fair play are, I shall argue, real and independent obligations, not derived from consent or promise. But current accounts of the conditions that are sufficient to generate the obligation leave doubts because they stop short of explaining the deeper basis for the duty of fair play. To uncover that basis I shall, in the second half of the chapter, turn to a different kind of example – one that has figured in recent debates over the nature of fair play and that does not so obviously depend on benefits conferred. Discussions of this example will help show how fair play is, in fact, best understood as yet another situation in which deference to the views of others may be morally required.

Constructing a Paradigm Case

Nonexcludability

If Mary could solve her dry air problem by installing a humidifier in her room alone, avoiding any beneficial spillover effects to common areas or Jim's bedroom, the problem of fair play would not arise. Her decision to invest in a larger-capacity humidifier that benefits both her and Jim would either be a gift

---

[3] I rely mainly on the perceptive discussions found in Klosko, *Fairness and Political Obligation*, and Richard J. Arneson, "Fairness and Free Riders," *Ethics* 92 (1982): 616. Both authors list similar sets of conditions as necessary and sufficient to create duties of fair play. See Klosko, id., 39; Arneson, id., 623.

or an example of what legal scholars call "officious intermeddling."[4] In neither case would Jim have a duty to share the expense. The reasons for this conclusion are now widely admitted but may warrant brief review here.

GIFTS. If Mary's service is a gift, no obligation to pay is created partly because none was expected by Mary – not, at least, at the time the gift was given. Why Mary cannot later change her mind and rightly demand payment after the gift has been made is a matter of some dispute in the literature, particularly since executory gift promises often *can* be retracted, at least in law. Most explanations for this difference in treatment between executed and executory promises depend on the claim that it is necessary to draw a line somewhere that explains when items become the property of another. In the previous chapter, we alluded briefly to this literature in attempting to explain the binding force of promise by analogy to a "gift of self." But however arbitrary the line between executed and nonexecuted promises is, the actual conferral of benefits, freely and without expectation of compensation, plausibly places such benefits on the other side of the property line: Recipients have no obligation to repay a donor who later regrets giving the gift. Possibly Jim should be grateful to Mary, but this only demonstrates that whatever requirements are imposed by the need to show gratitude, they belong to a very different category than, and are easily distinguishable from, the requirements imposed by moral obligation.[5]

OFFICIOUS INTERMEDDLING. If Mary does not intend the humidifier as a gift, but deliberately buys a larger one than she needs, presenting Jim with a bill for his share of the benefits, no duty results *even if Jim concedes that the bill is reasonable and that he desires the benefits*. It is easy to see why neither law nor morality supports the practice of first conferring benefits, where they are excludable, and later presenting the bill. Disputes about how much the service was worth and whether it was desired, along with other potential costs that are bound to arise if such conduct is rewarded, can all be avoided by the obvious alternative of requiring those who want to charge for excludable benefits to first obtain consent and establish a price through exchange.[6] Though

---

4 See *Restatement (Second) of Contracts* §10.1, p. 359.
5 Compare Klosko, "Political Obligation and Gratitude," *Phil. & Pub. Affairs* 18 (1989): 352 (discussing A. D. M. Walker, "Political Obligation and the Argument from Gratitude," *Phil. & Pub. Affairs* 17 [1988]: 191) with Walker, "Obligations of Gratitude and Political Obligation," *Phil. & Pub. Affairs* 18 (1989): 359. I ignore special cases where gifts are made in a society that understands them as triggering a duty to reciprocate; such cases resemble exchanges more than gifts in the ordinary sense.
6 This rationale for refusing to recognize obligations in the case of officiously conferred benefits also explains the exception that the law recognizes for altruistic intermeddlers: those who confer benefits expecting payment in circumstances in which (1) it is reasonable to think that agreement to pay would be forthcoming but (2) such agreement is impossible to obtain (e.g., the doctor treating the unconscious accident victim.) See generally George E. Palmer, *The Law of Restitution* (Boston: Little, Brown, 1978), §10.4.

this conclusion and its underlying rationale have long been known to the law, examples of officious intermeddling continue to appear in the philosophical literature, leading either to mistaken conclusions about the critical elements of fair play[7] or to conclusions similar to those reached by the law.[8]

Benefits

OBJECTIVE OR SUBJECTIVE. If Jim did not mind dry air, and would not have invested in a humidifier in any event, the problem of whether he should pay his fair share for benefits received doesn't seem to arise – there are no benefits. The major issue in applying this precondition for the existence of the duty is whether benefits here are to be measured objectively or subjectively. Suppose that Jim is wrong about the benefits of humidified air. Suppose that an objective appraisal of the health problems caused by dry air, compared to the cost of the humidifier, would lead a medical expert to conclude that the benefits of the humidifier were worth its costs to Jim. Jim, however, is simply unaware of, or doesn't believe, the medical evidence.[9] Does he have an obligation to pay?

It is easy to see why the subjective measure seems the more appropriate one. For one thing, a theory that imposes obligations on Jim despite his sincere (but mistaken) belief that the goods or services are not worth their cost to him will have little practical effect: Jim will not pay if he doesn't recognize the value, even though others accuse him of failing to do his duty. Of course, this is not a fatal objection. Any objective theory of ethics admits that people can be mistaken about their obligations and thus may act immorally despite their sincere but erroneous beliefs. But in the present context, where what is at stake is playing fair, it is easier to suggest that good-faith, sincere beliefs are more important than whether those beliefs are in fact correct. It is difficult, after all, to claim that Jim is free riding if he isn't enjoying the ride, even though others think he should be. If free riding is wrong in part because it shows a lack of respect for those who have provided nonexcludable benefits, that rationale

---

[7] See Nozick, *Anarchy, State, and Utopia*, 93–5 (the book-thrusting example is an obvious instance of officious intermeddling that Nozick incorrectly uses to conclude that fair play can never create obligations in the absence of consent).

[8] The fact that the law has long reached this conclusion (that no obligation is owed to officious intermeddlers for reasons mentioned in the text) tends to go unnoticed. See Garrett Cullity, "Moral Free Riding," 24 *Phil. & Pub. Affairs* 3, (1995): 10 (no duty to pay for shoe repair when "enterprising elves" confer the benefit and later present the bill).

[9] Some benefits (where mere matters of taste are involved, for example) may not lend themselves to objective measurement. If Jim is fully aware of the medical hazards of dry air but does not care about those hazards, it may not be clear whether the value of the humidifier can be measured objectively or is merely a matter of taste to be measured subjectively. Since I assume, for purposes of my argument in this chapter, that the benefit should be measured subjectively (since that assumption makes the strongest case for a fair play obligation), I shall not explore here the question of when objective measurements are possible.

ought to distinguish those who happily take advantage of nonexcludable benefits from those who would just as happily forgo the benefits if only they could.

It is possible to suggest a compromise between this choice of either an objective or a subjective measure of benefits – a quasi-objective approach to the issue according to which some dialogue between Mary and Jim is required if she thinks he benefits and he doesn't. One might suggest, for example, that infringing on Jim's liberty by requiring him to pay for goods he doesn't recognize as valuable means that Mary has the burden of proof in showing Jim that he is wrong (objectively), but that the burden then shifts to Jim if Mary makes a plausible case.[10] It is, however, unnecessary to decide whether there is any room here for a compromise between the objective and subjective approaches to measuring benefits. In line with the strategy of this chapter, I shall make the assumption that yields the strongest case for establishing Jim's obligation by applying the subjective measure of benefits to the humidifier example.

It is important to note what the subjective measure requires. It is not enough that Jim believes that the humidifier is worth its cost[11] to him. It must also be the case that his own priorities for spending money for all the things that might be worth their cost to him coincide with the timing of this particular spending decision. I might agree that installing a swimming pool in my backyard would be worth its cost to me. But I might have many other things I would rather do with my money before reaching the point where the swimming pool represents the next best marginal investment.[12] So here I shall make the strongest possible assumption about the subjective benefit of the humidifier: Not only does Jim agree that the humidifier is worth its cost to him, he also agrees that he was just about to purchase it himself if Mary had not already done so.[13]

SIGNIFICANCE. Many of the examples in the current literature involve benefits that seem insignificant or minor: broadcasts from public address systems, the aesthetic pleasures of a neighborhood flower garden, or the pleasure one might derive from watching well-dressed people stroll – or trains roll – by.[14] Indeed,

---

[10] Something like this approach is suggested by Klosko, at least as applied to what he calls "presumptive goods," i.e., goods that one can presume all members of the public want, whatever else they might want. See Klosko, *Fairness and Political Obligation*, 39, 48–50.

[11] Arneson, " Fairness and Free Riders," 623.

[12] The qualification made here, suggesting that the priority issue is separate from the net benefit issue, could perhaps be avoided if one included in the cost of the humidifier indirect (forgone opportunity) costs as well as direct costs.

[13] For purposes of the fair play argument, it is probably enough that Jim concedes that he would have been ready to pay half the cost of a humidifier if Mary had not already installed it. I will make the even stronger assumption that he would have borne the entire cost, if necessary.

[14] The examples may be found in Nozick, *Anarchy, State, and Utopia*, 93–5, and in Arneson, "Fairness and Free Riders," 621 ("Public goods are ubiquitous, but in many cases the benefits they supply are small change that is insufficient to justify imposition of coercion").

one could probably list with little effort numerous examples of daily unavoidable contact with the spillover effects (both pleasant and unpleasant) that result from the efforts of others. The idea that all of these encounters with beneficial effects generate a duty to contribute seems counterintuitive. Defenders of fair play obligations may explain the lack of obligation in these minor cases in several ways. First, one may suggest that the many examples of incidental beneficial effects cancel each other out; over the long run, I am just as likely to act in ways that unavoidably benefit others in minor ways as I am to be a recipient of such benefits.[15] Second, one may find that many of these examples do not involve expectations of compensation: They are gifts, either because the providers of the benefits are acting from generous motives and intend the benefits to be costless to recipients or because the providers are indifferent and don't care about contributions. Finally, one can simply bite the bullet and decide to limit the obligation of fair play to cases that reach a certain level of "significance" or "indispensability."[16] In line with the strategy of this chapter, I shall assume that the benefits of the humidifier in my example are significant in the relevant sense: Both Jim and Mary need the humidifier not just because it makes life a bit more pleasant, but because they would otherwise suffer medical problems they view as significant.

ACCEPTANCE OF BENEFITS. We can quickly dispense with the question of whether fair play duties arise only if recipients accept the benefits conferred. For those, like Nozick, who think that benefits that can't be refused can never be accepted in the relevant sense, fair play duties do not exist – only prior consent can yield an obligation to pay. Most of the initial response to Nozick's claim focused on softening this requirement, with Simmons suggesting that acceptance in the relevant sense occurs whenever (1) benefits are not forced on the recipient against his or her will and (2) the benefits are worth the costs.[17]

---

[15] In like manner, it is sometimes suggested that one reason no compensation is required for every trivial respect in which governmental regulations affect my use of property is that over the long run, I benefit from similar restrictions on others' property as much as I suffer from restrictions on my own. For a challenging argument that all fair play arguments, however significant the benefits, can be seen as similar trade-offs that cancel each other out in ways that do not generate a duty, see A. de Jasay, *Social Contract, Free Ride* (Oxford: Clarendon Press, 1989), 135 ("'free rider' and 'sucker' are, if looked at closely, more ubiquitous social roles than we tend to imply in ordinary discourse").

[16] See Klosko, *Fairness and Political Obligation*, 44–5. Klosko's explanation for why no duty arises where the benefits are slight is that the recipient may not find the small benefits worth the cost; but that explanation is just an application of the benefits requirement, not a reason for automatically excluding all slight benefit cases from the reach of the fair play argument. Arneson suggests another reason why no obligation arises in these cases, namely, that the costs of coercion to enforce the obligation would outweigh the value conferred. See "Fairness and Free Riders," 621. This suggestion seems to confuse the question of whether there is a moral obligation with the question of whether it is worth enforcing.

[17] John A. Simmons, *Moral Principles and Political Obligation* (Princeton: Princeton Univ. Press, 1979), 132.

As Klosko notes, these two conditions seem automatically to be met by a subjective approach to the measurement of nonexcludable benefits.[18] Certainly they are met under the assumptions we have made about Jim's acknowledgment of the benefit of the humidifier in our example.[19]

Fair Play, Tacit Consent, and Explicit Dissent

Those who think that fair play obligations arise only when there is prior consent are quick to reduce the apparent strictness of this conclusion by noting that consent need not always be explicit. One can "tacitly consent" to pay when one accepts goods knowing that they are offered with the expectation of payment and not as a gift. Thus there will be many cases where the "active acceptance" of benefits can be accounted for by straightforward theories of consent or promise, without the need for an independent duty of fair play. The natural countermove by defenders of an independent obligation of fair play is to make the recipient of the benefits explicitly deny in advance any consent to the scheme that provides benefits, so that any intuition that an obligation results cannot be accounted for as a case of tacit consent. Simmons gives the following example. Jones votes against a proposal to dig a public well, announcing in advance that he does not agree to the scheme. After the well is built, Jones takes water from it, continuing to deny that he consents to pay. According to Simmons, Jones has a benefit-based obligation to pay that cannot, in the face of Jones's explicit dissent, be derived from tacit consent.[20] Similarly, Greenawalt invites us to imagine owners of a condominium refusing to agree to a scheme for maintaining the condominium's tennis courts. When the owners subsequently play tennis on the courts after others have paid to maintain them, they now have a benefits-based obligation to pay their share of the maintenance expenses.[21]

The problem with these examples by defenders of fair play is that they ignore the requirement that benefits must be subjectively worth it to the recipient. Presumably, water from the public well cannot be made excludable (otherwise, Jones is simply stealing when he takes from the well – a violation of a different duty, not a duty of fair play). Similarly the condominium owners presumably

---

[18] Klosko, *Fairness and Political Obligation*, 51.

[19] Simmons also adds a third requirement, namely, that the recipient understand that the benefits have been provided pursuant to the cooperative efforts of others. It is not clear what the basis for this requirement is (Klosko concludes that it is "an unproved assertion." Id., 52). At most, it seems to raise questions not so much about whether the benefits were produced "through a cooperative scheme" as about the expectations of the benefactors: Did they confer the benefits with the expectation that all who benefited would pay their share or did they intend the benefits as a gift? I consider this issue, concerning the expectations of the benefactor and whether the recipient must know about them, in the next section.

[20] Simmons, *Moral Principles*, 126–7.

[21] See Kent Greenawalt, *Conflicts of Law and Morality* (Oxford: Oxford Univ. Press, 1987), 123.

have a preexisting property right of access to the common tennis courts. That being the case, the dissenters' existing rights cannot be compromised just by bestowing benefits that the dissenting condominium owners have explicitly declared in advance are not worth it to them. Of course, the benefits, being nonexcludable, may be happily accepted once they are provided despite the dissent; but that is the consequence of respecting the preexisting property rights of the dissenting recipients.

To make Simmons's and Greenawalt's examples work, we must suppose that Jones and the condo owners *do* believe the benefits are subjectively worth it in the relevant sense – as respects both the priority question and the net benefits question. Can one in this case, by announcing in advance a refusal to pay, avoid the fair play obligation? If Jim makes it clear to Mary just before she buys the humidifier that he hopes she isn't expecting him to pay for it, does this affect Mary's right to a contribution from Jim when she proceeds? When providers of benefits like Mary (or Jones's town or the other condominium owners) proceed in the face of explicit refusals to pay by nonexcludable beneficiaries, the providers do so presumably because the project is worth it to them, even without the dissenters' contributions. They are, in the law's terminology, "self-serving intermeddlers,"[22] and intuitions about whether they can somehow impose obligations on explicit dissenters are, at best, unclear.[23]

I focus on these examples because the case of explicit dissent in advance by potential beneficiaries points to the basic problem with fair play arguments even under the most plausible set of conditions: People may dissent from a proposed beneficial cooperative scheme not because they are trying to take advantage of others by free riding, but because they do not agree with the proposed method of allocating burdens and benefits. They may be quite willing to run the risk of losing the benefits, betting that others will give in first; but as long as they are willing to let everyone else play this same game of "bluff," they can hardly be said to be taking advantage when they win the bluff. I return to this basic problem later.

---

[22] For general discussion, see Philip Soper, *A Theory of Law,* (Cambridge, Mass.: Harvard Univ. Press, 1984), 72–4.

[23] The point is nicely made by John Dawson in his classic exploration of these problems in the law of restitution. Though I have quoted the passage before, it is worth repeating here as evidence that intuitions in these cases of self-serving intermeddlers are insufficiently clear to justify relying on them as self-evident examples of benefit-based obligations:

The underlying assumption, which at times seems almost to rise to the level of a moral judgment, is that self-serving enterprise ... should make its own way and is not entitled to subsidies. Discussion could end at this point if it were not for the source of the subsidy sought. If awarded, it would be drawn from those who themselves have gained without effort or contribution of their own and who can offer no more persuasive reason for refusal to contribute than: "We never asked for it." So there is always that underground spring of resentment that was so successfully tapped ... by the Book of Matthew, which described as a "hard man" one who reaps where he did not sow. J. Dawson, "The Self-Serving Intermeddler," *Harv. L. Rev.* 87 (1974): 1409, 1457.

Why the Paradigm Case Fails

Provider Expectations

Under the assumptions I have made, most defenders of the duty of fair play would, I believe, claim that Jim has a duty to pay Mary for his share of the benefits of the humidifier: (1) Mary has no choice but to provide Jim with the benefits (they are not excludable), and (2) the benefits are significant and worth their cost to Jim – by reference to his own subjective values. These two conditions, as analyzed more fully earlier, are the most important features in explaining why many would presumably conclude that fair play requires Jim to pay.[24] But there is one aspect of these conditions that warrants separate discussion, even though it has already been partly treated. We have noted that the motivations of the person providing benefits can be critical to the existence of a fair play duty: No obligation, for example, arises if the provider intends the benefits as a gift. Providers must expect beneficiaries to share their part of the costs, and this fact must presumably be made known to beneficiaries. This condition raises problems of timing and misunderstanding: When must Jim know of Mary's expectations, and what happens if he doesn't know?

Suppose that Jim thinks Mary is conferring a gift and discovers his mistake only after Mary presents him with a bill. If Jim refuses to pay, two situations are possible: (1) Mary may have proceeded even without Jim's contribution (the humidifier's entire cost is more than justified by its benefits to her) or (2) Mary would not have bought the humidifier without Jim's contribution (the benefits to her are not worth more than half the cost). In the former case, Mary has self-interested reasons for proceeding and, as just seen, it is not clear whether she is being treated unfairly if Jim leaves her bearing the entire cost of a project that, in the end, still represents a net gain to her. In the latter case, however, Mary has suffered a loss, having paid more than the humidifier is worth to her, and this fact may seem to strengthen the appeal of the fair play argument, particularly if all of the other requirements of the benefit condition are satisfied. If one thinks Jim would normally have an obligation to pay his fair share in this case, the only issue left is the effect of the misunderstanding on Jim's duty. If Jim was at fault for the misunderstanding (he should have known that Mary was acting only on the assumption that he would help pay), we can presumably continue to charge him with a duty of fair play, buttressed now by a duty not to be negligent. But what if no one is at fault for the misunderstanding (or both are equally at fault, which should come to the same thing)? Does Jim still have a duty to pay?

---

[24] Other conditions sometimes found in the literature seem to me either to be implicitly included in the preceding two conditions or are sufficiently obvious that they do not require separate discussion. The major other condition, variously described, is that the benefits and burdens must be fairly distributed (Jim must only pay his proportionate share of the expenses).

Consider an easier case. Suppose that Mary's expectations are clearly communicated to Jim at the outset. If Mary tells Jim she is purchasing the humidifier, expecting him to pay his share, Jim may consent to the arrangement (explicitly, or implicitly by saying nothing), in which case we do not need fair play to establish his duty because we now have consent.[25] Alternatively, Jim will explicitly dissent, leaving us in the situation discussed in the preceding section. At least Mary will be saved from a loss if the humidifier is not worth its entire cost to her; otherwise, she proceeds knowing full well that she'll have to bear the entire cost and realize a lesser net gain than if Jim had agreed to pay part, thus weakening the intuitive appeal of the fair play idea.

Most fair play examples seem to fall into a category that differs from this "easier case" because there is no opportunity for prior communication: Jim finds out after the fact that he is expected to pay, and it is nobody's fault that he wasn't explicitly given a choice to opt in or out at the beginning. Such situations are more likely to come about when the enterprise involves many people and collective efforts are needed to produce the good, which may explain why such "cooperative enterprises" figure so prominently in attempts to find paradigm cases of fair play and associated elements of a general theory. The difficulties of negotiating in advance with all who might benefit from cooperative enterprises that produce nonexcludable goods is just one of the well-known features of "public goods" that has led to the enormous literature on collective action problems. In these cases, it is plausible that people can discover they are receiving benefits that were (1) intended by providers to be paid for by all but (2) are made available under circumstances that do not permit advance negotiations to clarify just who is and is not willing to be a contributor. These features also coincide nicely with the situation people face in the context that motivates so much of the fair play discussion, namely, that of political obligation. We arrive in a state that is already in place, already providing the benefits that, it is argued, fit the requirements for generating fair play duties; but, of course, none of us had an opportunity to declare in advance whether we want to be in or out. The same reason that makes consent theories implausible as grounds for political obligation explains the attractiveness of fair play arguments that apply regardless of consent. Indeed, one can draw an analogy here to the same rationale that underlies the exception recognized in law for "altruistic intermeddlers"[26]: One has an obligation to pay for unsolicited benefits (even where they were excludable) if the provider reasonably thought one would have agreed to pay for them but consent under the circumstances was impossible to obtain. So, too, with the state. Those who cooperate and pay for the public goods that the state

---

[25] Even the law would assume that silence here, followed by receipt of benefits, would constitute acceptance of an offer and thus a straightforward promise to pay. See *Day v. Caton*, 119 Mass. 513 (S. Ct. Mass., 1876); *Restatement (Second) of Contracts* § 69 (1979).

[26] See footnote 6.

provides can reasonably assume that persons who can't yet be consulted about their willingness to pay would agree if they had the chance.[27]

Two Kinds of Dissent

The major point of the preceding discussion is that if prior negotiations *are* possible in advance of providing benefits (even nonexcludable benefits), we should always end up in one of the two situations already imagined: Either there is consent, so that fair play arguments are unnecessary, or there is explicit dissent by some recipients, creating doubt about why they should have any duty to pay if, with full knowledge of the dissent, providers (who are now self-serving intermeddlers) produce the benefits anyway. But the problems with the paradigm case are serious even if we assume that no possibility of prior negotiation exists. Though it is somewhat harder to see how this might happen in the simple two-person case we are considering, it is not entirely implausible. Mary might think, based on prior conversations about the importance of a humidifier, that Jim would pay his share if she purchased a humidifier; and it is easy to imagine that Jim might know that if Mary made such a purchase, she would not be intending to make him a gift. But there has been no explicit discussion about actually making the purchase. Once Mary makes the purchase (not consulting Jim in advance, either because there was no time or because she reasonably thought it wasn't necessary), we have the ingredients that explain how it could happen that neither party could be faulted for the absence of prior negotiations. Jim has no reason to know that Mary is about to make the purchase, and Mary has no reason to know that Jim would object if she did.

If all of this is conceded, do we now have a paradigm case for an obligation of fair play in Jim's case? We have assumed the following: (1) Jim agrees that the humidifier is worth its costs to him (and was, in fact, on his shopping list for tomorrow); (2) he knows that Mary never intended to make him a gift; (3) he recognizes that Mary was not acting unreasonably or negligently in failing to ask him first about whether he would pay his share.

To understand what is missing in establishing Jim's duty, imagine how Jim might explain to Mary why he doesn't think he should pay. Most of the fair play literature assumes that someone in Jim's situation can make only the unappealing sort of response that shows he is a free rider, a kind of grasping freeloader, happily availing himself of benefits just because there is nothing Mary can do to prevent his doing so. But Jim has another possible explanation, one that is far more appealing morally than the brute assertion of a willingness to "reap where one has not sown." Jim's explanation for why he thinks he shouldn't pay could reflect a different view of the principle that he thinks should be followed

---

[27] Klosko's definition of "presumptively beneficial" goods nicely fits into this rationale as well. See footnote 10.

in distributing the burdens and benefits of this particular collective good – a principle that is no less fair than the principle of proportionate payment by all who benefit that is presupposed by the notion of fair play.

Here is the major problem with the fair play literature. The literature assumes that the only legitimate grounds for dissent from a beneficial cooperative scheme is based on subjective disagreements about the value of the benefits – dissenters object because the benefits aren't worth it to them. Thus attention is focused on the benefits condition: If the benefits *are* subjectively worth it in the relevant sense, then, we are told, dissent that comes too late (and, as we have seen, even dissent that comes ex-ante, according to some) is dissent for the wrong reasons: It is a kind of selfishness, grabbing benefits just because nobody can now do anything about it. But dissent can also be based on disagreement about the principle of distribution itself that underlies the fair play idea. What other distribution principle might one suggest? At least two come to mind. The first is a lottery. Jim might say that when it comes to making major purchases for the apartment, he would prefer to draw lots, with the loser bearing the entire cost. The second distribution principle is what I referred to earlier as a "bluffing" strategy. "We both want the humidifier, and either of us might pay for it alone if the other doesn't agree, so we'll just see who can hold out longer."[28] There's nothing unfair about such a principle; indeed, since it allows either party to win, it satisfies a generally accepted condition for denying that any obligation to pay should result.[29] Jim may be free riding, but since Mary had the same chance to end up as the free rider, it is more appropriate to call him a "winning rider." This principle, to be sure, risks the possibility that both parties end up worse off (by suffering dry air longer than either would prefer), a problem that once again leads back to an enormous collective action literature. But the point is that there is nothing irrational or immoral about choosing to risk this particular disutility as long as it is at least offset by the possibility of winning: Depending on the particular circumstances (and one's willingness and ability to bluff), the expected value of the holding-out strategy could be positive.

So even the best paradigm case remains incomplete. We need to explain why Jim, if his dissent is in fact based on an honest disagreement about the appropriate distribution principle, should have an obligation to defer to Mary's different fair play principle. Though we are still some way, perhaps, from understanding the duty of fair play, we have made at least one significant change in our approach to the issue. In line with the thesis of this study, the fair play issue, according to the preceding analysis, is better approached by re-presenting it as a question of why one might have a duty to defer to the normative views

---

[28] By calling this the "bluffing" strategy, I don't mean to suggest that bluffing is inevitable, but just that it is permissible. It is possible that one could accept the bluffing principle simply because it might be a better way of seeing who cares about the humidifier more.

[29] See Klosko, *Fairness and Obligation,* 35 (there is unfairness only if "the advantages of non-cooperation cannot be extended" [to all]).

of others about how to distribute burdens and benefits in certain contexts. To answer that question, I shall first consider another recent example in the fair play literature that helps shift the analysis in a direction more closely related to this new approach.

Fair Play as Deference

An Example of Another Kind: Taking Turns in Queues

Anyone who does any freeway driving these days has experienced the following situation, presented recently by David Luban as another example of the fair play obligation:

> You are driving on a highway, and two lanes must squeeze into one.... You see that the cars in the two lanes are taking turns. You know (let us suppose) that this method advances the line of traffic most rapidly.... When you come to the head of the line, you ... skip ahead out of turn.[30]

Luban includes this example as well as another line-jumping case (you cut into the front of the line at a bus queue in London) as comparable to examples of the sort we have been considering. The illuminating exchange that followed between Luban and Wasserman reveals a different direction for fair play theory that helps fill out the basis for the obligation.[31]

The first question is whether we can even construe line-jumping as a case of taking advantage of nonexcludable benefits made possible through the efforts of others. Presumably, the attempt to make the cases analogous requires us to posit the following: (1) I could not have jumped in front if others had not lined up (thus I am taking advantage of the benefit of quicker mobility made possible only through the efforts of others; (2) those who lined up incurred a cost (they gave up the chance to cut in line ahead of where they are in the queue, but this cost was outweighed for them by the benefit of the more orderly procedure). Note that it is the second of these assumptions that is odd. In the case of Mary and Jim, there is no doubt that Mary incurred costs to purchase the humidifier. But to say that those who lined up incurred a cost seems to assume what is at issue: Maybe a Manhattan bus stop free-for-all would actually have benefited some people

---

[30] David Luban, *Lawyers and Justice: An Ethical Study* (Princeton, N.J.: Princeton Univ. Press, 1988), 39–40 (as quoted in D. Wasserman, Review Essay, "Should a Good Lawyer Do the Right Thing? David Luban on the Morality of Adversary Representation," *Md. L. Rev.* 49 [1990]: 392, 407).

[31] Compare Luban, "Freedom and Constraint in Legal Ethics: Some Mid-Course Corrections to *Lawyers and Justice*," *Md. L. Rev.* 49 (1990): 424, with Wasserman, *id.* Wasserman suggests that the blocked-lane case is different from (and more like the neighborhood cleanup cases than) the bus-queue case, because the former is simply an application of a principle determining how to proceed (take turns) about which we have strong antecedent beliefs. For reasons that will become clear, I treat both cases as essentially similar.

(the more aggressive). So those who don't like the free-for-all are just exhibiting their preference for a distribution principle that favors them. If I prefer the free-for-all principle, presumably it is because it favors me compared to lining up; but that does not distinguish me from those who are lining up: They prefer that procedure because it favors them compared to the free-for-all principle.[32] But there is a second problem with trying to explain intuitions about the fairness of line jumping in the way one explains free riding. As Wasserman notes, our indignation at someone who cuts in line does not seem to depend on whether the line jumper is actually gaining at our expense: We would feel the same indignation even if there was no gain or expense, as in the case of someone who cuts into a short line for a bus that has plenty of seats for everyone.[33] The same is probably true for the blocked lane on the freeway. Imagine that someone spurts ahead without taking turns like everyone else, but that under the circumstances (1) no measurable extra delay results for anyone else and (2) the line-jumping driver is not made better off than he would have been under a free-for-all scheme (i.e., he would have been first in line anyway, as the most aggressive driver). The point is not whether these two conditions are plausible. The point is that even if a case arose that seemed to fill both conditions, most people would still probably feel indignation at the driver who refuses, like everyone else, to take turns. The indignation does not so much reflect resentment over his exploiting our patience to benefit himself as it does resentment that he somehow thinks he is better than the rest and need not conform to the principle that requires turn-taking. Note that we might not feel the same resentment toward the motorcyclist who can more easily fill both conditions: She can pass the blocked cars on the shoulder and slip through the construction gap without either delaying others or benefiting herself at their expense. If similar resentment does not arise in her case (and one can even imagine reactions just the opposite of resentment: drivers waiting in cars might admire or envy the motorcyclist), it is because the motorcyclist already is distinguishable from ordinary drivers in ways that don't indicate that she is unjustifiably claiming to be better than us. Motorcycles *can* go places cars can't.

In some respects this is a familiar problem, treated at length in the collective action literature. If the lawn will be ruined if a certain number of people cross but will be unaffected by a few crossings, why should those who refrain

---

[32] Note how similar the argument here is to the argument that can be made about whether the state is better than a state of nature. Those who would win in the state of nature are arguably the strong and aggressive, whereas the weaker and less aggressive prefer the security of the state. This possibility of different attitudes about the value of the state helps explain the point of classical state-of-nature arguments in political theory. Those arguments aim to show that even the strong and aggressive stand to gain from the state (see Hobbes's emphasis on the relative weakness of even the strongest). It is not so clear that one could similarly establish that the first come, first served principle is best for everybody, though this forms part of the disagreement between Wasserman and Luban.

[33] See Wasserman, "Should a good Lawyer Do the Right Thing?", 409.

from crossing resent someone who takes the shortcut without causing harm?[34] Some attempts to answer this question fall back on generalization arguments (if everyone did that, the consequences would be disastrous; therefore no one should do it). But our line-jumping examples suggest a different explanation. Even if some people could cross harmlessly (or line-jump without hurting anybody), there remains the question of how to allocate that benefit. Lotteries and turn-taking provide one obvious principle; line-jumping suggests another, akin to the bluffing game mentioned earlier: "Let all who think they can jump over others without making everybody worse off try." If one is willing to universalize this principle, it is not clearly unfair; nor is it irrational, even though it carries the risk that errors can be made in inviting everyone to calculate whether they, too, can do the same without bringing about worse effects than taking turns.

What we need is an explanation for why the line jumper should defer to the distribution principle that everyone else has apparently accepted. Two possible answers suggest themselves. First, as Wasserman suggests in his exchange on this issue, one may conclude that some distribution principles, like "first come, first served" are in fact morally superior to others, and for that reason, failure to follow the principle is morally wrong, regardless of what others are doing.[35] The fact that others are observing the principle is not critical to creating the duty, but only to facilitating our ability to comply with the preexisting duty to observe the principle. The problem with this answer lies in its questionable assumption that only one principle (first come, first served) is morally correct in these situations. As Luban points out in his response, it is not clear that we would condemn as immoral, as Wasserman's assumption seems to require, the multiple-line queuing arrangements found in fast food outlets and supermarkets where customers take "the luck of their lane."[36] Luban's suggestion is that we have a duty to respect the principle already accepted by others as long as the principle is one of several possible reasonable principles. Luban reaches two important conclusions: (1) One need not receive benefits from a cooperative scheme in order to have an obligation to respect the principle that generates benefits *for others* under that scheme;[37] (2) the duty of fair play rests in the end on our duty to respect the power of others "to obligate us to participate in

---

[34] For a brief examination of this problem and an illuminating comparison of consequentialist and fairness attempts to account for it, see Klosko, *Fairness and Obligation*, Appendix I. For a complete and original treatment, see Donald Regan, *Utilitarianism and Co-operation* (Oxford: Clarendon Press, 1980).

[35] Not quite "regardless of what others are doing." If others are following the wrong principle (e.g., the free-for-all bus-queue principle), we may be excused from trying to follow the first come, first served principle because it would be impracticable to do so. See Wasserman, "Should a good Lawyer Do the Right Thing?", 409.

[36] Luban, *Lawyers and Justice*, 459 (quoting Wasserman, id., 410).

[37] "The role of benefits . . . in my argument is [indirect]. Only if a legally-created scheme creates benefits (for someone) does it make sense to regard noncompliance with the scheme as an expression of disrespect for our fellows. . . ." Luban, *Lawyers and Justice*, 458.

schemes with which we disagree – schemes that may not be utterly brilliant or maximally fair. . . . "[38]

Luban's conclusions provide strong support for the general thesis of this study. But there are two respects in which Luban's analysis is incomplete. First, as we shall see in the next chapter, the re-presentation of the duty of fair play as an obligation tied less to the receipt of unearned benefits than to the duty to respect the principles of others undermines Luban's claim that the obligation to obey the law is horizontal (owed only to the members participating in a particular, legally created, beneficial cooperative scheme) rather than vertical (owed to those who enacted the law in the first place). In this respect, the consequences of a respect-based view of the basis of the fair play obligation are more extensive than Luban recognizes. Second, Luban's failure to make any distinction between principles one has a duty to respect and the actual receipt of benefits overstates the fair play obligation: It fails to distinguish between mere rudeness and the violation of a moral duty. A complete respect-based theory of the duty of fair play is, in these two ways, both stronger and weaker than Luban's analysis suggests. To see this, let us return to our paradigm case and then, in the next chapter, apply this discussion to the problem of political obligation.

The Paradigm Case Explained

THE REASONS FOR DEFERENCE. The preceding discussion reveals the error in attempting to derive Jim's obligation to Mary from the fact that Jim is getting a free ride if he pays nothing. This traditional focus on an apparently ungrateful beneficiary overlooks the more basic problem of explaining why Jim, who may simply be following an equally plausible normative principle of his own, should defer to Mary's different principle about how collective benefits and burdens are to be distributed. Two cases can be imagined. First, Jim may also believe that the norm Mary is following – each beneficiary pays his or her proportionate share – is the correct norm and is "naturally" superior to all other possible principles. In this case, no problem arises: Jim is simply being inconsistent in failing to follow his own normative principle in a case in which he admits it applies. The free play issue becomes interesting only in the second case: Jim sincerely believes that a different normative principle ("we all take equal chances in seeing who can hold out longest") is the appropriate one to follow. If we assume that both normative principles are morally defensible, what reason does Jim have to defer to Mary?

The answer to this question requires reconsidering the type of relationship a roommate situation is and how the value of such a relationship affects the duties of those involved. If Jim and Mary were in a close relationship, it is plausible to

---

[38] Id., 461.

suggest that Mary's principle is naturally superior to Jim's bluffing principle, which invites dissembling and a kind of strategic maneuvering that can easily undermine the trust and affection necessary for a close relationship. But even if one could defend Jim's principle as consistent with these features of friendship, one might still urge deference to Mary's norm for reasons very similar to those that figure in attempts to establish her principle as naturally superior. Mary's norm, after all, is already the existing (accepted) norm; her principle has been adopted and acted on by the relevant community (in this two-person case, Mary is the only other person in the community); moreover, it was acted on under circumstances that do not permit one to charge Mary with fault for failing to discover that Jim actually believed in a different principle. The fact that the norm already exists provides a basis for the same kind of argument for deference that was available in arguing for the natural superiority of Mary's principle: Deference fosters a caring community; insistence on one's own principles (even if they are as good as or better than Mary's) fosters competition and antagonism.

It may now be easier to understand why fair play theory generates so much disagreement about whether the duty is genuine and distinct from promise. There is no clear answer in the roommate case to the question of whether Jim should prefer a caring community to a competitive one. The relationship of roommate is too general and permits of too many variations to allow one to draw the same conclusions about the ingredients necessary to its successful maintenance that one can draw in the case of a close relationship. Context here is crucial. Roommates in a sports fraternity may discover value in the kind of competitive community that Jim's principle promotes, whereas freshman college students, newly assigned to roommates in a dormitory, may make a serious mistake by not cultivating a cooperative community with those who have temporarily assumed the status of potential friend.

The main point is that the duty of fair play depends ultimately on a defense of the value of the relationship that the duty promotes – just as the duty to defer, in appropriate circumstances, to a close friend depends on understanding what friendship is and why ignoring or jeopardizing the value of friendship is a kind of moral failure. But where the circle of acquaintanceship broadens beyond that of a close friend – ranging from roommates, to next-door neighbors, to more loosely defined communities engaged in the production of mutually beneficial and nonexcludable goods – arguments about whether a cooperative or competitive community is preferable will be far less clear. Finally, it is important to recognize how much weight the duty of fair play seems to accord to the existing norm: Right or wrong, the fact that a norm has already been adopted and acted on changes one's own normative situation from what would have obtained if no decision about the operative norm had yet been made.

THE RELEVANCE OF BENEFITS. Though the duty of fair play has less to do with the receipt of benefits than is often thought, benefits do play a role in the theory. Explaining that role can help illustrate both why the focus on benefits dominates so much of the literature and why that focus needs to be redirected to the idea of deference.

Fair play duties ultimately depend on the obligation to respect the views of others, even where those views differ from our own. But the situations that seem to call for one to depart from one's own life pattern out of respect for others range far more widely than just the duties of fair play we have been considering. Assume, for example, that Mary dislikes soup-slurping, but Jim, having spent time in countries where slurping is a sign that one approves of the soup, continues to enjoy his noodles noisily. It is not hard to see why Jim might have reason to defer to Mary's custom. Indeed, the reasons for following rules of etiquette and adhering to strange customs in foreign countries ("when in Rome") can probably be explained in terms that "sound in respect" and thus resemble duties generated from the obligation to defer to others. One possibility is to treat all of these situations as examples of a "duty of respect," with no distinction between the trivial and the serious.[39] But there is a second possibility that probably more closely reflects existing practice: Rules of etiquette and the like may generate reasons for deference, but in these more trivial instances, we are likely to talk in terms of politeness and rudeness rather than duty and obligation.[40] If this is correct, the role of benefits in generating duties of fair play can be understood as marking the crossing from the trivial to the serious. Where property or valuable goods are at stake, particularly in the significant amounts that are necessary to generate the duty of fair play,[41] we are more likely to think that the error is one of moral failing rather than mere rudeness.

Thus, the ethics of deference is weaker in scope (a less extensive theory of duty) than the general requirement for civility or courtesy. On the other hand, where the duty to defer does apply, the force of the obligation is stronger than that of ordinary courtesy: Reasons to defer can outweigh not just self-interest in matters of etiquette, but strong principle in cases of moral disagreement. To see the full implications of this revised view of fair play, we turn now to the context in which fair play arguments have most often been used, namely, that of political obligation.

---

[39] Relevant here are recent discussions, noted earlier (see Chapter 1, footnote 16) suggesting a connection between courtesy and morality. See Cheshire Calhoun, "The Virtue of Civility," *Phil. & Pub. Affairs* 29 (2000): 251; Sarah Buss, "Appearing Respectful: The Moral Significance of Manner," *Ethics* 109 (1999): 795.

[40] See H. L. A. Hart, *The Concept of Law* (Oxford: Clarendon Press, 1961), 79–89 ("The Idea of Obligation").

[41] See the discussion at 145–6.

7

Political Obligation

Introduction

The previous two chapters illustrate some of the advantages to be gained from re-presenting familiar problems about the obligations of promise and fair play as problems of explaining why one might have reasons to defer to the normative views of others. This chapter attempts a similar re-presentation of the obligation to obey the law. I shall suggest that this problem, too, is best seen as a direct application of a theory that shows why citizens may always have reasons to defer to the legal norms of the state. But I shall begin by first attempting to apply the more traditional argument about fair play as a basis for political obligation. Since we have now shifted the focus of fair play arguments from benefits conferred to the duty to respect the normative judgments of others, it may be that this new focus will help solve standard problems in using fair play to establish a prima facie obligation to obey the law.

Political Obligation and Fair Play

I suggested earlier that fair play arguments for political obligation have become a popular alternative to arguments based on consent because they have the advantage of generating duties in exactly those cases where consent theories are weakest: namely, where citizens who derive benefits from living in a state cannot, by any reasonable interpretation of their conduct, be said to have agreed or promised to do anything in return. But application of fair play theory to such cases is problematic, revealing both the errors and the strengths of the standard analysis.

Begin with the strengths. The discussion in the preceding chapter shows how theories of fair play might be thought to establish a basis for political obligation. First, the benefits provided by the state – the value of security is the most obvious – are nonexcludable. Second, except for political anarchists,[1] any citizen will presumably admit that these benefits are significant, thus satisfying even the most stringent requirement that the benefits be measured subjectively. These two features are sufficient conditions in the view of some theorists[2] to ground at least a prima facie duty to obey the law.

The problems with this fair play argument, at least in its standard versions, have often been noted. The standard versions all focus on benefits conferred as the basis for the duty to obey – benefits that are conferred either horizontally (derived from the obedience of others) or vertically (derived from the value of having a legal system that establishes security). The horizontal arguments find the benefits that trigger the duty to obey in the fact that other citizens sometimes also obey the law, even when doing so is against their interest. This benefit, it is said, generates a duty on my part to obey in turn when it is against my interest to do so. The argument is unconvincing for two reasons. First, other citizens who obey the law are not voluntarily conferring a benefit on me comparable to the benefit conferred by those who willingly install devices for controlling air pollution. The law's sanctions make the motives for compliance by others too uncertain to make the analogy to free riding work. I am not free riding if I choose to risk sanctions that others are simply too timid to incur – they could have run the risk, too; instead they chose a different course. There is, then, no free benefit being conferred. Second, even if one could isolate those subjects whose compliance is willing (subjects whose obedience is not motivated by the sanction), the idea that they are benefiting me in ways that require similar restraint on my part is farfetched: How will my compliance with laws that are misguided benefit them?

This latter problem of explaining how obedience to bad laws can be said to benefit those to whom one owes a duty of fair play also haunts the vertical versions of the fair play argument. These versions focus, more appropriately, on the benefits derived from the existence of the state itself rather than the benefits that arise from the fact that others are law-abiding subjects. But even if one concedes the value of the state, it may well be that disobeying bad laws will actually prove more beneficial in the long run to a healthy state than obedience. Once again, it is difficult to see how one connects whatever obligation may be created by the benefits of living in a legal system with the specific obligation to obey all laws.

[1] I use the term "anarchist" to refer to those who deny the value of any state, preferring anarchy and the state of nature to any organized monopoly on coercion. Recent defenders of "philosophical anarchism" fall into a variety of camps that may mean to deny only the existence of a universal obligation to obey. See Chaim Gans, *Philosophical Anarchism and Political Disobedience* (Cambridge: Cambridge Univ. Press, 1992), 2. For a good discussion of various forms of philosophical anarchism, see A. John Simmons, "Philosophical Anarchism," in *For and Against the State,* eds. John T. Sanders and Jan Narveson (Lanham, Md.: Rowman & Littlefield, 1996), 19.

[2] See, in particular, George Klosko, *The Principle of Fairness and Political Obligation* (Lanham, Md.: Rowman & Littlefield, 1992).

Consider now how these problems with the standard fair play argument are lessened and may even disappear when the duty of fair play is re-presented as a duty to defer to the views of others. We have seen that fair play arguments may rest, in the end, on reasons to defer to the existing normative views of a given community about how benefits and burdens are to be distributed. As applied to the state, the first steps in establishing the duty to defer to legal norms parallel the steps in the standard fair play arguments: The benefits of living in a legal system are nonexcludable and subjectively valuable to most subjects. That being the case, the question of whether one has reason to defer to the existing norms of the state resembles the question explored in the preceding chapter. Deference to legal norms, even when those norms are wrong, may show respect for the values of the legal community in a way that strengthens the political bonds of society, just as deference to Mary's view about how to share the common benefits of purchasing the humidifier may promote a more desirable community than acting on one's own, equally valid, normative views. These arguments for deference, however, appear to be mostly instrumental: They point to the gains to be achieved in terms of a strengthened community by going along, even though one believes the community itself is making a mistake. But instrumental reasons for deference are subject to the same objections we have already noted in the case of standard fair play arguments. First, there is no clear answer in the case of the state, any more than in the case of the roommate situation, to the question of whether a cooperative or competitive community is preferable. Some subjects may be willing to disobey laws, paying the sanction if necessary and happily inviting others to do the same if they can, even though the consequence is a competitive attitude toward law that does little to foster a community of shared values.[3] To prefer such a competitive community in the case of law may not be clearly erroneous – any more than it is clearly erroneous to prefer line-jumping, or luck of the lane to first come, first served as principles for allocating benefits and burdens. Thus a subject who chooses the competitive relationship over the more fraternal cooperative arrangement will not have instrumental reasons to defer. Second, even if one does prefer a more cooperative relationship (or if it can be shown that cooperation is naturally superior), one still will not always have instrumental reasons to defer since not every act of disobedience will jeopardize the cooperative arrangement. Some acts of disobedience may even deepen community ties by leading others to recognize and change clearly unjust laws. Instrumental reasons to defer, in short, will always fall short of generating prima facie obligations to obey all laws for the reasons that we have already seen. Here, it seems, whether one is thinking of duties of fair play or of reasons to defer, context is everything: Sometimes obedience will have

---

[3] Ronald Dworkin, whose views I consider at greater length later, also suggests that certain forms of community ("de facto," and "rulebook" models of community) will unduly promote selfish interests rather than the kind of mutual concern necessary for political obligation. See Dworkin, *Law's Empire* (Cambridge, Mass.: Harvard Univ. Press, 1986), 208–16.

advantageous consequences for the community; sometimes it will not. To show that one always has some reason to defer requires an exploration of the other reasons for deference described at the beginning of this study and applied to the case of promise: intrinsic reasons, that appeal not to the consequences of failing to defer, but to one's own values and the respect that is due either to one self or to others based on those values. To understand the role of such reasons in the case of law requires a review of how intrinsic reasons for deference arise.

Political Obligation and the Ethics of Deference

Instrumental and Intrinsic Reasons Revisited

Many standard arguments for a universal obligation to obey the law are vulnerable to the problem discussed in the preceding section: Instrumental reasons are always context-dependent, which means that one can always imagine some contexts in which the values that may be jeopardized by disobeying bad laws are no longer at risk. The fact that the state is valuable, for example, does not by itself mean that one always has an instrumental reason to defer to legal norms for the simple reason that disobedience does not always threaten the state's existence – indeed, disobedience might even improve matters. It is for this reason that straightforward consequentialist arguments for the duty to obey fail; it is for this reason, too, that fair play arguments often fail, even when those arguments are recast in terms of the need to preserve or enhance a certain kind of community. To understand what more is needed in order to show how one might always have a reason to defer to legal norms, it will be helpful first to review briefly how the ethics of deference as we have now described it works in the case of our other paradigm examples: friendship, promise, and fair play.

We began by comparing this study to Hume's attempt to find, beneath consent theories of political obligation, a more basic and direct theory of ethics – in his case utilitarianism – that could then be applied to the case of law. In similar fashion, beginning with an analogy to friendship, we have now converted two standard and distinct arguments for political obligation – arguments from consent and fair play – into a single ethical theory of deference. Each of these paradigms is based, in some sense, on the duty to respect others and on the values of the relationship that such respect acknowledges.

With these two basic concepts in mind – respect for others in circumstances that implicate fundamental relationship values – we can present the normative argument for each of the four paradigm examples (including, now, that of political obligation) in pairs, each pair reflecting the kind of reasoning (instrumental or intrinsic) that most typically supports the duty to defer. The easiest case to defend is the case of close friendships. Here, the reasons for deference are often instrumental: Deference contributes to the preservation of the larger good represented by the relationship. Fair play arguments are closely related to friendship arguments: The reasons for deference here too are often instrumental, pointing to the consequences for the kind of community, competitive or sharing, that results from following one or another distribution principle. The comparison with friendship also helps explain why fair play duties are often problematic. The bonds between strangers, roommates, or neighbors will differ, depending on the context and the nature of the project that yields the nonexcludable benefits. The argument for the duty to defer will reflect these differences in two ways. First, the values at stake are more dubious, because the choice between competitive and sharing communities is likely to be genuinely open in a way that it is not within the more intimate context of friendship. Second, even where a sharing community seems preferable, the impact of the free rider on the value of such a community may be less easily demonstrated and less clearly seen as a sign of disrespect.

In contrast to duties of friendship and fair play, which seem amenable to explanation in terms of instrumental reasons to defer, political and promissory obligations often seem to require reference to intrinsic reasons for deference: The respect shown by deference in these cases is required not solely or even primarily because of the consequences if one fails to defer, but because of the intrinsic requirements for consistency in moral principle. Consider, again, the case of promises. Consequential arguments for the scope of promissory duties, as we have seen, inevitably produce cases where the benefits of breaking the promise outweigh the benefits of keeping the promise. But common intuitions balk at accepting the conclusion that these cases describe the limits of promissory duties. Attempts to account for these persistent intuitions by adding more consequences to the equation – the effect of the breach on the institution of promising, for example – miss the point. Even when all relevant consequences are accounted for, intuitions insist that the promisee has rights that survive the fact that breaking the promise would, in any particular case, produce the best consequences. The ethics of deference provides a basis for these intuitions by pointing to the value that is at stake in the decision whether to ignore the promisee's claim. When the promise is re-presented as a law passed by two persons, the question of whether one should keep the promise becomes analogous to the question of whether one should obey the legal norm enacted by one's own voluntary decision to enter this hypothetical mini-state. Even if all conceivable consequences favor disobeying the norm, one fact remains: The promisee presumably remains unpersuaded about the value of disobeying the norm (breaking the promise). One may think that the promisee is wrong, because he or she is miscalculating the consequences or is operating under a different theory of promise-keeping. The obligation to keep the promise under these circumstances (subject, of course, to the promisee's release) is the result of recognizing that one would expect the same if the situation were reversed, because one acknowledges the point of the practice of promising discussed in the previous chapter. Note that the argument here is not made exclusively in terms of the impact of disobedience (promise-breaking) on the promissory relationship. The relationship is, or can in some contexts be, too temporary to make the impact on future promissory relationships a critical factor. The argument for deference draws instead on the idea that respecting the wishes of the promisee is a means of respecting one's own principles – doing exactly what one would expect if the situation were reversed. Kant's notion of acting on norms that one could legislate for all, however mysterious in the abstract, gains meaning in the concrete case where one has in fact enacted a norm (promise) into law and now confronts an actual person (the promisee/legislator) who is demanding compliance with the norm.

Political obligation poses the same question as promissory obligation – why obey the legislative norm? The obvious difference is that the content of the norm in the case of the state is not usually the result of a voluntary choice on the part of the citizen. That fact weakens the consistency explanation for respecting one's own choice when confronted with the demand for compliance. In addition, consequential arguments have little purchase because the context and relationship have now been so diluted that no single act of disobedience is likely to have significant effects on the community. But these two ways in which the demand to show respect is weaker than in the case of promises are offset by a compelling difference between legal norms and promissory norms. In the case of law, the point of the state is evident: Legal systems are necessary in a way that making promises is not. Once again (with the usual exception for anarchists), the law's expectation of voluntary compliance corresponds to what I would also expect if I were the legislator. The duty to respect the legal norm is a reflection of the duty to respect the values I myself acknowledge in recognizing what a legal system is.

In summary, one can characterize the duty to defer in these cases along several dimensions. Friendship, fair play, promise-keeping, and political obligation are duties that are grounded in that order along a scale that moves from consequential explanations to increasingly deontological ones. The values of friendship and fair play are largely independent of consent, and the values that deference promotes in each case become more tenuous as one moves from the more intimate two-person relationship to larger communities. Promissory duties give strangers the same power as the state to demand compliance with self-created norms, but this power is constrained in scope and creation by one's own voluntary choice as to the content of the norm and the person of the promisee. The state's right to deference, in contrast, arises not from the subject's voluntary choice about the content of legal norms, but from the acknowledgment of the necessity of an enterprise that requires designated authorities to impose norms, in good faith, on the community at large.

Intrinsic Reasons for Deference to Law

The proceding review is meant to highlight the similarities and differences among our four paradigm cases of deference in terms of the relative importance of instrumental as opposed to intrinsic reasons in explaining why one has reason to defer. But it would be a mistake to assume that only one kind of reason is at work in any particular case. Though I have suggested that instrumental reasons are easiest to see as defining the grounds and limits of duties of fair play and friendship, it is important to recall that intrinsic reasons can also apply to these cases. We illustrated this possibility in Chapter 1, where we first discussed the difference between these two types of reasons. In cases of friendship, we said, it is possible that one has reason to defer to one's spouse not because of the consequences on the relationship, but because showing respect through deference is a way of acknowledging the value of the relationship.[4] We further suggested that the intrinsic reasons for deference in this sense may be either objective or subjective: The reasons are objective if in fact the relationship is objectively valuable in a way that is acknowledged through respect of the sort shown by deference; the reasons are subjective if, regardless of the objective value of respect, one's own values endorse this particular view of the point of the relationship. In that case, it is consistency with one's own values and self-respect that generates the reason to defer.

To complete the current argument for reasons for deference to legal norms, we must consider again the point of the state, the values that presumably generate either objective or subjective reasons for deference. In the case of promise, we accomplished this by imagining a state of nature for promises and suggesting that persons might recognize promise as a device not only for undertaking a commitment, but also for allocating decision-making authority in the case of dispute over the extent of that commitment. In the case of the state, the state-of-nature argument has been made too often to warrant anything more at this point than a brief reminder of at least one conclusion that we have assumed most people share: The legal system provides values of security that anyone will presumably acknowledge makes the state preferable to anarchy. But more is needed than just this particular value of the state in order to raise problems of consistency in failing to defer. One must also recognize what a legal system is; the inquiry in part I of this study returns to fill in the types of values at stake in the argument for deference.

The argument for deference in the case of law depends on the claim that subjects have reasons to defer to those who expect compliance even though subjects have different beliefs about the value of a particular state or different beliefs about the wisdom or morality of particular legal norms. As in our simpler

---

[4] See Chapter 1, "Substance: The Reasons for Deference."

roommate example, two possibilities arise. First, a subject may believe that no state is legitimate, and thus that no person or group of persons has the right to establish and enforce common community norms. Any subject who honestly held such beliefs would present a problem for political obligation under the ethics of deference because the benefits of the state would now have to be defended objectively rather than subjectively. Though an objective defense of the state as an alternative to anarchy is probably not that difficult to mount, I shall leave the question open and unaddressed here: Few people, after all, are sincere political anarchists, which means that most people will at least have subjective reasons to defer (even if the anarchist is right) so long as the state whose value they acknowledge is properly defined.

Equally unproblematic for our attempt to show reasons to defer is the citizen who concedes that the state is necessary but who disagrees with the merits of the particular state that expects his or her obedience. This citizen, too, will have subjective reasons to defer if he or she concedes the value of the state in general, which, by definition, as we have seen, only requires a good faith attempt to administer in the interests of all. That a particular norm is misguided or wrong is relevant only to the weight, not the existence, of the duty. Consistency in understanding what a state is requires one to concede that the enterprise that leads to the creation and enforcement of norms is a valuable one – as measured, once again, by one's own subjective views.[5]

We have assumed that a state expects citizens to comply voluntarily with its norms. Though we have argued that a state or a legal system does not claim that citizens have a moral duty to comply, as a matter of descriptive fact all states seem to expect voluntary compliance: Sanctions are wielded as an extra precaution and safeguard against those who will not so comply.[6] If one admits

---

[5] Certain forms of philosophical anarchism purport to recognize states as legitimate only if they conform to preferred substantive principles of political or moral theory – e.g., only if states are democratic or egalitarian. See Simmons, "Philosophical Anarchism," (distinguishing "weak" and "strong" anarchism). These claims do not represent disputes about what a state *is* but rather disputes about the claim to justice that particular states make. As long as the state's ideology or claim to justice can be defended in good faith, it remains an instance of what I take to be the basic value of the state that underlies the argument for deference: It is the attempt in good faith to impose norms claimed to be just on society that constitutes the idea, and represents the value, of the state. Disagreements about whether a particular state's claim to justice is correct must thus be distinguished from disagreement about whether the attempt itself is recognized as necessary and valuable. It is the attempt to rule justly that is valuable and necessary; whether one succeeds in the attempt is a question that deserves attention in trying to alter and improve a particular state, as well as an issue that will bear on whether the reason to defer in particular cases is outweighed by the immorality of the action required by the law. But these failures in execution do not undermine the claim that the *attempt* to rule justly is both an essential characteristic of what we mean by a state and an enterprise most people will recognize as valuable and necessary.

[6] Meir Dan-Cohen has argued that the state's reliance on coercion undercuts any argument for compliance based on respect for the state. See Dan-Cohen, "In Defense of Defiance," *Phil. & Pub. Affairs* 23 (1994): 24, 42–4. But his argument depends on an analogy with ordinary people who make requests accompanied by implicit or explicit threats if the request is not complied

that there are good reasons for the state to expect such voluntary compliance, then the argument for a universal prima facie obligation to obey is essentially completed: One will always have at least an intrinsic reason to defer to the state's normative judgments. Instrumental reasons for deference, we have seen, will reach only so far, leading to the conclusion that in many cases no such reasons exist. The impact on those who expect voluntary compliance in the case of law is even less immediate and far less obviously grounded in directly consequential considerations than in the case of ad hoc communities. The reasons for deference in the case of the law are Kantian in character, demanding that one avoid the same kind of inconsistency between one's action and one's own admitted norms that we saw in the case of Jim, who, under one hypothesis, agreed that Mary's distribution principle was preferable but decided to take his free ride anyway – just because he could. So, too, in the case of law. The question of why I should defer to the norms of the state is answered by reminding myself of the point of the state and the sense in which it represents values that I, too, endorse. The state is necessary, and it is the kind of entity that requires some to govern, in good faith, on behalf of all. Thus I, who could do no different were I in charge, have a prima facie reason to do as I would expect others in my situation to do. It remains for the last chapter to explore in somewhat greater detail this particular theory of ethics and compare it to other theories about the nature of political obligation.

---

with voluntarily. In these cases, the threat does seem to undermine any respect-based case for deference. The argument overlooks, however, that the state has an explanation for why it must use coercion that the ordinary person does not. I have discussed this aspect of the problem before. See Philip Soper, *A Theory of Law*, (Cambridge, Mass.: Harvard Univ. Press, 1984), 85; *id.*, "The Moral Value of Law," *Mich. L. Rev.* 84 (1985): 63, 73, n. 23 (The state's use of force differs from the gunman's [or the beggar's] in that there are good reasons for the former but not for the latter). See also William A. Edmundson, *Three Anarchical Fallacies* (Cambridge: Cambridge Univ. Press, 1998), 73–94 (discussing the "law is coercive" fallacy).

8

The Nature of Deference

The Logic of Deference

The Limits of Deference

My aim thus far has been to show that four recurring examples of human interaction – friendship, promise-keeping, fair play, and political obligation – can be re-presented as examples of the duty to defer to the views of others even if those views are incorrect or misguided. In this chapter, I consider somewhat more fully the normative basis for the argument for deference, including limits on the argument's reach. I also help illustrate and defend the argument by comparing other theories about the duty to obey the law that share similarities with the theory sketched here.

Forms and Varieties of Communities

In previous chapters, we considered two major types of community, competitive and cooperative, and indicated how the duty to defer may depend on the argument for preferring one or the other in particular contexts. I do not suggest that these broad types are exhaustive of the kinds of communities one might encounter, but only that they are particularly prominent alternatives that figure in the argument for deference. While it would be a mistake to assume that the four paradigm examples discussed here are the only examples that raise the question of deference, one must be careful not to so weaken the argument for deference that it collapses into a question of common courtesy. The varieties of relationships and occasions in which such questions might arise are as limitless as the human ability to imagine and form associations. Clubs, trade and business groups, religious and civic organizations, Internet user groups, school and workplace groups – the list could be extended indefinitely, with each group characterized differently in terms of the strength and the kind of bond that exists among the members. The argument for deference defended here will not extend to most such groups, even though common civility will, in many of these cases, require conduct that often appears similar to deference. We encountered a related problem earlier, noting that the requirements of courtesy and etiquette often constrain one to act against one's own interests or instincts in order not to offend others. But courtesy and civility are not the same as the obligation to defer. The ethics of deference is a requirement for giving weight to the normative judgments of others even against one's own judgment about the correct action to take – a step that the principle of autonomy makes clear is far more extraordinary and requires more justification than ordinary civility. The requirements of courtesy may chafe against self-interest, but they do not require acting against principle. Indeed, in most associations, it would be rude to expect deference on any serious matter. Where groups, for example, operate democratically by voting on serious issues, deferring to a colleague's request to vote a particular way, against one's own better judgment, undermines the whole point of the vote as a means of determining members' views. Of course, the rules of organizations may designate authorities to make decisions with the expectation that all will defer to them, but here, too, the ease of exit from such voluntary associations when one does not like the decision leaves the principle of autonomy mostly intact without requiring deference.

Associative Obligations Compared

In some respects, the normative basis we have described for the ethics of deference resembles the argument for associative obligations that has figured prominently in recent legal and political theory. Ronald Dworkin is, perhaps, the most explicit recent proponent of the view that political obligation is a form of the special responsibilities that arise not through consent, but simply because of "membership in some biological or social group."[1] As in our own example of the case of friendship, Dworkin's claims for the duties that are required in order to show respect in such groups are strongest when the relationship is close and personal, and weakest when the emotional bonds weaken as the relevant group grows larger and more diverse. Indeed, the strongest criticism recently of the attempt to assimilate political obligation to the theory of associative obligations is mounted by Simmons on precisely this point:

It is simply not true, either in our own political community or in any others with which we are familiar, that most citizens feel with respect to all of their fellows a deep and abiding concern. In the interest of realism, we must acknowledge that the divisions between religions, ethnic groups, races, political parties, castes, economic classes, and so on run

---

[1] Ronald Dworkin, *Law's Empire* (Cambridge, Mass.: Harvard Univ. Press, 1986), 195–6. For other examples of arguments that find political obligation in theories of membership or association, see Yael Tamir, *Liberal Nationalism* (Princeton, N.J.: Princeton Univ. Press, 1993); Margaret Gilbert, "Group Membership and Political Obligation," *Monist* 76 (1993): 119.

too deep for this claim to be convincingly denied. Where one might find the kind of closeness and concern necessary for Dworkin's account of associative obligations, of course, will only be in groups far smaller than the large-scale political communities with which Dworkin claims to be concerned.[2]

Dworkin's response to this criticism is that the personal, emotional bond found in close relationships is mirrored in the political context by a shared interpretive bond. The concern that is required "is an interpretive property of the group's practices of asserting and acknowledging responsibilities... not a psychological property of some fixed number of the actual members."[3] Simmons suggests that this response is inadequate for two reasons. First, the response is "bizarre" in suggesting that an "interpretation" of a practice can play the same role as actual personal concern in the absence of any shared emotional bonds. Second, even Dworkin seems to recognize the need for a personal emotional bond when he concedes that "a group will rarely meet or long sustain [the conditions for obligation] unless its members by and large actually feel some emotional bond with one another."[4]

This dispute provides an opportunity for explaining how the ethics of deference resembles and differs from standard theories of associative obligations. In the latter cases, the insistence on a personal bond in order for associative obligations to arise reflects the tendency to rely on an instrumentalist account of the obligation: It is the impact on persons whose expectations I have reason to honor, and the effect on the relationship if I ignore those expectations, that ground the duty. As we have seen, however, the ethics of deference is based not simply on respect for others, but also on respect for one self and one's own values and choices. The move from the personal context to the impersonal confrontation with the state requires deference – not to one's neighbor or friend but to a legislator who is doing exactly the job I would do if I were in his or her place: expecting compliance with norms enacted in good faith for the good of the community. What I confront when I consider breaking the law is not (necessarily) an actual person whose potential disappointment or concern triggers the duty; rather, I confront a hypothetical person in the character of an actual or ideal (but personally unknown) legislator who shares and is acting on values that I also share if I admit the need for and the nature of the state.[5] Dworkin's

---

[2] A. John Simmons, "Associative Political Obligations", *Ethics* 106 (1996): 247, 260. Similar objections can be found in Richard Dagger, "Membership, Fair Play, and Political Obligation," *Political Studies* 48 (2000): 104, 107–8) (contesting the analogy between family and polity); Christopher Wellman, "Associative Allegiances and Political Obligations," *Social Theory & Pract.* 23 (1997): 181; Leslie Green, "Associative Obligations and the State," in *Law and the Community: The End of Individualism*, eds. Allan C. Hutchinson and Leslie Green (Toronto: Carswell, 1989), 93.

[3] Dworkin, *Law's Empire*, 196, 201.

[4] Simmons, "Associative Political Obligations," 259–60, quoting Dworkin, id., 201.

[5] Heidi Hurd suggests that any defense of influential authority based on the "moral importance of attending to another's will" requires a commitment to intentionalist theories of interpretation that

mistake is to tie the interpretive conditions that lead to political obligation too closely to the particular practices of a community, requiring those practices to reveal at some level a continued sense of equal concern for all members. But the only practice that is needed to yield the obligation on the account defended here is the practice of the state itself. Simmons's mistake is to insist that associative obligations can only exist where the bonds are personal. While that insistence makes sense where the association is causally affected by the actions of members, the argument developed here, as we have seen, relies on intrinsic reasons for deference even in the case of strangers in certain special contexts where no long-term personal relationship is implicated (the state, or the voluntary partnership created temporarily with a stranger through promise).

It may be helpful to illustrate these differences between associative obligations and the ethics of deference by considering a case that is often presented as a counterexample to the claim that there is a universal duty to obey law – namely, a case in which the law can be disobeyed in secret without anyone finding out. If I can conveniently run the stop sign when it's clear that no one is observing and there is no risk, what possible reason could I have for obeying the law? Consequential explanations that stress the uncertainties of discovery or the possible abuse of the precedent in future situations will always ring hollow at some point: One can always manipulate the hypothetical facts so that the only reasonable conclusion is that the probable gain outweighs the probable risks. So consequential explanations of the duty to obey will not work – whether based on direct appraisals of harm and benefit or on the impact of disobedience on the expectations of others and thus on the possibility of disrespect undermining community values. Note that the same might also be said of promises. The teenager who promises his parents never to drive on a freeway without prior permission might reasonably conclude that his parents will never find out about a particular breach of the promise. One might think that in this latter case, instrumental explanations for why breach of the promise would be wrong have more force: Secretly breaking a promise requires hiding the secret

have been largely discredited. See Heidi Hurd, *Moral Combat* (Cambridge: Cambridge Univ. Press, 1999), 150. I do not believe it is necessary to examine the debates about interpretation that underlie Hurd's claim for two reasons. First, the theory defended here only requires that subjects understand that some definitive action is required of them by the law. How one decides what that action is will require one to take account of accepted theories about how to interpret legal norms. Thus it is not so much the "will" of an actual identifiable person or legislature that one respects in deferring: It is the "ideal" will represented by the legal norm, where the question of how to find that will is open to the full range of debates about appropriate theories of interpretation. Second, even if one believes that deference to authority under the current account does entail a commitment to some kind of intentionalist approach to interpretation, it is far too soon to conclude that such approaches are indefensible. See, e.g., Andrei Marmor, "Authority and Persons," *Legal Theory* 1 (1995): 337, revised as "Authority and Authorship," in Marmor, *Positive Law and Objective Values* (Oxford: Clarendon Press, 2001), 89 (defending a personal conception of authority); Larry Alexander and Emily Sherwin, *The Rule of Rules* (Durham, N.C.: Duke Univ. Press, 2001), ch. 5 (defending a theory of interpretation that relies on "inchoate intent").

in the future in ways that can undermine the trust between child and parents in unpredictable ways. But with appropriate manipulation of the hypothetical case, it will again seem farfetched to think that the wrong committed by secret breaches of promises can be accounted for entirely by reference to such potential impacts on the relationship. Much more compelling is the alternative Kantian-like explanation. The teenager knows that his parents expect his compliance, and that he accepts the value of the promissory convention that underlies this expectation. By keeping the promise, he shows respect for a hypothetical other (what his parents would want if they were present) and respect for himself in the values that he himself acknowledges. So, too, with law. Running the stop sign shows disrespect for hypothetical others (legislators who won't know but whose expectations are clear), as well as for one's own values (I would expect the same if I passed this law, whether or not disobedience could ever be discovered). Associative obligations, in short, at least as understood by people like Simmons, arise out of the impact of acts of disrespect on actual persons, whereas the obligations of deference arise out of the impact of my acts on actual others *or* on hypothetical others whose values I share.

Related Arguments

The difference between the obligations that arise from personal associations and those that arise more generally from the ethics of deference helps explain a variety of other strains in contemporary political thought. I consider here a very brief list of some of these alternative attempts to explain political and/or associative obligations – a list drawn primarily from Simmons's recent critique – with the aim of showing how these arguments relate to the ethics of deference.

CONCEPTUAL ARGUMENTS. A persistent strain of thought in political theory claims that the obligation to obey the law follows analytically from the concept of the state or the legal system.[6] One version of the argument claims that it is contradictory to acknowledge that a state has authority but to deny that one has an obligation to obey. Simmons's objection seems to be that the obligation to obey cannot be derived analytically from the concept of a state, for that would mean that anarchists and others could not meaningfully deny the authority of the state. Such denials, even if wrong, are not self-contradictory.[7] This study helps give the conceptual argument its due. First, the "authority" of the state that can be derived from the concept itself is only the authority to enforce norms, not the

---

[6] Hanna Pitkin's may be one of the best known of these conceptual arguments, see "Obligation and Consent, II," *Am. Pol. Sci. Rev.* 60 (1966): 39. Simmons also credits the argument to Margaret MacDonald, "The Language of Political Theory," in *Logic and Language*, 1st ser., ed. A. Flew (Oxford: Blackwell, 1963), 184; and Thomas McPherson, *Political Obligation* (London: Routledge & Kegan Paul, 1967), 64. See Simmons, "Associative Political Obligations," 253.

[7] Simmons, id., 254.

moral authority that claims a right to obedience. The moral authority that results in a duty to obey is synthetic, not analytic.[8] In this respect, critics like Simmons are correct: The concept of a state or legal system does not entail analytically the obligation to obey. (Indeed, as we have seen, legal systems do not even claim that subjects have an obligation to obey.) Second, understanding what a legal system is *and admitting that it is valuable* does entail a recognition that one is being *morally* inconsistent in denying that deference is due to the state's norms.[9] The anarchist does not contradict himself in denying the authority of the state, because the anarchist denies that the state is valuable or needed. But others, who admit the nature and necessity of the state, are morally inconsistent in denying any reason to defer to state judgments. "Moral inconsistency," of course, is not the same as logical contradiction. People may, and do, act in knowing violation of norms that apply to them. In doing so, they are being immoral, not acting incoherently. So the conceptual theorists were on the right track: There is a conceptual connection between understanding and accepting the value of the state and the obligation to obey. It is not the analytic kind that leads to self-contradiction, but the moral kind that leads to a form of Kantian hypocrisy.

THE NORMATIVE POWER OF THE ACTUAL. The possibility that a social practice can generate normative duties simply because the practice exists finds a remarkable number of reputable proponents[10] – remarkable, in part, because of the apparent bluntness with which this view seems to ignore the fact–value distinction. The possibility that associative obligations might be based on such a "normative independence thesis" attracts the most sustained critique from Simmons's perceptive analysis.[11] Simmons insists, in my view persuasively, that examples used to support the claim that a local practice can generate an

---

[8] See Joseph Raz, *Practical Reason and Norms* (London: Hutchinson, 1975), 164–7 (distinguishing "definitional" from "derivative" approaches to linking law and morality).

[9] John Finnis's arguments for the obligation to obey law may also serve as an example of what I am here calling a conceptual argument. See Finnis, "The Authority of Law in the Predicament of Contemporary Social Theory," *Notre Dame J. Law, Ethics, & Pub. Policy* 1 (1984): 115, 116n.4 (". . . arguments capable of justifying a claim to moral authority to make and enforce the law would . . . equally (or by addition of only uncontroversial premises) justify the claim that there is a generic moral obligation to obey that law").

[10] Michael Oakeshott's emphasis on the importance of existing traditions in understanding political duty may be an example of this approach to political theory. See, e.g., Oakeshott, "Political Education," in *Philosophy, Politics and Society*, 1st ser., ed. Peter Laslett (Oxford: Blackwell, 1975), 1, 13 ("What we have to do with is something less imposing than logical implications or necessary consequences; but if the intimations of a tradition of behaviour are less dignified or more elusive than these, they are not on that account less important"). Simmons suggests that a similar belief in the "normative power of local practice" underlies the arguments of role-related theories of obligation. See Simmons, "Associative Political Obligations," 252 (citing, inter alia, John Horton, *Political Obligation* [Atlantic Highlands, N.J.: Humanities, 1992]; F. H. Bradley, "My Station and Its Duties," in Bradley, *Ethical Studies* [Indianapolis: Bobbs-Merrill, 1951], 110; Michael Hardimon, "Role Obligations," *J. Phil.* 41 [1994]: 342, 344, 353).

[11] Simmons, "Associative Political Obligations,".

obligation to conform either fail to persuade or prove in fact that the obligation is not independent of external moral principles. If the local practice is wicked, it is difficult to see why the mere fact that it is in place creates any obligation other than one to resist. Thus, the test case must be one of practices that are neutral or relatively harmless. But these cases, if they generate a duty to conform, do so for reasons that are obviously based on external principles – the disutility, for example, that is caused by disappointing or defeating the expectations of those who observe the practice.

The ethics of deference accounts for both ideas – the *apparent* normative force of the existing practice and the fact that the force derives, ultimately, from external moral principles. The most obvious context for apparently independent normative force occurs in the fair play examples. The mere fact that my neighbors have undertaken a project that I admit benefits me under the assumption that all would pay their fair share (an assumption that could not reasonably be presented in advance for beneficiaries' consent) forces me to decide whether I have reason to defer to their principle of distribution. An affirmative answer to this question gives the examples the appearance of normative power for "whoever goes first." But the reasons for deference draw on external principles: a consideration of the relative merits of the two kinds of community that will result from my decision on whether to defer or to insist on my own equally plausible principle of distribution.

MERE EXPECTATIONS AND ENTITLEMENTS. Simmons's critique of the attempt to assimilate political obligations to associative obligations includes a reminder that we cannot generate obligations from the mere fact that someone will be disappointed if we don't act in ways that he or she expects. The example he uses is Kant's daily walk through Königsberg, taken so regularly that housewives set their clocks by his passing. Surely, Kant incurred no obligation to continue walking at his regular time merely to avoid defeating their expectations.[12] The example is so obvious that it helps to reinforce the normative basis we have been sketching for the ethics of deference. First, the question is not whether one has a prima facie duty to please others. The problem posed by the principle of autonomy is whether one can ever be expected to defer to the judgment of others about what should be done. It is highly unlikely that housewives formed the judgment that Kant should continue to take his walks at the same time each day (and even if they did, Kant would have no reason to defer). The housewives here are in the same position as people who rely on predictions by weather forecasters: Knowing that the prediction is just that – a prediction, not a promise – they realize they are assuming the risk in relying on it. The obligation of deference is limited to rare situations: (1) I have a special relationship that elevates moral judgments and their associated expectations to a level that

[12] Id., 258.

requires me to heed them; (2) I have deliberately created a special relationship (through promise) that includes the obligation to defer to the promisee's views when there is disagreement about the extent of my commitment; (3) I have reasons to defer to the distribution principle that is in place and that has resulted in benefits I acknowledge as valuable; (4) I confront expectations for deference in a context that I concede is simply the application of a general theory of the state that I accept as valid.

The Structure of Deference

Partial or Absolute

Questions about the structure of deference are questions about how much deference is required and about the method for determining the answer to those questions in particular cases. I consider here the first question: How much deference is required.

Absolute deference is most easily illustrated in the context of closed, rule-governed systems. Legal systems provide the most familiar example: Rules typically designate both the institutions that are to decide disputes initially and the principles of finality that indicate which institutions are to have the final say in determining which norms shall be enforced. It is commonly supposed in the United States, for example, that lower courts must always defer to higher courts; but this question is obviously an empirical one about how to interpret the rules actually in force in a particular society.[13]

The ethics of deference, of course, is a moral theory, not the product of artificially promulgated rules. The whole point of the theory is to explore questions about the reasons for deference in any context – including contexts that purport to foreclose such inquiries. No system of promulgated rules can foreclose these inquiries, because any attempt to do so simply raises again the question of why one should defer to such a demand for deference. Promulgated rules are simply facts that cannot by themselves dictate answers to the moral questions raised by the ethics of deference.

So it is to moral theory that one must turn to decide whether the deference that is due in appropriate cases is absolute or partial. This study assumes that the deference at stake is partial, not absolute. Partial deference is already difficult

---

[13] For the argument that lower courts in the United States might not be required in certain circumstances to defer absolutely to higher courts, see Michael Stokes Paulsen, "Accusing Justice; Some Variations on the Themes of Robert M. Cover's *Justice Accused*," *J. L. & Religion* 7(1990): 33. For a response see Evan H. Caminker, "Why Must Inferior Courts Obey Superior Court Precedents?", *Stanford L. Rev.* 46 (1994): 817. See also Larry Alexander and Frederick Schauer, "On Extrajudicial Constitutional Interpretation," *Harvard L. Rev.* 110 (1997): 1359. As these contrasting arguments make clear, the question of whether and how much courts should be required to defer to higher courts is a policy question, not a logical necessity, in the design of a legal system.

enough to defend in light of the principle of autonomy. Absolute deference implies that no matter how wrong the normative judgment of those to whom one defers, action in accordance with that judgment is morally required. Common sense suggests that such an account of morality is implausible. Partial deference poses the issue in the familiar terms of a prima facie obligation that dominate most of the discussions of political obligation. Though the concept of a prima facie obligation has complexities of its own,[14] at least it points in the correct direction: The obligation to defer must be measured against the harm my act of deference causes. I am, after all, acting by hypothesis in a way that would be wrong but for the alleged overriding reason to defer.

Assigning Weights

Deciding how to compare prima facie obligations that point in different directions is notoriously difficult. And it is unrealistic to expect that a precise formula could be developed for determining the correct balance in all cases. The most that one can hope for is a general indication of the factors to take into account in making a final decision. Two factors in particular suggest themselves in deciding how much weight to assign to the reason to defer to another's opinion: (1) the relative intensity and (2) the nature of each person's conviction. The first factor suggests a quantitative comparison: How much does each person care about the matter at issue? The second suggests a qualitative comparison: Does the matter involve an issue thought to affect fundamental principles of morality or is it one that affects only self-interest? Whether one of these factors dominates the other is also a matter that is unclear. It is sometimes suggested, for example, that moral reasons always outweigh reasons of self-interest, which suggests that the nature of the conviction is the more important factor, with questions of relative intensity to be used only when both parties are acting for either moral or self-interested reasons. But the claim that moral reasons always trump self-interested ones is not self-evident. For one thing, drawing the line between the moral and the self-interested is itself difficult: Some moral theories, in fact, make no such distinction. Second, even if one were confident that a clear line could be drawn between moral reasons and reasons of self-interest, it is not clear that a matter of minor moral significance should always outweigh very strong reasons of self-interest.

We can illustrate these vague suggestions with examples drawn from each of our four paradigms of the duty to defer. In the case of political obligation, the two dimensions of quantity and quality of conviction are perhaps easiest to illustrate,

---

[14] See M. B. E. Smith, "Review Essay: The Obligation to Obey the Law: Revision or Explanation?" *Criminal Justice Ethics* (Summer–Fall 1989): 65. For a brief review of how moral obligations may be overridden, see Paul Harris, "The Moral Obligation to Obey the Law," in *On Political Obligation*, ed. Paul Harris (London: Routledge, 1990), 151, 154–7.

even if difficult to measure. The state commonly gives clues to the intensity of its convictions about the norms it enforces in two ways. First, the sanctions are rough guides to how serious the proscribed conduct is thought to be. Second, the distinction between *mala in se* and *mala prohibitum* may sometimes help distinguish conduct that is thought by the state to involve moral error, as opposed to acts that are wrong merely because the state in its coordinating role declares them to be. Thus less deference is required in the case of traffic laws – less in terms of both the kinds of reasons that might justify disobedience and how strong the reasons must be. So running red lights in the middle of the desert may well be justifiable. As long as one recognizes the need to offer a justification that includes giving some weight to the state's opposing view, many cases of justified disobedience will still arise. Conversely, where the state's decision is based on its view of basic moral values or fundamental principles, more is required to justify disobedience. Again, one needs to be careful in assuming that a precise calculus can be supplied to determine either the strength of the reason or the kind of reason. If the state wrongly prohibits abortion, one who disagrees with the state typically disagrees on the basis of the same kinds of fundamental moral reasons that underlie the state's decision: The claim that abortion is the woman's choice is a claim about the principle of privacy – a claim that the woman has the right to make the decision for any reason (including what might be called reasons of self-interest) and a corresponding claim that the state is morally wrong to impose its choice on the woman. That disagreement will often lead correctly to the conclusion that disobedience is justified, even after one gives weight to the state's opposing judgment.[15]

The question of how to weigh opposing views in the case of promise presents different issues that do not lend themselves so easily to the balancing metaphor. We have assumed that deference primarily explains the case for strictly performing; other theories can explain why the promisor is responsible for the harm caused to the reliance and expectation interests of the promisee. We have also suggested that deference is required even though the promisor (correctly) believes that no uncompensated harm will be caused by breach. Presumably, the promisee disagrees: Some dispute about how failure to perform affects the

---

[15] One critic of my earlier effort to explain how to balance such conflicting duties suggests that a woman who believes that an abortion would "drastically change her life for the worse" would be acting on reasons of "mere self-interest or convenience," and thus would not be entitled under my argument to oppose the state's ban on abortion, which is presumably based on moral reasons. See Smith, "Review Essay: The Obligation to Obey The Law," 64. The criticism overlooks the fact that disagreements with the state on this issue are typically on fundamental moral grounds: The state is violating the privacy interests of the woman, which give her the right to decide *for any reason* whether to have an abortion. The case of the woman who acts on mere self-interest would be, e.g., one who does not believe the state is invading such fundamental privacy rights but who nevertheless finds it temporarily inconvenient to carry the fetus to birth. It is also misleading, I think, to suggest that wanting not to have one's life drastically changed for the worse, even if it is thought of as a self-interested reason, could never outweigh moral reasons.

promisee's interest must explain why the promisee doesn't simply release the promisor. The dispute could be over whether and how to measure harm, or it could be over the general question of how trust and confidence might be affected, or any of the other kinds of interests that presumably underlie the promisee's continued disappointment. How shall we compare the relative strength of these different views about the reasons for performance? One might suggest simply considering the magnitude of the cost of performing: If performance will be too costly, deference is not required. But that suggestion does nothing to help one determine just why and how much importance the promisee places on performance. We can't simply compare the promisor's costs to the promisee's gain, because by hypothesis the parties disagree about that calculation; the promisor already believes (we even assume correctly) that failure to perform won't cause any additional harm to the promisee, so, a fortiori, acting on his judgment about the relative costs and benefits results in never deferring. Conversely, if we decide that the promisee's interest must be considered without regard to harm, we risk suggesting that performance is always required – simply because the promisee insists or has not released the promisor. What we need is some way to reflect the idea that the promisor has an obligation to take into account the promisee's views before simply acting on his or her own view of the matter.

One possible way to illustrate how the ethics of deference might work in these cases is to borrow from a notorious example in contract law. In *Peevyhouse v. Garland Coal & Mining Co.*,[16] the court was asked to decide what damages to award when a coal company breached an agreement to restore Peevyhouse's land after the company finished its strip-mining activity. The harm caused by the breach as measured by the market value of Peevyhouse's land, the court assumed, was minimal – approximately $300. On the other hand, the cost to the coal company if performance was required was $25,000. Assuming that it had to choose between one of these ways of measuring damage, the court chose the lesser award. But $300 surely undercompensates Peevyhouse just as much as $25,000 overcompensates.[17] Commentators have suggested that one solution would be to order specific performance, on the understanding that the parties could negotiate a settlement: The coal company would pay Peevyhouse something less than $25,000 to release them from the decree of specific performance; Peevyhouse would have an incentive to settle for something more than the market value ($300) but less than the full $25,000.[18] While the contract case

---

[16] 382 P.2d 109 (Okla. 1962), cert. denied, 375 U.S. 906 (1963).

[17] The Peevyhouses apparently had declined to accept $3,000, which the company offered during negotiations for the lease if no restoration work was required. See Judith L. Maute, "The Ballad of Willie and Lucille," *Nw. U.L. Rev.* 89 (1995): 1341. On the other hand, one doubts that the Peevyhouses would have spent $25,000 on restoration.

[18] See Robert L. Birmingham, "Damage Measures and Economic Rationality: The Geometry of Contract Law," *Duke L. J.* (1969): 51, 69–70. The jury's award of $5,000, which the court noted was more than the entire value of the Peevyhouses' farm, may not have been much different from what a settlement would have produced.

is meant for analogy only, there is perhaps some reason to think that it points to a possible explanation of how the duty to defer would play out more generally in the case of recalcitrant promisors. The duty would at least require some willingness to hear the promisee's case and some mechanism for accommodating the promisee's reasons for insisting on performance. With the requirement of good faith in the background, the possibility that a duty to defer can function in many cases like a duty to negotiate in good faith over the reasons for and against performance may be plausible.

How to weigh the duty to defer in the case of fair play also raises unique problems based on the argument for why deference is required. Normally, we have seen, deference here is a result of discovering that others have acted on a principle of distribution that assumes that each will pay a proportionate share for the benefits received. If one's own preference is for a different principle, one that fosters competitive rather than sharing communities, when would one's view be strong enough to outweigh the views of those who have already acted and conferred benefits? It is possible again to suggest that the question simply requires comparing the relative intensity with which both parties hold their views. We have assumed that the sharing principle is not naturally superior to alternative principles; otherwise, one could defend the duty to pay one's fair share directly, without the need for arguments from fair play or the ethics of deference. If it is not naturally superior, then the only way to judge the strength of the duty to defer seems to be by comparing the relative perceived importance of the values fostered by these alternative principles of distribution. In the end, this may be the only plausible response. If I care more about distributing by a principle that allows for the possibility of free riders, with the competition such a principle fosters, than others care about the sharing principle, it is difficult to see why deference is required. This conclusion may help explain why there is so much doubt about the fair play principle. On the other hand, there are several factors that help explain why more than just a comparison of relative intensity of conviction might be relevant. First, even if both distribution principles are equally defensible, one group has already acted in circumstances that made prior consultation impossible. The "normative force of the actual" reappears here in suggesting that an additional element of disharmony or discord is created when one confronts a fait accompli that has come about through nobody's fault. One may decide to give extra weight to the principle that has been acted on because, even though one would normally be happy with a competitive community, in this case an additional perceived insult results from the fact that the benefits can no longer be taken back: Others, who acted in good faith on the assumption that the sharing principle would prevail, never had a chance to see who would win under an alternative bluffing distribution principle. This fact may warrant deferring to the sharing principle in a particular case, even though it would not be one's normally preferred principle. In the end, it seems, the strength of the duty to defer is likely to reflect the strength of the argument that establishes the duty in the first place: The fair play duty is, along with the duty to defer in the case of friendship, the one most amenable to consequential arguments and instrumental reasons for deference. Accordingly, how important it is to defer may simply reflect how important it is to maintain a community of one sort (sharing) rather than another (competitive). Fair play, in short, is the most likely case in which the duty to defer is likely to be all or nothing rather than merely prima facie.

Finally, in the case of friendship, the question of how to weigh the duty to defer against the duty to do what is right defies neat capture. One could, of course, suggest that the question is once again one of comparative intensity of feeling (how much does it matter to each partner?) and quality of conviction: Is it a case of perceived fundamental values (should we send the children to private schools when public schools need our support) or of mere economic concerns (public schools cost less)? No doubt friends do have a rough intuitive sense along both of these dimensions. (The theoretical inability to demonstrate interpersonal comparisons of utility seems largely beside the point in most close relationships.) These rough calculations of comparative concern (how much does it matter to each partner, and why?) could be used to decide how much deference is required in a particular case. But algorithms have a hollow ring in this setting, partly because friendship seems to resist being reduced to calculations that "prove" who is entitled to deference. In this setting, too, as in the case of fair play, the argument for the duty to defer is amenable to consequential explanations: What counts, in the end, is the relationship and the effect on that relationship of deciding which partner will prevail when only one can. While it is likely that an intuitive sense of relative degrees and type of conviction are often the key to who defers, there is no reason to assume that this must be the case. In the end, it is the relationship that is at stake, and if other forms of compromise in response to the duty to defer can be devised (e.g., taking turns), then there would be little point in insisting on one particular method of deciding who prevails.

The Value of Deference

The Appeal of Deference

We have been mainly concerned with defending the ethics of deference by showing how it helps explain settled intuitions and resolves puzzles that cause trouble for standard theories. But showing that a theory helps make practices more understandable or coherent is not, of course, the same as proving that the theory is "true," whatever that might mean. The difficulty of knowing how to prove that a moral or legal theory is true has led recently to a different tactic in attempting to establish the plausibility of a normative theory: We will ask not (only) whether the theory is true, but (also) whether it is "attractive."[19] While

---

[19] See Dworkin, *Law's Empire*, 186.

one might object that there is no connection between arguing that it would be desirable that something be the case and concluding that it is the case,[20] there is some point in considering what effects a theory might have if it were accepted and acted on as if it were true. At the very least, a theory that would have negative effects – requiring, for example, superhuman efforts to comply or leading to behavior that clashes with widely accepted human values or needs – should raise doubts about whether the theory could really be a plausible prescription for human behavior. What is there about the ethics of deference to recommend it? What happy or unhappy consequences, if any, might result if people accepted it as true and acted accordingly?

The most obvious difference that the ethics of deference makes is that it shifts the moral focus in deciding what one ought to do from the evaluation of the action in question to a consideration of the interests of the person to whom deference is owed. The primary value that underlies the theory is respect for others; in some cases, as in our argument for political obligation, it is respect for oneself as well and for the implications that follow from one's own understanding and acceptance of the value and nature of law. Among the consequences of such a shift in focus, the following may be the most important. First, where the duty to defer exists, dialogue and discussion, as opposed to unilateral action, are promoted, with the result that conflict may be avoided or postponed. Second, the duty to defer underscores the need for humility in assuming that one's own view of the matter in question is correct, particularly as respects matters involving moral judgment or questions of value. Third, the duty operates as a kind of default rule determining who shall have the prima facie right to decide when disagreement continues – a rule that often applies, under our analysis here, to cases where an impasse seems to require some resolution. Dialogue, after all, however desirable in the abstract, cannot go on forever. Sometimes action must be taken and decisions made.[21]

The Dark Side of Deference

It might be thought that the disadvantage of acknowledging a duty to defer is simply the price one pays for the advantages just discussed: In return for increased harmony, greater social concern, and more efficient allocation of decision-making authority, one sacrifices acting in ways that would normally be correct and preferable to the action required by deference. Of course, if the theory of deference is correct, this is not a sacrifice but a necessary condition of making sure that the action one takes, in the ultimate sense, is correct. Instead of

---

[20] See Donald Regan, "Authority and Value: Reflection on Ray's Morality of Freedom," *S. Cal. L. Rev.* 62 (1989): 1036–9; id., "Reasons, Authority and the Meaning of 'Obey': Further Thoughts on Ray and Obedience to Law," *Can. J. L. Jurisp.* 3 (1990): 23–8.

[21] See J. Waldron, *Law and Disagreement* (Oxford: Clarendon Press, 1999), 7 ("the point of law is to enable us to act *in the face of disagreement*").

just repeating the arguments for the ethics of deference, the disadvantages of acknowledging the duty should be sought elsewhere – in the effects on other aspects of human behavior. One possibility is that duties of deference are subject to abuse. First, it is possible that deference will be demanded or expected where it is inappropriate. Many of the clubs, social organizations, workers' unions, civic associations, and other groups that form part of everyday life have hierarchical structures that can easily appear to confer authority on individuals in ways that might seem to require other members to defer where no such deference is warranted. In bodies that are organized on more or less democratic principles, with equality among members, deference to leaders who establish basic policies outside of normal democratic procedures may not only be unwarranted but could have the opposite effect on social relations: Expecting deference where none is appropriate can be perceived as an insult rather than an occasion for showing respect. Second, knowing that one is owed deference can lead one to ignore the reciprocal nature of the duty. Deference requires good faith on the part of the state, the promisee, those who have conferred benefits in the expectation of payment, and friends. I have described elsewhere some of the problems of finding good faith in the case of political obligation and the state.[22] In the case of promisees, good faith means, in part, that the promisee considers the promisor's case for release from the promise and engages in the dialogue that results. Those who confer benefits on others, expecting payment, must at least be able to justify the failure to consult potential beneficiaries in advance to see if they agree with the distribution principle they expect to be observed. Friends, no doubt, will naturally consider each other's conflicting views, even if one in the end deserves deference; otherwise, they would probably not be friends. In all of these cases, an ethics of deference could lead to neglecting the central question of trying to decide what action is correct. If one knows that deference is due, even if one's view is wrong, the incentive to try in good faith to reach the correct decision may be diminished.[23]

A Final Defense

While it is possible that one might need law to coordinate activity, even in a "society of saints,"[24] the point of moral and legal practices would change drastically in the absence of conflict or disagreement. At the very least, much

---

[22] See Philip Soper, *A Theory of Law* (Cambridge, Mass.: Harvard Univ. Press, 1984), 119–25.

[23] I have discussed this problem previously in suggesting that Socrates' strong claim about the obligation to obey the law can be plausibly understood as an example of what I have here called the ethics of deference. See Philip Soper, "Another Look at the *Crito*," *Am. J. Jurisp* 41 (1996): 103, 130–1.

[24] See Regan, "Law's Halo," *Soc. Phil. & Policy* 4 (1986): 15, 26; Gregory Kavka, "Why Even Morally Perfect People Would Need Government," in *For and Against the State*, eds. John T. Sanders and Jan Narveson (Lanham, Md.: Rowman & Littlefield, 1996), 41.

of the motivation for engaging in arguments about morality and justice would be lost if people did not disagree over fundamental issues of value and about what to do when such disagreement cannot be resolved before action must be taken. Modern attempts to defend theories of justice despair over the possibility of reaching agreement on ethics and accordingly suggest that process, rather than substance, offers the key to harmony. We will not abandon the search for truth in ethics or condemn it as nonsense, but we will set it aside temporarily while we engage in dialogue, or while we hope that our disparate truths will converge in an "overlapping consensus" that will permit some decisions to be made without undue rancor, whether or not they are correct. We are told that the other possibilities for harmony hold out false hope: We cannot hope to persuade others "to abandon their errors and adopt our truths," or "convince them that toleration is in their self-interest," or "induce them to sympathize with us, despite the error of our ways."[25] Instead, we must engage in "neutral dialogue,"[26] hoping that by removing bias and similar impediments to good faith, we will arrive at least at consensus, which may be the only alternative to truth.

The final appeal to be made for an ethics of deference is that it offers a modest alternative to the resigned acceptance of process or dialogue in lieu of substance in ethics. To be sure, the motivation for the modern movement toward process over substance – despair over the possibility of persuading others of our truths – also motivates the argument for deference. But the argument for deference is not an argument designed to foster tolerance or sympathy for erroneous views; nor is it simply a call for more dialogue and debate. The argument for deference is an argument about *duty* – a claim about the *obligation* to defer, while dialogue continues and the jury remains out on the question of truth. Though the theory is partial, it remains a substantive theory – not simply a plea for more process, however enlightened, however constrained. For those who fear that the abandonment of substance for process celebrates, in the end, the claims of those who deny that there can be truth in ethics, the ethics of deference may offer a way back.

[25] Bruce Ackerman, "What Is Neutral about Neutrality?" *Ethics* 93 (1983): 372, 389–90.
[26] See id.; Ackerman, *Social Justice in the Liberal State* (New Haven, Conn., and London: Yale Univ. Press, 1980).

Index